CHRIST AND ANALOGY

CHRIST AND ANALOGY

THE CHRISTOCENTRIC METAPHYSICS OF HANS URS VON BALTHASAR

JUNIUS JOHNSON

Fortress Press
Minneapolis

CHRIST AND ANALOGY

The Christocentric Metaphysics of Hans Urs von Balthasar

Cover design: Alisha Lofgren

Library of Congress Cataloging-in-Publication Data is available

Print ISBN: 978-0-8006-9995-6

eBook ISBN: 978-1-4514-6523-5

The paper used in this publication meets the minimum requirements of American National Standard for Information Sciences — Permanence of Paper for Printed Library Materials, ANSI Z329.48-1984.

Manufactured in the U.S.A.

This book was produced using PressBooks.com, and PDF rendering was done by PrinceXML.

CONTENTS

Abbreviations

CD   Barth, Karl. *Church Dogmatics*. 14 vols. G.W. Bromiley and T.F. Torrance, eds. Peabody, MA: Hendrickson, 2010.

DS   Denzinger, Henricus. *Enchiridion Symbolorum Definitionum et Declarationum de Rebus Fidei et Morum*. Barcinone: Herder, 1973.

CL   von Balthasar, Hans Urs. *Cosmic Liturgy: The Universe according to Maximus the Confessor*. Translated by Brian E. Daley. San Francisco: Ignatius, 1988.

GL   von Balthasar, Hans Urs. *The Glory of the Lord*. 7 vols. Edited by Joseph Fessio and John Riches. San Francisco: Ignatius, 1982–1989.

H   von Balthasar, Hans Urs. *Herrlichkeit: Eine Theologische Ästhetik*. Freiburg: Johannes Verlag Einsiedeln, 1961–1969.

LA   von Balthasar, Hans Urs. *Love Alone Is Credible*. San Francisco: Ignatius, 2004.

TD   von Balthasar, Hans Urs. *Theodrama: Theological Dramatic Theory*. 5 vols. Translated by Graham Harrison. San Francisco: Ignatius, 1988–1998.

TDg   von Balthasar, Hans Urs. *Theodramatik.*Freiburg: Johannes Verlag Einsiedeln, 1973.

TLg   von Balthasar, Hans Urs. *Theologik.*Freiburg: Johannes Verlag Einsiedeln, 1985.

TL   von Balthasar, Hans Urs. *Theologic*. 3 vols. Translated by Adrian J. Walker and Graham Harrison. San Francisco: Ignatius, 2000–2005.

TH   von Balthasar, Hans Urs. *A Theology of History*. San Francisco: Ignatius, 1994.

TG   von Balthasar, Hans Urs. *Theologie der Geschichte: Ein Grundriss*. Freiburg: Johannes Verlag Einsiedeln, 1959.

PREFACE

In *The Glory of the Lord*, Hans Urs von Balthasar speaks of the need to find an "index of interpretation" when we come to the task of attempting to understand God's self-manifestation in the world. The inadequacy of any worldly form to be this index of interpretation should be clear from a proper understanding of the nature of God, and yet in many ways it is the argument of the first volume to make this inadequacy clear. God's appearance is not the necessary appearing of creaturely being; it is entirely at God's own discretion and therefore the result of sovereign freedom. This makes it "lordly" and transcendent of any worldly measure. The only adequate measure would be one that is of the same provenance that is itself delivered in the moment of the appearing.

In like fashion, as I began the process of writing a dissertation, it was my goal, in the face of such a large corpus and so much confusion about where to begin with von Balthasar, to provide an index of interpretation. In the interest of respecting his right to speak for himself, I sought this index not outside of his writings but within them. This search led me to the belief that his doctrine of analogy is the key concept that unlocks the rest of his system. For even though Christ is at the center, one may still go on to ask what type of Christ von Balthasar has. And it quickly becomes apparent that Christology turns upon the doctrine of analogy.

In pursuit of this index of interpretation and the project of explicating it, I discovered that many passages were illuminated and a thoroughly rich read of von Balthasar was enabled. The outlines for a thorough study of the central moments of his theology began to emerge. However, the more I tried to bring these discussions to the center of the study, the more I realized that we were ill-prepared to talk about them. Too many terms and concepts have such specific meaning within the Balthasarian horizon for us to dare to leave them unexamined; we invariably would be translating von Balthasar into a foreign language without even realizing it and losing much of what is both distinctive and decisive, to borrow some of his favorite words. A study of his theology that would be sufficiently subtle seemed to me to first require an equally subtle study of his metaphysics.

It quickly became apparent that this was a type of task that has not really been done, and I was encouraged by the opportunity to contribute to the ongoing project of critical reflection on this great theologian by being the first to try my hand at so daunting a task. I did not, however, fully realize even at the time that I completed the dissertation the extent to which this study is meant to enable the later study. Only subsequent reflection has shown how much that is true and has allowed me to more properly cordon off issues that do not properly belong to this study.

This volume obviously revises the material found in that dissertation. But the greater difference between this study and that one is in the reorganization of the material, and the addition of much deeper discussion of the major themes. About forty thousand words have been added over the initial project, with an aim to strengthen the usefulness of this volume as a guide to von Balthasar's metaphysical intuitions and commitments. The result is an argument that is the same as the original, but is drastically different in form, presentation, and depth.

Many people have encouraged me along the path to the completion of this task. First I need to thank my *Doktorvater*, Miroslav Volf, who kindly and insistently sent me back to the drawing board again and again until I was face to face with the fundamental choices that lead to this project existing at all. I am also indebted to my student Aaron Butler for his close reading of and careful commenting on the final draft of this book, and for a very enjoyable lunch during which, in painstaking detail, we combed through his thoughts and reactions. I am indebted to the University of the Free State in Bloemfontein, South Africa—where I am have been a Research Associate during the writing of this book—for their continued support, as well as to the community of scholars at the Rivendell Institute at Yale, whose belief and sharp minds have greatly benefitted this project. The debt I owe to Yale University, which nurtured my doctoral studies, and the Yale Divinity School, where I have been fortunate to teach among the best imaginable colleagues and students, is not able to be repaid. I am grateful to have had the chance to teach twice on von Balthasar in that remarkable community of scholars, a place that has come to me more than any other to feel like home. Last and above all I would like to thank my wife, without whom I proved incapable of finishing the dissertation, and with whom I have found the ability to continually deepen and sharpen my engagement with von Balthasar.

It is my wish that this book will open more extensive dialogue on von Balthasar's metaphysics. But above all, I have written it in thanks to him for his many years of intellectual labors, both creative, editorial, and as a translator. The gift he has left behind for us is a legacy of which any son of the Church should feel proud, and I gratefully acknowledge my own debt to his efforts. *Requiescat in pace.*

Junius Johnson
New Haven, Connecticut
June 2013

1

Introduction

The history of theology has left us no small number of examples of intellectual genius coupled with remarkable industry attesting to that genius. Even among such a rich company, however, the contribution of Hans Urs von Balthasar stands out. Not only the amount of text he produced (as writer, compiler, and editor), but also the scope of topics and literature that he ranges over set him apart as one of the most learned and daunting theologians of any time.

This is, of course, at one level, a scholar's dream. von Balthasar has left us an enormous playground on which to chart our own concerns and values, and in which to find the room for our analytical speculations (whether faithful or "interpretive") to roam. It is therefore paramount that any scholarly reflection on von Balthasar define in the clearest possible terms what its own nature is to be: what type of study is it, what relationship does it intend to have with the original Balthasarian material, what topics are central and what peripheral to its aims?

In this chapter I intend to introduce, as specifically as possible, the nature of the current project, and to situate it within the web of issues relating to the interpretation of von Balthasar. In order to do so, this chapter will also have to mark several issues and themes in von Balthasar which themselves have exercised a controlling influence on the shape of this project, and which must to some extent be taken into account in any reflection on von Balthasar that seeks to be analytical rather than constructive (which is the type of project this one is). This includes some reflection on von Balthasar's sources and influences as well as on the issues involved in interpreting von Balthasar across different genres (most notably, his historical vs. his constructive works).

I. Theology's Handmaid

Von Balthasar is a theologian, and, in spite of the attraction he offers to those in other fields of study, he is of primary interest to theologians. It is my ultimate desire to interpret von Balthasar theologically in light of the most central and pressing claims of Christian theology: the Trinity, Christology, and grace. However, the specificity of his theology in these loci is difficult to demonstrate apart from the nest of assumptions, commitments, and conclusions that inform even the meaning of such basic words as *love*. In the case of many theologians, the explication of these philosophical issues can form an introductory chapter to the theological analysis proper. However, in von Balthasar's case, sustained reflection on the philosophical themes which are evident throughout his works is necessary if we are to avoid interpreting him in light of someone else; for he has labored hard (if not precisely or concisely) to specify a conceptual language that is to be deployed in the explication of the theology. We cannot learn this language from anyone other than von Balthasar, because it is *his* language. As a language, it is not without antecedents or analogues, but it is nevertheless *sui generis*.

Accordingly, the ultimate theological horizon of Trinity, Christology, and grace has to be deferred until a later study. The current study, which will serve as necessary preparation for the other, will occupy itself with the explication of von Balthasar's metaphysics. However, it is important to realize that any attempt to defer theological questions to the subsequent study would deeply caricature von Balthasar's thought, which sees a deep connection between the two.[1] Metaphysics can only be discussed in conversation with theology.

Terms like *metaphysics* and *theology* have been used and misused so frequently that one often wonders if the concept the speaker and the hearers have of these words are at all similar. So what do I mean by *metaphysics*, and what do I mean by *theology*?

A. WHAT IS METAPHYSICS?

Metaphysics is the philosophy of first principles. It includes under itself ontology and epistemology. Therefore, all ontological and epistemological questions are *de facto* also metaphysical questions. However, metaphysics is not simply co-extensive with the conjunction of ontology and epistemology, but has its own questions. What are these? If all ontological and epistemological questions are set aside as included within metaphysics broadly speaking but not part of metaphysics proper, what is left?

One answer to the question is logic. Logic is neither ontology nor epistemology: it is the rules by which we judge thinking to be correct, the formal principles that guide our whole process of thinking and reflecting on the world. Is logic then co-extensive with metaphysics? Or is it something other than and prior to metaphysics?

The identification of logic with metaphysics would be a reduction, and an unwarranted one. For while in actual practice logic has the upper hand on metaphysics (as can be seen from the fact that at the very beginning of metaphysical reflection, logic is already at work controlling what can and cannot be said), this is more a methodological priority than a "logical" one. For logic, closely examined, will be found to depend upon certain claims about the way the world is, and so is founded upon a certain ontology. Or, if it is not founded on "beings" or "Being" but on some other dynamic in the world, even if it is taken to simply be a description of the fundamental structures of rationality, logic is still founded upon something which itself belongs properly to the field of metaphysics.[2] For this reason, von Balthasar's use of the word *logic* in the Triptych[3] is largely a way of referencing *metaphysics*.[4]

If logic also is a part of metaphysics with its own proper content distinct from ontology and epistemology, is anything left to belong to metaphysics proper? Yes: what is left are questions of the structures that obtain between beings, or between different modes of knowledge. That is to say, the conditions of the possibility of being and knowledge, causality as such (which may require being but is itself no part of the field of being, nor is a robust understanding of beings obviously sufficient to ground a robust understanding of causality). Ontology thus seems to be not all questions whatever about being, but the study of the nature of being; *whether* there is a being and *which* beings there are seems to belong more properly to metaphysics than to ontology.

Thus, the fundamental questions of metaphysics are: "Why is there something rather than nothing?" "What accounts for the fact that there are many things and not just one thing?" "What types of things are there?" "What types of causality are there?" "What is the nature of causality considered generally, and in its particular types?" "What is necessary and what is contingent?" There are of course more.[5] But this should serve to give some sense of what I mean by metaphysics. It is these properly metaphysical questions that are my focus in the following pages, precisely because such questions are deeply informed by and have deep significance for theological questions.

However, there is a certain passage from *My Work in Retrospect* in which it seems that von Balthasar wishes to distance himself from metaphysics. What he is really concerned with, he says there, is meta-*anthropology*: "It is here that the substance of my thought inserts itself. Let us say above all that the traditional term 'metaphysical' signified the act of transcending physics, which for the Greeks signified the totality of the cosmos, of which man was a part. For us physics is something else: the science of the material world. For us the cosmos perfects itself in man, who at the same time sums up the world and surpasses it. Thus our philosophy will be essentially a meta-anthropology, presupposing not only the cosmological sciences, but also the anthropological sciences, and surpassing them toward the question of the being and essence of man" (*My Work in Retrospect*, 114). This seeming challenge to considering von Balthasar's philosophy under the heading "metaphysics" doesn't actually say as much as it seems to. What von Balthasar has offered here is an attempt to shut down the possibility of moderns taking the anthropological dimension as subsequent to or excluded from the basic philosophical question. His point is that the microcosm is found in humanity, and so humanity isn't defined over and against an impersonal metaphysical backdrop, but is right at the heart of it.[6] We catch already a hint of the distinctive note von Balthasar will sound, that *personhood* will play a much larger role in metaphysics than is traditional. But at the end of the day, this is not an argument for meta-anthropology instead of metaphysics, but simply for a certain broadening (or resistance to the shrinking) of the *scope* of metaphysics.

B. WHAT IS THEOLOGY?

What is theology, then? Theology is that discourse which is primarily concerned with the proper conceptualization and articulation, as far as it is humanly possible, of truths about God. Theology is not anthropology, or physics, or literature, yet it will deliver much that is true which will drastically alter the reflections of all other disciplines. Thus, if we know that God is of such a sort (Creator, good, worthy of worship), we will also know a lot about humanity. Or better, we will have to exclude certain theses about humanity (our self-sufficiency, for instance).

Thus, the central theological topics are the Trinity (who and how God is in Godself), Christology (the identity of God in a person who willed not to exclude but rather to include creation in Godself, and the work of God in recovering lost humanity for Godself), and grace (the general and specific character of God's actions toward those beings to whom God owes nothing). From these midpoints, theology will expand to include a doctrine of creation (including angelology, demonology, anthropology, and theology of nature), a theology of history, and other such things. But it does not thereby *become* history, or the natural sciences, precisely because these disciplines study their objects in themselves, while theology looks at such things in their relation to God. True, it is a claim of theology that its view is a privileged one, that it sees things most clearly; but more premises would be required to reach the further conclusion that this in any way impinges upon the dignity and value of the sciences and humanities in their own right.

C. THE RELATION OF METAPHYSICS AND THEOLOGY

If metaphysics and theology are understood as I have said here, then it becomes clear that a strong separation between them is not really possible. Metaphysics lies "exposed" to theology both because it receives fundamental information which it is not privileged to question from theology (if the metaphysician is also one committed to the truth of Christian theological claims) and because it must hold itself ready to be judged, and, if necessary, corrected at all times by theology. Its proper space of exercise is the identification, proper distinction, and clarification of conceptuality that will enable theology to speak more accurately and authentically, to more fully and coherently translate its divine message into human terms. These ways taken together define metaphysics in its role as the handmaid of theology.

This dynamic, as with theology's relations to the other fields of human knowledge, does not take away from the proper exercise of metaphysics, or its right to work in its proper field; it does, however, point the work of metaphysics toward theology, and precisely when it is to be used by a theologian: "Thus we may conclude that the whole unabridged metaphysics of the transcendentals of Being can only be unfolded under the theological light of the creation of the world in the Word of God, who expresses himself in divine freedoms as a sensate-spiritual man. But in asserting this, we do so without implying that metaphysics itself needs to become theology" (*Epilogue* 78).[7] This is important for understanding the notion of the relationship between theology and metaphysics as von Balthasar sees it. He has a fundamental commitment to the idea that reality is only the way it is because God is the way God is (thus, God is not self-identical because the law of non-contradiction requires it, rather the law of non-contradiction itself holds because God is self-identical). This is in effect to refuse to submit God to any outside standard, but rather to make God the determiner of every standard. This means that the immanent (Trinitarian) being of God as such is the ground of metaphysics.

That this is true places metaphysics in a necessary relation to theology. For in taking the being of God as the first principle of metaphysics, one in fact asserts that the immanent being of God is as such beyond the bounds of metaphysics as a ground that conditions but is not conditioned by the dependent system. Before creation, there is no metaphysics at all, just God and the all-sufficiency of the divine essence. Only once there is creation are there implications of that essence which are more than merely hypothetical, and thus metaphysics proper. Only creation is subject to metaphysics, and at the head of creation stands not merely the divine essence, not even the Trinitarian God, but the archetypal Son in imitation of whom creation obeys the rules of the being of God.

Metaphysics, therefore, while the height of philosophy, stops short of theology. In other words, philosophy takes creation for its object, theology takes God for its object. The incarnation is therefore the most significant event in the life of the relationship of these two disciplines, and on that analogy philosophy is not destroyed by theology, but perfected by it (*gratia non destruit, sed perficit naturam*).

It is this relationship that also gives metaphysics a sort of priority, as von Balthasar expresses at the beginning of the *Theologic*: "By its very nature, theological insight into God's glory, goodness, and truth presupposes an *ontological*, and not merely formal or gnoseological, infrastructure of worldly being. Without philosophy, there can be no theology" (*TL* I.7). Or again, "In order to be a serious theologian, one must also, indeed, first, be a philosopher; one must—precisely also in the light of revelation—have immersed oneself in the mysterious structures of creaturely being (and the 'simple' can do this just as well as, and presumably better than, the 'wise and understanding'" [Mt. 11:25]) (*TL* I.8). Von Balthasar goes on to discuss the nature of the philosophical problem of worldly being as the theologian will encounter it; ultimately it issues in the question of the way in which finite being is an "image and likeness" of absolute being. He concludes: "But this question becomes meaningful, indeed, urgent, only insofar as our horizon is theological and trinitarian" (*TL* I.11).

Thus it is clear that metaphysics cannot get "puffed up"; in order to understand itself properly it will have to look beyond itself: "Creaturely logic can only have a correct estimate of itself if it sees itself as participating analogously in an absolute Logos that traces its origin backward to the Father and forward to the Spirit of freely given love who pours forth from him and from him who is his source. Formal creaturely logic, too, is grounded in the Trinity and molded by it" (*TD* V.65). The reciprocal dynamic of philosophy and theology, where each claims its own sort of primacy, may thus be summed up for von Balthasar by reference to Klaus Hemmerle: "If mankind is to understand God's word that is uttered to the world, philosophy is presupposed; conversely, this means that man's finite reason must exhibit an openness beyond itself if it is to be receptive to the divine speech" (*TD* V.73). He calls this a "reciprocal a priori of philosophy and theology."[8]

Given that this is so, I will not try to bracket theology to such an extent that it is not an integral part of the discussion: this would violate the entire schema presented here, to which von Balthasar is deeply committed. Nor will this bracketing show up most properly in the bracketing of topics discussed (for our analysis reaches fulfillment in a consideration of the Trinity and Christology). Rather, theology will be bracketed in the sense that some ideas will not have their full explication here, because the final dimension of all topics is their explication as it is found in God, which crosses the threshold from metaphysics to theology. It is simply true for von Balthasar that everything in the metaphysics could be transposed into the theological realm, and that in fact, properly understood, metaphysics is just a transposition into the creaturely realm of what is properly theological. This is the boundary we shall constantly resist crossing, from the metaphysical to its theological transposition. As a result of this, the discussion presented here may be thought to suffer in places from incompleteness: something important has been left out, or something has not been discussed with the depth it could have been. It is my hope that such thoughts will only arise precisely at those places where the deeper explication of the topic in question would require a more explicit and rigorous theological analysis. Such analyses will have to wait for a later study that will complement and expand upon this current volume.

Consider an example from von Balthasar's book on Maximus the Confessor, *Cosmic Liturgy*:[9] "It would be an anachronism, in dealing with a thinker like Maximus (or with any patristic or early Scholastic writer), to try to make a distinction between philosophy and theology when the subject is a thoughtful interpretation of God and the world and their relationship to each other, as if to suggest that trinitarian issues are not connected to the purely philosophical problem of positive and negative theology. The fact that Maximus grounds both the natural law and the positive moral teaching of the old covenant in Jesus Christ, as Word-to-be-made-flesh, excludes such an approach, as does the way he always considers all the "philosophical" problems of the emergence and return of the world exclusively within the concrete, supernaturally grounded order of sin and redemption" (*CL* 100). To the extent that this is also true about von Balthasar, it could be read as a serious criticism of the current project. This project should, the criticism would say, treat metaphysics and theology together; the attempt to separate them only introduces caricature. This objection is not Balthasarian, however: he has no problem treating metaphysics separately, as is shown by *Theologic* I.[10] What this passage does delineate are the reasons the boundaries between the philosophical and theological projects will not be drawn with strict lines. This is not metaphysics with theology bracketed, not even to the extent that *Theologic* I is; it is an explication of a metaphysics which must not only always be open to theology but will actually always be inviting theology in to precisely the extent that the metaphysics is conditioned by the theology.

As to its own nature, therefore, this study does not properly belong to the discipline of philosophy, because its treatment of von Balthasar's metaphysics always treats it in the realm of and with an eye to theology. My goal here is to present the metaphysics precisely as an introduction to a serious study of his theology. In spite of the focus on philosophical themes, this work remains a work of philosophical theology.

D. SACRED METAPHYSICS

Von Balthasar's statements about not just the mutual *a priori* of theology and metaphysics, but also the necessity that a theologian also be a metaphysician and that all metaphysics in fact understand itself theologically, leads to a further question: to what extent is it possible to talk about a "sacred metaphysics?" What I mean by "sacred metaphysics" is a metaphysical system that is internally marked as being Christian. Thus, it is not simply a metaphysical system that has been influenced by Christianity, nor one that is hospitable to Christian claims; rather, it is one that has been thought through from the first moments of its reflection in the light of Christian truth claims. Such doctrinal claims would form an integral part of the material that is taken as given by the system: while it may be confirmed by later deduction, it is foundational to such an extent that it is never really in question. Can von Balthasar allow for such a conception?

It seems to me that not only can he allow such a conception, but also that only such a conception can really satisfy the demands he has placed, to the point of near polarity, on these two disciplines. Further, not only can he allow such a conception, he must, at least in part, be involved in the effort of trying to construct such a sacred metaphysics; partly in order to be consistent with his own claims about the role of metaphysics in theology, and partly because of his strong exemplarism. To think that he, as one who has faith in Christ, could attempt a metaphysic that would not be sacred, given his understanding of Christ's role in creation, would be ridiculous.[11]

As an example, let us take another passage from *Cosmic Liturgy*. There he describes Maximus as placing his metaphysics in the light of a *Biblical* synthesis. Metaphysical reflection has the job of explicating the positivity of creation as other than God so that it is strengthened against all attempts to dissolve it back into the divine (a tendency von Balthasar feels that Maximus, as an

Eastern theologian, would above all have to face).[12] von Balthasar concludes that: "Only such a metaphysic lays a foundation deep enough to bear an all-inclusive synthesis and strong enough to let different elements of Eastern spirituality be added to the structure without endangering either its cohesion or its meaning" (CL 55). But a careful reading of the sort of metaphysics he has claimed Maximus has won reveals that it is one that, by thinking through the implications of Monophysitism and Monotheletism, the assumptions of Origenism, and the entire Platonic prejudice against created reality, has become a sacred metaphysic. That this is how he reads the development of Maximus's thought becomes clear a few pages later, when discussing Chalcedon: "These texts are enough to give us a notion of the way the Christological formula [of Chalcedon] expands, for Maximus, into a fundamental law of metaphysics" (CL 70). This is a clear example of metaphysics based on material delivered as a given by theology: what I am calling sacred metaphysics.

On the other hand, any claim that von Balthasar is self-consciously attempting to construct a sacred metaphysics must deal with his relation to his previous sources, particularly his dependence on Plato, Aristotle (through Aquinas), Hegel, and Heidegger. These sources will be discussed individually later;[13] what is relevant here is that if von Balthasar is constructing a sacred metaphysics, it is not a project that attempts to start from the beginning, to rethink for itself all that must be thought. Rather, in accordance with his principle that a theory shows its power by its ability to include other theories in itself,[14] he will attempt to incorporate what he believes to be the genuine insights of other metaphysical systems. He is further enabled in this by what he considers the Christian response to the reality that "the supernatural has impregnated nature so deeply that there is simply no way to reconstruct it [nature] in its pure state (natura pura)," namely, to "acknowledge and accept the indelible presence of such theologoumena at the heart of concrete philosophical thinking" (TL I.12).

This allows us to recognize that the distinction between a sacred and a secular metaphysics is not going to be so very significant for von Balthasar, precisely because of his exemplarism. For if Christ stands at the head of the world as its exemplar, then the difference between a sacred and a secular metaphysics is reduced to whether or not a) the creatureliness of all things is recognized and b) the relation of those things, if they are seen as creatures, is seen in light of their origin. This does not mean that all metaphysics are in some way sacred; the failure to reflect on these two themes is a deep failure that will place a limit on how accurate the system can be.

However, since von Balthasar does not exclude these things, however much he may borrow from secular sources, this project is an attempt at sacred metaphysics of a sort. I say "of a sort" because it seems to me that serious questions remain about the extent of any possible isomorphism between a metaphysics that is secular in this sense and a properly sacred use of it. Isn't it just possible that there remains a character that is stamped upon every individual proposition in the metaphysics (which is always understood in the web of its relations to the rest of the system) that at least makes it very difficult to extricate the proposition and migrate it into a new setting? Perhaps it is as hard for philosophical propositions to change systems as it is for Aristotelian accidents to change subjects.

II. NEVER-CEASING FOUNTAIN: VON BALTHASAR'S SOURCES

I mentioned in the previous section von Balthasar's use of prior philosophical systems. It is important to reflect on the general character of his relations to his sources and on the nature of his relationship to some of his most important sources.

What strikes the reader who ranges widely across von Balthasar's corpus is the inconsistency of evaluation of sources. A particular figure may be treated quite sympathetically in one place and quite negatively in another. Plotinus, for example, receives a positive evaluation in *The Glory of the Lord* IV,[15] but virtually everywhere else in the Triptych he is mentioned negatively, almost to the point of villainization. On the reverse end, Bonaventure, whom I will argue is the most important of all of von Balthasar's sources, is praised and depended upon universally through the Triptych, except for *Theologic*III, where his understanding of the Trinity must be firmly denied in favor of von Balthasar's developing Spirit-Christology.

The reason for this inconsistency is not difficult to identify: von Balthasar will at some point attempt to retrieve something valuable from everyone he has read, and at such times a positive evaluation is the inevitable result. But he also must be clear when he is distancing himself from others so that his own voice may be heard.

In itself, there is nothing unusual about this. What is peculiar to von Balthasar is that he does not try to balance his accounts. Many other writers, when praising an aspect of a thinker they largely disagree with, will qualify their praise so that it is clear that their overall evaluation is negative, even if there is something positive that deserves special consideration. Von Balthasar by contrast will indulge in unfettered praise, even though he really only likes one very small thing, and otherwise thinks the author quite pernicious or bankrupt. Likewise, when he offers criticism, it is not typically mitigated by what may in fact be an overall positive estimation. This means that one must attend to a particular figure's fate over the whole of the Balthasarian corpus and not merely in particular spots, or one risks getting exactly the wrong impression of von Balthasar's feelings about that figure.

There is also another type of interaction with his sources in which von Balthasar punctuates his own text with the words of others, as if all he has been saying is merely a gloss of what they had said. *Theologic* I, for example, is filled with references (especially to Aquinas) in which von Balthasar cites the original formulation in support of an idea he has just presented.

For example, he says: "Being coincides with consciousness and self-consciousness, thus becoming its own object. This is the true meaning of the *cogito ergo sum*" (*TL* I.93). It is very unlikely that this, as von Balthasar means it, is what Descartes meant. Often in such cases, the Balthasarian claim that is getting summarized by these quotes (often signaled as quotes because they have been left in their original language by the translator) are, in actual point of fact, *not* the same as the idea that is being referenced.

This seems strange at first: why so much desire to read his philosophy back into the great thinkers of the western intellectual tradition? The answer is one we have already encountered: it is precisely because he believes that the best way to replace a system of thought is by showing that its insights have already been included, but with a broader vista, in the new system of thought. He wants us to see, for example, that his understanding of the reciprocity of activity and passivity in the intellect is a fuller and deeper understanding of what Aquinas was after with the Aristotelian concepts of active and passive intellect; he wants us to understand that subject–object mutual interpenetration is what makes best sense of the Aristotelian claim that the intellect is in a certain way all things.

It is therefore to some extent a rhetorical strategy. But, it is worth asking to what extent this may be read as *merely* a rhetorical strategy, that is to say, whether at the end of the day it turns out that there is not actually any correspondence between von Balthasar's view and that of his source. To affirm this would be, I think, too facile. Von Balthasar seems to believe that there is substantive agreement and not merely cosmetic agreement, and our interpretations must start from that premise. Of course, we may still decide after careful consideration that only a distorted reading of Aquinas would allow von Balthasar to conclude that there is concord: that would have to be determined on a case by case basis.

We turn, thus, to a brief consideration of some of von Balthasar's specific sources. Von Balthasar is notoriously well read; to go into all of his sources, even in brief detail, would require a lengthy study of its own and more erudition than most of us can claim. I intend only to point out the sources which are most important for the development of his metaphysics. This shrinks the field down to Plato, Aquinas, Hegel, Heidegger, and Bonaventure. Of course, the make-up of the list can itself be disputed; such dispute would in fact be a substantive disagreement with the interpretive reading offered here. Even in that case, however, I think the figures chosen have to appear on any list of von Balthasar's most important sources of his philosophical thought; whether they suffice or not, they must surely be recognized.

A. PLATO AND THE QUESTION OF PLATONISM

Von Balthasar maintains throughout his works a sharp distinction between Neo-Platonism and Platonism. The two are not the same, and he is most certainly a Platonist and not a Neo-Platonist. Yet, he is aware that there is sufficient confusion about what the distinction between these two might be that his works would run the risk of getting him classified as a Neo-Platonist.[16] What is the difference?

Briefly (the difference will be discussed at more length later),[17] Platonism parses the relationship between God and the world with analogy, while Neo-Platonism parses it with identity. Neo-Platonism is therefore, in his view, some form of pantheism. Thus he can refer casually to the "pantheistic dress of Neo-Platonism" (CL 29).

Von Balthasar's relation to Platonism, on the other hand, is one of the most undeniable of his philosophical influences. The very conception of the Triptych rests upon a positive valuation of the Platonic understanding of being as qualified by transcendental properties. Further, participation plays an important role in his metaphysics, and this is a favorite theme of Platonists. Other Platonic intuitions are clearly present, including certain notions about mediation and the nature of causality (as expressed in the exemplarity borrowed from Bonaventure).

In spite of this, there are also some very important ways in which von Balthasar will want to distance himself from Plato and Platonism, even going so far as embracing an Aristotelian view instead. There are two specific disagreements with Plato: the first is concerning the positivity of the non-ideal world, and the second is concerning the ideal world itself.

Plato's valuation of the world of ideas is such that it reduces our world to a world of shadows, a lack of reality; it is the realm of becoming, and as such it is unstable and insecure. It is the result of a fall: in truth, we belong with the gods, contemplating the forms, and we have fallen into these bodies as tombs due to our inattention. This is, for von Balthasar, unacceptable. Part of the reason is Christological: the fact of the Incarnation tells a different story about not just corporeality but also historicity. But beyond this, more fundamentally, the problem turns out to be trinitarian in nature. Because Plato has not understood the Trinity, he has not been able to find a way to affirm that the other, even the non-divine other, is good in itself.[18]

All positivity has migrated to the ideal world, the world of forms. This too comes in for strong critique by von Balthasar. It is, in fact, the most consistently critiqued Platonic notion. The specifics of this critique will be covered later;[19] for now, it is enough to note that this is the point where von Balthasar thinks we must follow Aristotle rather than Plato.

These two claims are of course no small part of Platonism; von Balthasar's disagreement with them constitute a serious departure from the Platonic program. Thus, while the influence of Platonism on von Balthasar's thought is fundamental and undeniable, he must at best be considered a modified Platonist. The term cannot be applied to him without serious qualification.

B. AQUINAS

Aquinas is a major player in von Balthasar's thought. He dominates the first volume of the *Theologic*, and makes a good showing at the opening of the second volume before getting drawn into a conflict with Bonaventure (*TL*II.161–70) from which Bonaventure ultimately emerges victorious (*TL*II.174 ff.). There is thus no shortage of literature on the importance of Aquinas to von Balthasar's project.[20]

Yet it is undeniable that Aquinas does in the end get superseded. The final evaluation of him is not as negative as that given to Plotinus or even Plato, but there is a palpable sense of disappointment in the treatment afforded him in *The Glory of the Lord*: "Beauty is seldom a central concern for Saint Thomas Aquinas, and for the most part his discussion is dependent on material presented to him by tradition. He calmly reviews this inherited material and tries to harmonize the elements that pour in upon him from Augustine, Denys, Aristotle, Boethius, and his master, Albert, without, so it would seem, making an original contribution of his own to aesthetics in the strict sense" (*GL*IV.393). The disappointment is obviously relative to the particular concern of the beautiful in the realm of theology: von Balthasar is critiquing Aquinas for not seeing its importance. Is this then why von Balthasar is not more of a Thomist? Hardly; von Balthasar will go on to say that it only *seems* that Aquinas has not made an original contribution. His actual contribution is his understanding of the real distinction between essence and existence, which will transform all subsequent thought about beauty.

The real distinction is, to von Balthasar's mind, the greatest Thomistic achievement. He praises Maximus for anticipating it,[21] and it is the main reason Aquinas gets pride of place in *Theologic* I. The role of this distinction in von Balthasar's thought will become apparent in what follows; but it rescues Aquinas from what otherwise may well have been a bored dismissal.[22]

In spite of this significant accomplishment, Aquinas is constantly playing second fiddle to Bonaventure in the Triptych. In some ways, it is because Aquinas is not enough of a Platonist.[23] But ultimately, it all comes down to the disagreement between Aquinas and Bonaventure over the choice of the formal object of theology: for Aquinas, it is God, while for Bonaventure, it is Christ.[24] This is decisive: von Balthasar's Christocentrism and exemplarism mean that it must be Christ who stands atop the system. This difference between Aquinas and Bonaventure colors their relative understandings of the analogy of being, which is of prime concern for von Balthasar; this means that Aquinas's doctrine of the analogy of being will not be sufficient for von Balthasar's purposes.[25]

Lastly, Aquinas does not escape the suspicion of semi-nominalism, the idea that the divine essence is something which lies behind the divine persons.[26] This is a suspicion that is much harder to pin on Bonaventure.[27] If the formal object of theology is God and not specifically Christ, the door is not so thoroughly shut on semi-nominalism as von Balthasar would wish.

C. HEGEL

Von Balthasar's relationship with Hegel is, if anything, even more complicated than his relation to Aquinas. On the one hand, Hegel is an example of the entire Neo-Platonic stream that von Balthasar not only criticizes, but from which he must take care to distinguish himself. He is most likely to be misunderstood to be one of them, and so he must give special attention to show how this is not the case. Hegel is, in fact, the highest exemplar of this stream, the true successor to Plotinus, and so is to be harshly criticized.

On the other hand, Hegel has deeply shaped von Balthasar's understanding of freedom, and there are many other Hegelian marks on the Balthasarian system. Von Balthasar will in fact speak of the "enormous harvest" of German idealism,[28] and it is particularly Hegel who heads this stream.

This is a sensitive point in the evaluation of von Balthasar's achievement. A deep theological analysis would be required to show the pivotal role that freedom plays in von Balthasar's system; yet already here in the present study of the metaphysics we will see that freedom is a significant feature that does a lot of systemic work. But the understanding of freedom that von Balthasar applies is one that owes much to Hegel. This means that a large amount of reasoning power is given over to Hegel by transitivity, and more of von Balthasar's system than would at first appear stands or falls with a positive valuation of Hegel's notion of *Geist*.

Thus, whether positively or negatively, Hegel looms large. He is treated several times at length in the Triptych.[29] The complicated relationship appears very clearly in *Theologic* III, when von Balthasar, on his way to constructing what he calls a "Spirit-Christology," turns to Hegel as one who has done most in this area. Hegel receives a generally sympathetic treatment before being booted out of the realm of true Spirit-Christology. It is particularly Hegel's understanding of the Spirit that disqualifies him (namely, that it is not personal); but this is really a Christological disagreement at heart: such a person-less Spirit within a philosophical system controlled by the concept of *Geist* shows that personhood, and particularly personhood in Christ, has not yet become the ground of philosophical reflection.

D. HEIDEGGER

There is much less direct interaction with Heidegger than with Hegel. However, there is perhaps no less noticeable a dependence. It is difficult to imagine how the phenomenological analysis of worldly truth in *Theologic* I could be carried out apart from Heidegger's thought. From the opening assumption of truth as unveiledness to the dynamics of the subject-object structure, Heidegger has left a deep and indelible mark on the Balthasarian edifice.

Unlike Hegel, Heidegger does not receive extended treatments in the Triptych. He is most often recognized from the assumption of his language, though occasionally his name comes forward to quickly move the discussion along. We see him mentioned both positively and negatively in the same breath in the following passage: "Wonder at Being is not only the beginning of thought, but—as Heidegger sees—also the permanent element (ἀρχή) in which it moves. But this means—contrary to Heidegger—that it is not only astonishing that an existent being can wonder at Being in its own distinction from Being, but also that Being as such by itself to the very end 'causes wonder,' behaving as something to be wondered at, something striking and worthy of wonder" (GL V.614–615).

In spite of this strong dependence, the final word on Heidegger taken as a whole is negative. He is ultimately lumped in with Hegel as insufficiently clear on the distinction between God and the world: in other words, he belongs to the Neo-Platonic stream, and so has failed to ground his thinking in a principle of analogy.[30] This is also, as we shall see over the course of this study, a Christological failing.[31]

In the end, all of the thinkers mentioned above, in spite of the great influence they have on the final shape on von Balthasar's thought, fall short. He ultimately takes leave of each one of them, and the underlying reason is always the same: their systems are insufficient to ground a Christology of the sort he desires.

E. BONAVENTURE

That brings us to Bonaventure. Surely it will not be the case that Bonaventure, the most Christocentric theologian of the Scholastic tradition, will be rejected on Christological grounds. And in fact, he is not. It is to a large extent the robust Christology of Bonaventure that gives him pride of place among all of von Balthasar's sources.

It is difficult to understate the importance of Bonaventure to von Balthasar. Von Balthasar will turn to him again and again, borrowing both conceptuality and language. The conceptuality he borrows is the exemplarity that becomes central to von Balthasar's own understanding of the analogy of being, the key concept in all of Balthasarian thought. Bonaventure is in fact so key to von Balthasar's thought that any invocation of him is sure to be a sign of a major moment in the system. So much so that the reader is cued to pay close attention to the idea being developed whenever the name of Bonaventure appears in the text.[32]

Bonaventure receives the lion's share of attention in *The Glory of the Lord* volume 2, where he is offered as the great synthesizer who says better what the other authors in that volume have said: and, as has been mentioned, Aquinas is constantly transcended in the direction of Bonaventure in *Theologic* volume 2. It can be said without hesitation that no substantive mark on the theological vision is deeper than that of Bonaventure. The ways in which this colors the fundamental metaphysical choices will become clear in this study: the version of the Analogy Thesis von Balthasar adopts, the relation of trinitarian procession to creation (*proportionalitas*), and therefore the idea which is above all Balthasarian, that Christ is the concrete analogy of being. All of this only becomes possible in the light of Bonaventurean commitments.

But even Bonaventure can take von Balthasar only so far. They too ultimately part ways, but not this time over the question of Christology. Instead, it is the Spirit that causes them to separate. Bonaventure's understanding of trinitarian processions is not robust enough to ground the Spirit-Christology of the final volume of *Theologic*, and therefore he too must be dismissed. But he is the last of von Balthasar's sources to go: he has survived longer than any other, and is the clearest antecedent to von Balthasar in the theological tradition.[33]

Before leaving this question of von Balthasar's influences, I want to say a word about one of von Balthasar's habits, namely that of making broad, sweeping generalizations or characterizations, like "Asian religion."[34] This is of course distasteful to the contemporary scholar. Usually such unfortunate excesses may be corrected by the demonstration that the reality in question is in fact more complex than the author has allowed for, which is usually done by means of reference to more text than the author has examined. But von Balthasar's erudition gives us pause here; whatever we think we might urge against him to show that he is wrong is something he has likely read. We are forced to conclude that these pronouncements do not proceed from ignorance. We may of course still choose to dismiss them as intolerable intellectual vanity, but it is worth at least considering just what von Balthasar thought he was conveying by such claims.

If one stops to look longer in this way, the most charitable conclusion is that such statements are the result of the synthetic process, which sees beneath all things deeper unity and connection than casually appears. In that way and for that reason von Balthasar may not be as wrong as our contemporary tastes might like to hastily conclude. More importantly, such synthetic moments, whatever their adequacy or inadequacy with reference to their objects, tell us an enormous amount about the synthesizer, precisely because he has synthesized in *this* way and not another.

This is important to bear in mind if we are not to bring a series of criticisms to bear on von Balthasar which would be fair if we were to take von Balthasar as attempting to do work in a field not his own, but which are in fact not at all to the point. If the task is to understand von Balthasar, it is only marginally interesting whether or not his reading of Hölderlin gets the poet *right*;[35] what is much more important is that von Balthasar thought that *this* type of material could be drawn from *this* type of poet.

III. Point of Departure

We have already spoken of the vast nature of the Balthasarian oeuvre. As a consequence, his legacy is in a somewhat confused state of disarray: no small number of studies of his thought are extant, many of which quite excellently elucidate their chosen theme. Yet among them all, taken singly and collectively, there is a lack of synthesis in evidence. And so we begin to see, as a second stage of scholarly reflections, short guides and primers designed to initiate one into the towering edifice that is von Balthasar's thought.[36] There is clearly a need, acknowledged by all, for help in approaching von Balthasar.

The problem is created by von Balthasar himself, and in particular, by two aspects of his work. The first is, as has been noted, a problem of *scope*. Both the amount of material he wrote and the range of topics covered make the bar for entry into a scholarly understanding of his work dauntingly high. But there is a second aspect which complicates our ability to assess and assimilate his works into a scholarly discourse, and that is his method. Not only the way in which he expresses particular ideas, but even the nature of the ideas he discusses and the number of them expresses a certain lack of attention to a proper (or even reasonable) ordering of material. He is far from the first to speak theologically in highly poetic, rhetorical, and metaphorical ways. But he is in very exclusive company in speaking in this way about such blatantly philosophical topics as the problem of universals. The result is that he often speaks in an incomplete or non-precise way about topics that seem by their very nature to require the utmost precision.

This of course has led some to despair of any systemic principle which could be used to organize the disparate material: von Balthasar is simply not a systematic theologian, and must be read in a different way; the result of his work is not a theological system, but a series of interesting studies and reflections, or explorations, and so on.[37]

It might seem that von Balthasar shared this opinion of his own work, based on the following comment: "All this is what every Christian knows in a spontaneous and unselfconscious way and what he strives to live out. What I am trying to do is to express this in a form in which all the dimensions and tensions of life remain present instead of being sublimated in the abstractions of a 'systematic' theology" (*Retrospect* 98–99). However, to take this in support of the claim that there is no Balthasarian system would be contrary to the whole thrust of the essays that make up *My Work in Retrospect*, which are concerned to *organize* the enormous material von Balthasar has produced. This desire does not decrease with age but increases, such that in the final reflection (written in 1988, the year of his death), von Balthasar sets himself to the question "what, fundamentally, was I trying to say?" (*Retrospect* 111). He attempts to answer this question by laying out a *post facto* logic of the development of central themes in his thought: this is, in fact, the closest von Balthasar ever got to the type of project I am pursuing here. The enemy in the above passage is thus not a system *per se*, but the type of systematic theology that abstracts from historicity, losing itself in the realms of ideal abstraction.

So, while it is certainly true that von Balthasar's style of writing and argumentation is not what we would call "systematic," such that the three volumes of *The Glory of the Lord*, *Theodrama*, and *Theologic* do not constitute a systematic theology, it is a fundamental assumption of my project that these do in fact constitute a theological *system*. It does not follow from the fact that von Balthasar eschewed the systematic approach to presenting and arguing his theology that he therefore also abandoned any desire or intention of unity and completion in the presentation of the theological vision. The very form of the work, spread as it is across three parts, each corresponding to a transcendental property of Being which, taken together, are united in the meta-transcendental unity of the fullness of Being, disallows such a conclusion.

But there is more: one of the reasons why the quest continues for a synthetic reading of the Balthasarian corpus which would at the same time be accessible to the non-specialist is that the experience of reading von Balthasar belies the claim that there is not a unified, coherent vision that is being presented. We are everywhere, from the opening salvos of early works such as *The Cosmic Liturgy* to the closing pages of the *Epilogue* struck by the sense that we have entered into a singular project oriented toward a particular focal point, which ought to be able to lend coherence and structure to the whole once it has been brought into view.

Scholarly attempts to bring this whole into view flounder largely on what turns out to be an organizational principle. Von Balthasar rarely thinks things from their ground to their conclusion, subsequently laying them out in this order for us to see. Rather, he moves organically from topic to topic, and when it is clear that something must be said about the philosophical grounding to establish his argument, he often interrupts himself to do so (or just as often, tells you to look somewhere else in his vast oeuvre for it). Thus, any attempt to construct a synthesis will have to take a wide view of the corpus, but also will have to wander from text to text, reconstructing what is, in effect, the proper logical order of ideas. Such a method can leave one with the suspicion that the interpreter is picking and choosing passages that suit the argument at hand; the only way to sufficiently assess such claims is by an examination of the passages in their original contexts to see if they really do seem to say what the interpreter claims they are saying.

I have painted a picture of von Balthasar as a synthesizer who has a greater eye on the use to which he can put the work than to the original situation of the work itself. In many ways, comments he has made about others may be understood also about his own project. A few of these are instructive, and perhaps serve as helpful warnings:

> How ridiculous those grumblers are, who typecast a Christian thinker with some particular label—for example, Christocentrism—and then stamp as tasteless excess whatever they cannot arrange, in an obvious concentric way, around not simply that theme but the very term itself. The freedom of the mind proves itself not least in one's unshakable ability to change perspective, to see things at one time from behind, at another from below or from above. It also consists in the possibility of changing one's mode of expression, of saying the same thing in different ways, and in the ability to take the depths of conceptual perspective into consideration so that one does not always speak on the same level. [. . .] Thinkers of the class of Maximus Confessor are not simply trivial compilers or passive reservoirs; they are creators, who can work, surely, with additional material but who also know how to arrange the pieces according to their own architectural design (*CL* 57).

The following is said of Bonaventure: "At a superficial level he could indeed appear simply to occupy a privileged place of convergence and confluence of all the theological tendencies that from many sources water the mid-thirteenth century and make it fruitful: he could appear as the heart, wide as the world, that offers a place of shelter to each influence, that synthesises them all" (*GL* II.261).

In addition, the following statements, made about Karl Barth's theology, could also be used to describe von Balthasar's theology: "Because Christ is the measure of all things, no contradiction between God and the world can break in upon the depths of this compatibility" (*Barth* 114); "now the thought of the incarnation takes over and determines all questions of method" (ibid.).

With this last, we arrive at the question that marks the true "point of departure" for von Balthasar, the person of Christ. Von Balthasar's favorite metaphor for this privileged position is "midpoint" or "center."[38] Involved in this choice (though who can say which direction the causality flowed) is the importance von Balthasar will place on mediation. Christ, as the one who is the midpoint between God and humanity, not by being partly each and therefore other than each, but rather by being in himself entirely and internally what each of them is, is therefore able to communicate something significant between them. *Communication* here is closer in sense to modern English *transmission*—something of what God is has been given over to humanity, and humanity in its innermost possibilities is lifted up into the Godhead.

This notion of communication bases itself on the fundamental conceptuality of how causality works: participation. Only that which is the midpoint and therefore capable of mediating between two realities is capable of creating a space of participation (*mitteilung*, a sharing along with another in which one is not sharing something extrinsic, as when two children share a toy, but something intrinsic, as when husband and wife share the fullness of who they are). Ultimately, the picture is Platonic;[39] and to von Balthasar only such a picture is able to allow sufficient room for the theological claims required about the work and, more importantly, the person of Christ.

These claims can be best seen in concrete form in *A Theology of History*. This book is concerned with the problem of grounding the value of the unique, which is in effect to ask how it is possible to have a robustly positive view of historicity. Philosophy produces an unsolvable problem, namely that it is "philosophically impossible for one human person, who as such is nothing other than one specimen of the human genus or species (the species whose dignity it is that all its members are unique persons)—it is impossible for one such person to be raised to a position of absolute dominance and hence, fundamentally, to become the center point of all persons and their history" (*TH* 13–14). It is a result of this philosophical reflection that we recognize that any path to salvation "could be historical only in an external sense: if it is really to have validity for all, to be a universal and valid way, its basis would have to be in essentiality: the essence of man, of destiny, of the cosmos as a whole" (*TH* 14).

The action of God in the wonder of the Incarnation steps into this philosophical quandary, exploding it from within. Here, a single man is raised to the level of the unique while remaining consubstantial with other humans, our brother. The uniqueness required for his universal validity cannot be such that it endangers the commonality between him and us.[40] Here is the solution to the quandary: "It is evident that if one of us is existentially one with God's word in God's redeeming act, he is thereby, in his uniqueness, raised to become the norm of our being in the normal of our concrete history, both that of the individual and that of the race" (*TH* 17).

This has, it turns out, direct consequences for metaphysics: it means that metaphysics cannot go on about its business as if this hadn't happened, nor can it hold itself impervious to the methods of sacred science, remaining aloof in its own independent right to study the one object of metaphysics and theology with the proper tools of metaphysics.[41] Finally, it cannot simply become theology either,[42] because this would ultimately not respect the integrity of the creaturely and historical realm; it would be the triumph of essentiality over history. There is an incommensurability between theology and every other discipline;[43] but because this does not ground the collapsing of all disciplines into theology, it means that every discipline must go to theology to learn its norm. That norm, in all things, is Christ.

This means that von Balthasar is out to construct a system that is metaphysically and theologically Christocentric; it will be, as Barth said of his own *magnum opus*, grounded in "Jesus Christ as its basis, goal and content" (*CD* I.1.6). Therefore, it is Christ as midpoint and first principle that will be the point of departure for the Balthasarian metaphysic. Once this has been seen and taken as a truth by the theologian, it is not possible to simply return to secular metaphysics and take the remaining necessary assumptions from there; from this point forward, every metaphysical assumption, deduction, or utterance of any kind must be re-examined in light of this new norm.

Now, insofar as metaphysics is concerned with first principles, and takes as its point of departure that which is most fundamental, it is worthwhile to consider why it is Christ specifically and not the Trinity that holds the first place. At first glance, the Trinity has a good claim to this place: it is more fundamental than Christ because the fact of Trinity is the condition of the possibility of the person of Christ; the Trinity also contains reference to that person in the Godhead who is related to Christ as origin, and therefore seems to be (at least in the order of logic) more fundamental than Christ. After all, once every specter of subordinationism has been laid to rest, there is still a discernible priority among the persons, which in the Western tradition has run from Father to Son to Holy Spirit. Von Balthasar himself would say that the Trinity is the first "moment" in the life of God—why then is this not chosen as the basis for the metaphysic?

The answer is equally simple and crucial for the right understanding of von Balthasar's thought: metaphysics is concerned with creation, that is to say, with created realities, and thus its primary reference is to that which is the archetype of all creation. Christ's archetypal relationship to creation will be considered at length in the next three chapters; for now, it is enough to assert that it is Christ who is this archetype, and it is in virtue of this that he occupies the central role. The Trinity, properly speaking, is *above* the metaphysic, while at the same time grounding it (to the extent that it grounds the reality of Christ). Thus, though God three-in-one is the most fundamental reality, it is that person who took on created being and is its archetype who stands at the center.[44]

It must be noted at this point that Christ is only distinguished from the Father and the Holy Spirit by virtue of his person—in all else they are not merely equal, but in fact identical. Therefore, if the midpoint of the metaphysic is to be Christ and not the Trinity, we must infer that it can only be as *person* that Christ occupies the central place.[45]

If, therefore, the midpoint or first principle of the metaphysics is a person, it follows that personhood has been placed squarely at the center of the metaphysics. And if the first word in metaphysical discourse is personality, then we are dealing with a metaphysics that is personal in a way that causes it to differ distinctly from the major metaphysical competitors.

This difference between von Balthasar's metaphysic and those he inherits is a point that unfortunately may receive only passing mention here. The results are of fundamental importance, however; for however much there may be a Platonic theology in intimate conversation with the transcendental qualities of being, and whatever room is left for the truly theological dimension after the ontological reductions of Heidegger's later work, the divine as *personal* remains a subsequent interpretive move, whether made by the author or by the reader. For, while one may attempt to identify the Platonic form of the Good with a personal God, the texts themselves are ambiguous and patient of multiple interpretations. Heidegger forces us to work even harder to identify the ontological first principle as it appears in the moment of phenomenological encounter with any sense of personality, and certainly offers no clear and unambiguous claim that such a reality is the first moment of the system.[46] Even Aristotle, with his emphasis on the particular realities, universalized the particulars, thereby stripping them of their concretivity.[47] At best, this approach could enshrine personality *as such* in the first place, but never a single, concrete *person*.

However, when, as with von Balthasar, a person becomes the center, then the metaphysics is not just built on personality, but is characterized as *personal*. The immediate advantage is that now the theological reality, an absolute being who is three persons and one God, is not forced to submit to a greater principle in order to make an appearance within the metaphysical realm. No longer are the rules based upon transcendent goodness, to which God must conform at the risk of imperiling the very fabric of reality. Now it is God, in the Trinitarian specificity of personhood (and therefore *this* divine person and not *that* one), that is the inviolate and inviolable principle of all things. This is a step he saw prepared for him in Maximus: "Still, with the appearance of a new emphasis on existence and person, alongside the classical Greek concern with essence (οὐσία), an important step had been taken in the direction of an ontology of created being" (*CL* 64). In such a system, because of the unity of their first principles in one person, we will speak not of a *rapprochement*between theology and metaphysics, but rather of a *unity* whose character will turn out to be one, not of identity, but of analogy.

IV. The Road to Be Travelled: Methodological Comments

Any reading of von Balthasar must despair in its beginning of attaining any sort of comprehensive scope. Even if the entire corpus is able to be brought to bear as subject matter and source, many critical passages will have to go undiscussed due to the simple limits imposed by the unity of a single study. One must embrace this up front, and endeavor to say things that are true and representative such that they will be continually confirmed by further reading, rather than weakened or challenged.

In light of this, it is necessary to say a few words about the scope of text that will be used to substantiate the claims about von Balthasar in this book. I have in large part confined myself to the books which some might consider more academic: that is to say, many of the delightful little books about various topics from Mary to meditation do not come in for much discussion here. I believe these books may be taken as applications to particular cases of general principles to be found elsewhere in the corpus.

The bulk of the text examined comes from the Triptych, the volumes comprising *The Glory of the Lord*, *Theodrama*, *Theologic*, and the *Epilogue*. This is von Balthasar's mature constructive work, and even his own reflections on his productivity focus our attention on it. However, several other works are important and will be referred to extensively: *Cosmic Liturgy*, *The Theology of Karl Barth*, and *A Theology of History*. These are not exclusively the texts that will be used (as a glance at the bibliography will show), but they form the core of the texts from which the argument will be developed.

Thus, the central texts could be divided between primarily historical works (*Cosmic Liturgy*, *The Theology of Karl Barth*) and constructive works (*A Theology of History*,the Triptych). The division may not be neat, given the depth of historical engagement throughout the Triptych and especially in *The Glory of the Lord*, but it is important. For the type of historical engagements to be found in the constructive works differ from the historical engagements of von Balthasar's earlier period, and precisely in this way: the former are engagements which are carried out with an eye to the synthetic, constructive project. They are more concerned with the usefulness of the text to von Balthasar than to explicating the text in its own context. This gives them a certain priority.

The historical texts are of great importance because in them we see von Balthasar doing the type of analysis on others that I am doing on him in this book. The way von Balthasar reads Maximus and Barth may be taken as a guide to how to go about reading von Balthasar. To this end, it is worth reflecting at a little more length on von Balthasar's work with Maximus.

What von Balthasar describes through the first chapter of *Cosmic Liturgy* is the way Maximus builds his metaphysics on Christology. The particular outlines of Maximus's system are not those of von Balthasar's; but what von Balthasar has found in Maximus is someone who is engaged in the same type of project as von Balthasar will eventually engage in. This is the reason so much of what is said about Maximus, Bonaventure, and Barth could be said about von Balthasar as well. He is praising them for doing the thing that he himself sees as needful.

Thus, in the section in *Cosmic Liturgy* on God, we see the tight interconnectedness of analogy, the God–world relation, and the Trinity in von Balthasar's thought. Analogy measures the distance between the Creator and the creation, and as such it grounds the real distinction between essence and existence on the Trinitarian distinctions. This section thus constantly anticipates what is said about the Trinity in *Theologic* II, but it also contains *in nuce* what is to be the final statement of both the likeness and the greater unlikeness between God and creatures, namely aseity expressed in the identity (in God) and non-identity (in creatures) of essence and existence. Von Balthasar clearly thinks that analogy is the great accomplishment of the Maximian synthesis: this is stated as the conclusion to the whole section on Maximus's doctrine of God.[48]

This project, similar to von Balthasar's historical projects, aims primarily at explication. I intend to show the structure of von Balthasar's thought on its own terms. This reading will therefore be sympathetic, as I believe understanding is fundamentally an act of sympathy. It will not be slavishly so, for sympathy need not be blind; but my goal is more to get von Balthasar right than to determine whether the reader should approve of the particular choices made or not.

As a last word of introduction, I ought to comment on the translations used in this volume. Von Balthasar is known to the English-speaking world through the very detailed translations available from Ignatius press. The amount of labor and erudition that went into the production of these volumes is in itself a worthy imitation of von Balthasar's own intellectual labors. However, some problems in the published translations are significant enough to warrant reference to the original German texts. Whenever possible, I have used the published English versions of von Balthasar's works. When it seemed that reference to the German text was advisable, I have included both the German text and my own English translations.

Notes

1. For von Balthasar, there can be no theologian who is not at the same time a metaphysician: "Da die Frage nach dem Sein als solchem die Grundfrage der Metaphysik ist, ist sie für den Theologen nicht zu umgehen, für ihn folgt daraus bloß, daß er ex professo kein Theologe sein kann, ohne zugleich Metaphysiker zu sein, wie . . . eine Metaphysik, die sich weigerte, Theologie zu sein, ihren eigenen Gegenstand verkennen und verleugnen würde" (*TLg* II.159). [Because the question of being as such is the fundamental question of metaphysics, it is not to be passed over by the theologian. For him it simply follows that he *ex professo* can not be a theologian without at the same time being a metaphysician, as . . . a metaphysics which refused to be theology would misunderstand and disavow its own proper object.] (All translations not from a published volume are mine.)

2. This seems to be confirmed by von Balthasar in *TD* V.65, where logic is subordinated to God. The inescapability of referencing some logical intuitions in the first moments of building a metaphysical system does not change this fundamental situation; it only points out how difficult the task of building metaphysics is. If the Cartesian/skeptical value of starting metaphysical reflection from a blank slate (or as close as one can get) is rejected and some evidence is permitted as given, primordial, and so on, then the fact that one cannot begin reflection without some intuitions and premises in hand is much less distressing.

3. That is, the combined masterwork whose parts are *The Glory of the Lord, Theodrama, Theologic*, and the *Epilogue*.

4. Logic is not truth as an epistemological reality, nor is it the beings on which this knowledge rests; it is rather the inner *structure* of truth, the system of relations that create truth as such.

5. Von Balthasar himself identifies the first of these as the most basic question of metaphysics: "The direction of the meandering historical paths of western Metaphsyics becomes straightforward and simple if we centre the chaotic fragments around the authentic metaphysical question: 'Why is there anything at all and not simply nothing?'" (*GL* V.613).

6. Carefully considered, this passage only asserts that, following both the etymology of "metaphysics" and the changed nature of the science of physics, the original referent of "metaphysics" can no longer truly be designated by that word. The whole point of introducing "meta-anthropology" is not to talk about something different, but to *make sure* we do not end up talking about something different.

7. Thus, in von Balthasar's view, metaphysics is never in fact free from theology; however, it makes a great deal of difference whether metaphysicians are aware of the theological situation that conditions their work or not.

8. See also *TL* I.15: "Integration: a program of this nature requires rigorous collaboration between philosophy and theology, but such collaboration is possible only if both disciplines are intrinsically open to each other. But this intrinsic openness is itself possible only on the condition

that we recenter our intellectual effort on thinking through the analogy between the divine archetype and the worldly image from both sides."

9. This book will be important throughout our study, for reasons that will be explained later (chapter 1, IV).

10. See also this passage from *Cosmic Liturgy*, where ontology stands in for philosophy and metaphysics stands in for theology: "The synthesis we have just described is a genuinely transcendental one—or, if one wants to distinguish between ontology and metaphysics, a metaphysical one, which concerns the ultimate basis for created being as such. The syntheses that follow attempt rather to describe created being from within; they are, in a more narrow sense, ontological syntheses. Still, the two realms cannot be cleanly divided. An 'immanent' theory of being finds its final explanation and illumination only in metaphysics, which sets created being against the background of absolute being" (*CL* 154).

11. The question whether he has succeeded or not is not, however, ridiculous.

12. "Maximus' whole philosophical undertaking [with regard to Christology and soteriology], which we have described, stands in service of this highest synthesis, which is purely biblical; its function is to prevent the creature, understood in its essential identity, from being overwhelmed and dazzled in this loving encounter with God, openly or implicitly, to such a degree that it is reduced merely to the level of an 'appearance.' By preserving the metaphysical rights of humanity—in the human nature of Christ and in the ordinary human person—Maximus provides the support for man's right to grace as well" (CL 55).

13. Chapter 1, II

14. This is a version of the German proverb "Wer mehr Wahrheit sieht, hat mehr recht" ("Whoever sees more truth is more right"). Von Balthasar quotes this proverb in *Epilogue* 15. This idea is fundamental to von Balthasar's whole project, but can be seen most distinctly at work in *Truth Is Symphonic: Aspects of Christian Pluralism* (San Francisco: Ignatius, 1987) and *In the Fullness of Faith: On the Centrality of the Distinctively Catholic* (San Francisco: Ignatius, 1988).

15. *Glory of the Lord*, 280–313.

16. H III.1.1.17, footnote 4: "Ich mußte darauf gefaßt sein, ehe man mich auch nur ausreden ließ, zum alten neuplatonischen Eisen geworfen zu werden." [I had to be prepared to be thrown out as an outdated Neo-Platonist before anyone let me finish speaking.] He goes on to quote H.-E. Bahr, who does just that, saying that von Balthasar is in pursuit of a Neo-Platonic Christian mysticism.

17. Chapter 3, I.A.

18. The ground of the positivity of otherness in the Trinity is discussed in chapter 3, especially section II.A, and chapter 6, I.A.1.

19. Chapter 4, II.A.

20. For a few examples, see: Steffen Losel, "Love Divine, All Loves Excelling: Balthasar's Negative Theology of Revelation" (*Journal of Religion* 82, no. 4 [Oct. 2002]); Larry Chapp, *The God Who Speaks: Hans Urs von Balthasar's Theology of Revelation* (San Francisco: International Scholars, 1996); Nicholas J. Healy, *The Eschatology of Hans Urs von Balthasar* (Oxford: Oxford University Press, 2005).

21. *CL* 71.

22. Peter Henrici warns that von Balthasar's relationship to Aquinas is very complicated: "von Balthasar's relation to Thomas is neither that of an enthusiastic admirer and follower, nor a mere exercise in ecclesiastical duty" ("The Philosophy of Hans Urs von Balthasar," in *Hans Urs von Balthasar: His Life and Work*. Edited by David Schindler [San Francisco: Ignatius, 1991], 162).

23. Thus, when Larry Chapp says that "the old Platonic-Plotinian concept of a direct participation in divinity by way of God's 'emanations' is changed by Thomas into a mediated participation, that is, God's 'emanation' of Being must not itself be hypostasized, must not be 'divinized'. […] If God's emanation of Being to the world was hypostasized, then we would be right back to a metaphysics of identity and this is unacceptable to Christian philosophy" (*God*, 72), the problem is not so much a misunderstanding of Thomas as a misunderstanding of *Platonism*.

Because we have, to von Balthasar's mind, lost the language of analogy (that which separates Platonists from Neo-Platonists), it is doubly challenging for us to untangle von Balthasar's complicated relation to Platonism.

24. "Thus, whether one defines God (Thomas Aquinas) or Christ (Bonaventure) as the formal object of theology [. . .]" (*TL* II.28).

25. "In den Dienst dieses zentralen Satzes stellt Bonaventura seine ganze Lehre von der *Seinsanalogie*, die sehr anders lautet als bei Thomas" (*H* II.297). [Bonaventure places his entire doctrine of the analogy of being, which runs very different than in Thomas, in the service of this central statement.]

26. *TL* II.128 ff., which begins with an appeal to Aquinas, but ends with severe doubts about Aquinas' ability to bring the trinitarian persons into proper focus. The question of nominalism will be discussed in chapter 4, II.A.

27. The central theme of Bonaventure's *Disputed Questions on the Mystery of the Trinity* is that all divine attributes are not only compatible with tri-unity, but in fact must be re-thought according to tri-unity to be properly understood. This is close to von Balthasar's own belief that divine attributes are not the attributes of an essence, but of the persons, and so are modulated by the eternal personal life of the Trinity (cf. *TD* V.66).

28. "Solowjew steht am andern Ende der idealistischen Philosophie, deren gewaltige Ernte er in die christliche Theologie einbringt" (*H* II.17). [Soloviev stands at the other end of idealistic philosophy, whose enormous harvest he brings into Christian theology.]

29. *GL* V.572 ff., *TD* I.54 ff., *TD* I.578 ff., *TD* V.224–27, *TL* III.41ff.

30. See *GL* V.628–29.

31. Perhaps the most noteworthy passage on Heidegger comes in a footnote on *TL* II.134. There, Heidegger's onto-theological problematic is rejected as applying to the trinitarian logic von Balthasar is developing. It is interesting because the immediate context is Aquinas and Augustine, whom von Balthasar is both praising and critiquing; but to the extent that von Balthasar's use of the Trinity to free Aquinas and Augustine from Heidegger's concern is valid, it will be clear that he is even less subject to Heideggerian criticism than they on this point.

32. Among those who recognize the fundamental nature of the Bonaventurean debt, two are worthy of mention: Aidan Nichols says that "Balthasar prefers to take his cue here not from Augustine (and Thomas after him) but from Thomas's Franciscan contemporary, Bonaventure" ("The Theo-logic," in *The Cambridge Companion to Hans Urs von Balthasar*, edited by Edward T. Oakes and David Moss, 158–71. [Cambridge: Cambridge Univ. Press, 2004], 166); this is seconded in John O'Donnell, who says that "Balthasar nevertheless finds himself in disagreement with certain tendencies in [the Augustinian-Thomistic] tradition and aligns himself rather with Bonaventure and the Franciscan school of theology" ("Truth as Love: the Understanding of Truth according to Hans Urs von Balthasar," *Pacifica* 1:2 [1988], 200). Bonaventure is then invoked on the procession of the Holy Spirit (*per modum liberalitatis*), which is a bit ironic, as this is where von Balthasar will ultimately part from Bonaventure. This is, unfortunately, the extent of the acknowledgement of the Bonaventurean debt in O'Donnell's article.

33. In this study, the Trinity in its proper dimension remains beyond our reach, for there metaphysics must give way to theology. We will therefore also stop short of the rejection of Bonaventure. Our field of inquiry is one in which, for von Balthasar, Bonaventure reigns supreme.

34. See the section on "East and West," *CL* 44ff.

35. See Martin Simon, "Identity and Analogy: Balthasar's Hölderlin' and Hamann" in *The Analogy of Beauty*, John Riches, ed. (Edinburgh: T&T Clark, 1986), 77–104.

36. Aidan Nichols, *A Key to Balthasar: Hans Urs von Balthasar on Beauty, Goodness, and Truth* (Baker: Grand Rapids, 2011); Stephen Wigley, *Balthasar's Trilogy* (T&T Clark: London, 2010); Rodney Howsare, *Balthasar: A Guide for the Perplexed* (T&T Clark: London, 2009); Karen Kilby, *Balthasar: A (Very) Critical Introduction* (Eerdmans: Grand Rapids, 2012).

37. See Thomas O'Meara, "Of Art and Theology: Hans Urs von Balthasar's Systems," *Theological Studies* 42 (Je 1981): 272–76; also, cf. John O'Donnell: "at last Balthasar has completed

the theological synthesis which he proposed over twenty-five years ago. No doubt it is a synthesis. At the same time it is hardly a system" ("Truth as Love: the Understanding of Truth according to Hans Urs von Balthasar," *Pacifica* 1 [1988]: 189).

38. It may rightly be argued that this places von Balthasar's project squarely in the realm of those types of projects Derrida had in his sights in "Structure, Sign and Play in the Discourse of the Human Sciences." It is, it must be noted, a project that is unashamed of metaphysics and ontology, and is equally in violation of onto-theological critiques as that of Jean-Luc Marion in *God without Being*. It is imperative, however, that we do not allow these more recent critiques to control our reading of von Balthasar. For these are not unfortunate features of his system that are to be excised in an attempt to rehabilitate him—they are fundamental structural characteristics without which the entire system collapses. The refusal to allow them would not so much constitute a refutation of von Balthasar as a refusal to enter into conversation with him at all. Von Balthasar explicitly notes Marion's removal of God from the realm of being as a misstep (*TL* II.163, note 9). Von Balthasar's disagreement with Marion will be seen in its proper light in chapter 2, II.B.

39. For von Balthasar, this is developed primarily from the *Symposium*, when Socrates repeats what he heard from Diotima. In von Balthasar's own summary of this passage, Socrates comes to understand that: "Eros is neither God nor man but 'something in between' (μεταξύ), 'a great *daimon*' therefore, 'for the whole of the *daimonic* is between divine and mortal'; he has the task of 'interpreting and transporting human things to the gods and divine things to men'" (*GL* IV.189). He goes on to say that according to this view, "God does not mingle immediately with men: all communication goes through [the *daimon*]" (ibid.).

40. *TH* 16.

41. "We cannot carry on with natural metaphysics, natural ethics, natural jurisprudence, natural study of history, acting as though Christ were not, in the concrete, the norm of everything. Nor can we lay down an unrelated 'double truth', with the secular scholar and scientist on the one hand and the theologian on the other studying the same object without any encounter or intersection between their two methods" (*TH* 18–19).

42. "Nor, finally, can we allow the secular disciplines to be absorbed by theology as though it alone were competent in all cases because Christ alone is the norm" (*TH* 19).

43. "Precisely because Christ is the absolute he remains incommensurate with the norms of this world; and no final accord between theology and the other disciplines is possible within the limits of this world. Refusal of any such agreed demarcation on the part of theology, though it may look like and be called arrogance, is really no more than respect for the methodological demands of its subject" (ibid.).

44. Although the Father is more fundamental than the Son, this does not affect the Son's privileged place with reference to creation: "daß die 'Unterordnung des Sohnes unter den Vater' (von der Paulus spricht) in keiner Weise seine Absetzung von seiner Herrschaft über den Kosmos besagt" (*TLg* II.142). [That the "subordination of the Son under the Father" (of which Paul speaks) in no way means his demotion from lordship over the Cosmos.]

45. What "person" means for von Balthasar here may be illustrated from a passage in the *Theology of History*, where he glosses "personality" as "the psychological center of man's free and reasonable acts, which would not be a center were it not so ontologically" (*TH* 15, note 2). Thus, while on the one hand he seems to be accepting the modernist tendency to read person psychologically, on the other hand he is grounding this in a prior ontological reality. The claim is thus that personality is ontologically central, and as such forms the center of the psychological faculties. It would be a typical Balthasarian deduction to say that this is the appearing in the created realm of that principle on which it is founded, and thus a reflection of the personhood that stands at the metaphysical center.

46. For Heidegger, metaphysics transcends "beings" in rising to ask the question about "Being" as such. His is a perpetual struggle against the way in which beings obscure their ground, annihilate the question about Being. However much the later Heidegger may indicate a connection between Being and God (and even more stringently deny it on onto-theological

grounds), philosophically speaking personhood as such doesn't play a role in grounding the relation of Being to beings, nor in the dynamics of concealedness and openness. See Martin Heidegger, *Introduction to Metaphysics*, Gregory Fried and Richard Polt, trans (New Haven: Yale University Press, 2000). Von Balthasar seems to indicate that he interprets Heidegger as disallowing such a personal principle at the heart of reality in *Epilog* 21.

47. This is clear from the fact that it is *particulars* and not a *specific* particular that is the privileged location for philosophical analysis.

48. "At this point, the whole theory of unity returns to the simple scheme of analogy of being between God and the world: to the absolute transcendence of God and his immanence in created being" (*CL* 114).

2

Exemplarity and Expression
Rejection of the Pure Difference Thesis

At the outset, our task must be to draw von Balthasar's ideas back to a few fundamental ideas that can be taken as foundational for everything else. This requires an examination of the basic metaphysical questions in order to discern where von Balthasar's primary interest (the incarnate Christ) falls. What are the basic metaphysical questions?

Classically speaking, metaphysics must account for the basic ontological questions ("Why is there something rather than nothing?" "What accounts for the fact that there are many things and not just one thing?" "What types of things are there?" and so on), but also for more abstract questions about the types of relations that hold between those realities: causal, formal, ideal, or whatever else (how the list itself is populated is already internal to the frame of reference of some metaphysical system). A sacred metaphysic, or even just one that is involved in a non-polemical conversation with theology, starts with some of these questions already answered, or answered in certain directions. Such a system does not need to busy itself with the question of what the first principle is, or with proving its existence: the first principle is God, and the existence of this first principle is delivered to the system from outside. Now, as we have seen, for von Balthasar this first principle is specifically God in the incarnate Christ, which shows that it is still possible to further nuance this first principle. Such a possibility means that there is at least the possibility of multiple sacred metaphysics with different visions of the one starting point; and, as has been often noted, a small difference in the beginning becomes a large difference in the end.[1]

Nevertheless, the result of this is that von Balthasar's metaphysics will begin *in medias res*, as it were. The first question that can profitably be asked is one that assumes the first principle in God and goes on to ask about the relation that obtains between that which is the source of all reality and those dependent realities themselves. The guiding question must therefore be: [Q] "What is the nature or character of the God-creature relation?" This question is of primary concern for us as we lay the foundations for the Balthasarian system.

I. What Is the Nature of the God-Creature Relation?

Von Balthasar conceives of three ways to answer the question of the nature of the God-creature relation [Q]. One may say that (1) they are totally different, with absolutely nothing in common, (2) they are totally the same, with no difference, or (3) the relationship is somehow in between these two extremes. I will call (1) the Pure Difference Thesis, (2) the Identity Thesis, and (3) the Analogy Thesis.

Here we might wish for more subtlety, expressed in the acknowledgement of more than three options. Isn't it at least plausible to think *a priori* that to create two extremes and then lump everything else in as a *via media* is very likely to caricature the range of possibilities that lie between the two extremes? Put another way, what reason is there to believe that there is only one real way to be neither totally different nor totally the same?

In some sense, von Balthasar could allow the objection, but respond in the following way: even granted that there may be a bewildering panoply of options that fall under the third category, that is a question which must be settled at a later stage of intellectual reflection. In these early moments, the choice is really between genres: what will the general *character* of the metaphysical system be? We will in fact see that it is not only the Analogy Thesis, but also the Pure Difference and Identity Theses that have a vast variety of possible interpretations.

What is gained by such an abstract consideration? It allows one to claim *a priori* but not without evidence that if the Pure Difference Thesis is ruled out as a fitting type of Christian system, then every system that is an example of the Pure Difference Thesis will face the same objections to admission as a sacred metaphysic. But at least as important for von Balthasar is that this schema, to his mind, accurately describes the actual historical options: every attempt to think the problem, whether along with or apart from the question of religion (and there are many fewer of the latter attempts than we might think, according to von Balthasar), must give an answer which may be seen to fall under one of these three types. In other words, he thinks that every historical answer to Q reduces to one of these three types of answers.

No explicit argument is given for this: in some sense, the onus is on the objector to come up with a counter-example. However, throughout von Balthasar's life we see him consistently reducing every possible system to fall under one of these three categories. It is worth mentioning that these three categories line up with the linguistic analysis given by Thomas Aquinas in the *Summa*, where he says that words may be used equivocally (1), univocally (2), or analogically (3).[2] Von Balthasar, like Aquinas, will think that his linguistic analysis correctly cuts reality at its joints, and so these are not just the linguistic possibilities, but also the metaphysical ones. Thus, there is a significant historical precedent for this way of dividing the options.

Returning then to the three options that are answers to Q, we may make a further comment about this preliminary stage of questioning. At this early stage the specifics of von Balthasar's claims about the first principle may be safely bracketed. For while it will ultimately make all the difference that the first principle is not the divine essence or God the Father but Jesus Christ,[3] this first move has more to do with classifying the *type* of system we will be dealing with, and is still patient of many different sorts of content. It will become clear later that only one answer *can* make sense for the particular conception of Christ that von Balthasar has, and it is in fact that conception which is more fundamental: it decides Q, it is not decided by the choice made in response to Q. Nevertheless, once that choice has been made, it becomes the logically (though not causally) prior moment of explanation of the metaphysical system.

Such a bracketing of the specificity of Christ should not cause us concern. von Balthasar himself was willing to follow this very same method in his own constructive work. The first volume of *Theologic* is in fact controlled by the bracketing of the question of the necessary ground of worldly truth in divine truth. Likewise, the third volume of *Theologic* brackets the question of the personhood of the Holy Spirit until its second section. This latter bracketing is very analogous to the type of bracketing our analysis requires here.

A. THE ANALOGY THESIS

Thus, we return to Q, and may say that von Balthasar consistently and emphatically rejects the Pure Difference and Identity Theses and chooses the Analogy Thesis. Over the following chapters I will examine in detail the way he argues historically against each of these, as well as his logical reasons for and against each of these. This will clarify both what von Balthasar wants to safeguard and what he wishes to rule out in the articulation of his metaphysics.

The negative shades (those things that are ruled out) are important to the full vision of the depth and nature of the positive claims about analogy.

The task of articulating this vision within the confines of the Triptych fell necessarily to *The Glory of the Lord*, which, as the first statement in this monumental work, had to lay the groundwork for the whole in addition to revitalizing the theological discourse about beauty. In the first volume, von Balthasar was concerned to argue that divine revelation must be considered not only as true and good, but also as beautiful. He argued that everything in the world is beautiful, and therefore bears a relationship of analogy to the self-revelation of God in history. Thus, the very project of restoring the dimension of the beautiful is to some extent also an apologetic for the choice of the Analogy Thesis over either the Pure Difference or Identity Theses. The entire purpose of *The Glory of the Lord* was to set the stage for an understanding of what precisely the *character* of the likeness and unlikeness that holds between God and creature is.

B. SOURCES

Therefore it is from this project that we will draw von Balthasar's historical rejection of the Pure Difference and Identity Theses and his acceptance of the Analogy Thesis. But where in these seven volumes to look? In the first volume, von Balthasar attempts to sketch the abstract propositions that would guide the entire project, that in fact form the kernel of the vision of the entire project. His next task was to fill these abstract propositions out with historical garb.[4] He intends to present various theologies that "having been marked at [their] centre by the glory of God's revelation, [have] sought to give the impact of this glory a central place in [their] vision" (*GL* II.13). Each of the theologies examined is therefore *representative*, is a historical instance of the abstract principles developed in the first volume. These principles therefore form at best a fundamental theology large enough to embrace the others within itself; at the very least, they form the ground required for such theologies. In either case, von Balthasar is not simply offering a summary of prior theological visions, and then offering his as another in the long line—he is in fact explicating *through* the earlier theologies the conditions necessary for their existence as the sort of theologies von Balthasar's project can approve.

The second volume of *The Glory of the Lord* therefore forms an excellent starting place for our examinations of the roots of the Balthasarian metaphysic. Nevertheless, even so fitting an entry point requires that a few comments be made about scope, for after the theologies of the second volume, there follows a volume on the history of metaphysics proper, and then a volume on the Biblical witness to divine glory. All of this may be taken as various evidence in the historical realm of what was presented abstractly in the first volume. The evidence is massive, and it is a matter of individual judgment whether the sheer volume of it adds in any way to its compellingness. However, as our task here is to trace the systematic outlines and not to recapitulate the mass of Balthasarian evidences, we need only take so much of it as material as will serve to make clear the heart of the system.

The question which then presents itself is this: Which of these three *types* of evidences—theological, philosophical, or Biblical—ought we to take as central for our study? Since our goal is the illumination of the midpoint of the metaphysics, it might seem that it is the volumes on the history of metaphysics that should interest us. Yet because that midpoint is asserted to be Christ, the history of metaphysics can only approach it obliquely, under the codename *being*. Again, it may seem that the Biblical witness, where Christ is revealed to us, presents a strong case. Yet here we have the events presented in such a way that reflection on their relationship to the whole meaning of reality is only incipient—the metaphysics is too far in the background to be properly examined here.[5]

Therefore it is to the theological survey that we must turn. The English edition splits this volume into two volumes after the chapter on Bonaventure, following a distinction von Balthasar himself makes between theologies developed by "official" church theologians and those developed by lay theologians like Dante. The former were preferenced, because they "were able to treat the radiant power of the revelation of Christ both influentially and originally, without any trace of decadence" (*GL* II.15). He goes on to note that "after Thomas Aquinas, theologians of such stature are rare." At that point, the vision is to be found chiefly in the works of lay writers who, though enriched by theological culture, are not engaged in theology as such. von Balthasar points out that this "dividing-line" is not intended to be polemical; "it simply corresponds to an unfortunate but incontestable fact" (ibid.). There is, therefore, such a dividing line in his thought, and a distinction may be made between the theologies that precede it and the theologically informed creative writings that follow it. No more than von Balthasar do I wish to denigrate the achievements and usefulness of the literary works that follow in the succeeding volume; however, for our purposes, theological discourse remains the best suited to the task of illuminating the character of the metaphysic and its influence on the theological system.

These chapters will therefore concern themselves with the first half of the second volume of *Herrlichkeit*, or what is published as the second volume of the English *The Glory of the Lord*, which begins with Irenaeus and goes through Bonaventure. This is not an attempt to read this volume exhaustively; rather, we are after the conceptual high points that bear on the development of the metaphysic. Along the way we will not be concerned with the accuracy of von Balthasar's readings of the figures discussed, but rather with the way he uses his theological material in building his own vision.

It is worth stating that it is precisely the question of the God-creature relationship [Q] that the second volume of *The Glory of the Lord* is ultimately trying to address. The "high points" of the volume are concentrated around statements about the relationship between Creator and creature, a relationship that is ultimately thought to rest in a certain suitability that exists between God and the creature. This key insight, of which all of the theologies represented are worthy instances in von Balthasar's judgment, must be developed through his readings of Irenaeus, Augustine, Denys[6] and Anselm, all to be ultimately surpassed by Bonaventure.

We will not, however, be able to follow von Balthasar's order of presentation. At the end of the day, von Balthasar's understanding of these theologies is not that they all say the same thing, but that they all witness to the same reality. He is after a synthesis arising from them, in which the best insights of each theology may find itself welcomed and even transformed into a higher meaning. But because these insights are derived from an original glimpse of the divine glory, rather than from discursive reflection on fundamentally propositional data, the temporal order of their appearing will not necessarily indicate their logical order. Thus, though Irenaeus wrote before Augustine, the Irenaean insight von Balthasar is interested in requires as a logical prerequisite part of the Augustinian insight.

II. Historical Form of the Rejection of the Pure Difference Thesis

The Pure Difference Thesis, as has been stated, is the claim that the relationship between the Creator and creatures is best described in terms of pure difference. This may be expressed in various ways: a common one is Derrida's *tout âutre*,[7] "wholly other," but one may also arrive at this notion by means of a Heideggerian critique of onto-theology[8] or the type of radical transcendence asserted by most negative theology.[9] What is the common claim is that God is so different from creatures that it is not appropriate to look for any similarity between them. Even when we think we have noticed some similarity, it is in fact only condescension to the feebleness of human understanding. The best theological practice therefore proceeds by negation, and if it must say something positive, it is careful to immediately "unsay" it by qualifying or (in some cases) directly contradicting it.

As mentioned, the Pure Difference Thesis is one that von Balthasar wishes to reject. What this looks like in the form of a historical argument is a deduction of a relationship of exemplarity between God and creatures. Given that there is such a relationship, the Pure Difference Thesis is ruled out. We will follow this deduction in detail before returning to ask what von Balthasar's logical concerns with the Pure Difference Thesis are.

A. ESTABLISHING THE ARCHETYPE

We are at the beginning of von Balthasar's analysis in a historical key of the question with which we opened this chapter, namely: "What is the nature or character of the God-creature relation?" Two methodological paths open themselves to us in this analysis: the path of ana-logy, which is a bottom up approach that begins from created realities and argues from them upward to the divine reality, and the path of kata-logy, which begins with the divine being and then makes deductions about creatures here below. It is clear from the centrality of Christ in the thinking of von Balthasar that the last of these, the katalogical, is to be preferred. Nevertheless, to start there would be to jump straight to the conclusion, and much of what is fitting and consonant about the steps in the argument that lead to that conclusion would be lost. At this early stage, therefore, our approach must be analogical.[10]

1. THE ANALOGICAL APPROACH: FIRST CAUSE FROM BELOW

It is therefore fitting that we begin with Augustine, whose path, von Balthasar says, is "from a lower to a higher aesthetics" (GL II.95). Augustine follows an obviously analogical path at times, moving from the beauty of the world to eternal beauty; more often, he prefers to "see in the light of God's beauty the beauty of the world revealing itself to the person who loves God" (GL II.100).[11] Yet this latter is not yet katalogical; it is not to see first the light of God, and then by means of it to see all other things. Rather, it is to recognize *in the seeing* of worldly things that it is God's light by which one is able to see at all. The starting point remains here below, and the direction of inference remains from inferior to superior, and so it is still an analogical approach in the final analysis.

If we are to follow this approach, we too must first bring created realities into view. It is true that contemplation of the beauty of created things ought not to rest in itself, dwelling on inner-worldly beauty; rather, the mind is intended to use these created realities as a means to go beyond them to their uncreated ground, as a "flight to the immortal and eternal."[12] But the first step in that journey to the infinite remains the contemplation of created realities.

a. Created Realities and Causation

Von Balthasar spends little time on setting up the nature of this contemplation, assuming a strong familiarity with the strategies and theories of Plato and Plotinus alike in his readers.[13] To motivate and explicate the nature of this "flight to the eternal," and indeed to pick up the theme that will resound most impressively through the various authors considered here (which will turn out to be the way in which the *nature* of created being declares its own createdness), it is necessary to spell out more fully than von Balthasar has the logic he sees underlying Augustine's conception here. This will be to offer as an explication for the passage cited from Augustine above an examination of the moment in which the contemplation of creation first turns to that which is above it. In this contemplation of creation, it becomes clear that creaturely being is not self-caused, but rather is externally caused. This is in fact, as it seems, a species of an argument for first cause, and the logic of it is the following.

For any created reality x, it is a condition of the possibility of x that there be a cause of x. Were this not so, x would not be a *created* reality.[14] That it has a cause is further confirmed if x is a being that is a) not the sufficient cause of anything like itself and b) is prone to pass out of existence, for the following reasons.

(a) If x is not the sufficient cause of anything like itself, then it seems unlikely that x could be the cause of *itself*; at the very least, we would have no reason for believing x to be capable of such causal activity. The term "sufficient" is decisive here; an animal causes something like itself in procreation, but most animals are not *sufficient* to cause something like themselves: They require a host of cooperating causes, not least an animal of the opposite sex.

Here we may object that there are creaturely instances of something that is the sufficient cause of something like itself, namely cell division and other analogous asexual methods of reproduction. Perhaps in these cases, we might entertain the notion that the cell is the cause of itself, because it has shown itself capable of causing a reality that is of its own sort and nobility?

But that which is created is not the cause of itself for the simple reason that before it was created it was nothing, and nothing has no causal power (it is, in fact, non-existent). Thus, while that which is not the sufficient cause of something like itself shows that it is likely also not the author of its own being, even that which *is* the sufficient cause of something like itself still does not seem likely to be its own cause. Therefore it is likely that it was created, and therefore caused, by another.

In the latter case, the conclusion could be avoided by supposing the entity in question (a cell) was eternal. In that case, it might be thought to be the cause of itself. And that is where the second criterion comes in.

(b) If x is a being that is prone to pass out of existence (speaking here of a natural end to its being and bracketing the possibility that its existence be ended by violence), this would seem to be an indication that it is not truly self-sustaining. For if x is self-sustaining, what would cause it to cease the activity of sustaining itself? It cannot be any change in an external factor, for this would mean that x was not *fully* self-sustained, but rather sustained by itself and by another in such a way that without the external help it could not continue in existence. If x ceases its activity of self-sustenance due to some internal change, then this change must have been either voluntary or involuntary. If this internal change was involuntary, then x is shown to be not fully self-sustaining, for something has been able to constrain its sustaining activity. If it is something voluntary, what could convince a being to cease its own existence? And if it is voluntary, then it does not necessarily happen, and so we would expect (at least statistically if for no other reason) to see some x that has chosen not to allow or suffer a natural end to its existence. x is not capable of sustaining itself indefinitely, and therefore x is not self-sustaining *simpliciter*, but only up to a point. Such a being, it seems, obeys a law outside of itself, and by that fact demonstrates the likelihood that it was caused.

These two confirming reasons, which do not issue in a necessary deduction, but rather in a likelihood, serve to underscore what may be considered the principal point here: The creature, insofar as it is a creature (which is to say, insofar as it is not self-caused and not self-sustaining) declares by its ontological status that it is not the absolute, that it is in fact only a creature. It is a matter of no small importance that when the intellect questions a creature, asking what it is, the creature responds necessarily "I am a creature"; this response is coded into it from the very beginning, and thus the possibility of the recognition of something higher than it in the causal order is also coded into it. It may be, to be sure, only the possibility of recognition, for the reasons followed earlier do not lead to *necessary* conclusions. If they did, then the creature could be said to not just declare its creatureliness, but to scream it. As it is, even in the mysteriousness of the non-disclosure allowed by the space of doubt left open in the earlier arguments, creatureliness still offers itself to the intellect precisely as likely to be creaturely, and thus brings in the likelihood of something like a Creator.

Thus, we have a version of an argument for a first cause, and one that is both familiar within the Greek philosophical milieu and modulated by its encounter with Christian theology. This is the situation von Balthasar celebrates in Augustine, the mutual conditioning of philosophy and Christian theology. "These two things," he says, "come into his field of vision simultaneously, philosophical form and the content it frames and structures, Christian teaching" (*GL* II.96). But the insight von Balthasar wants to pick up here does not rest at the level of a demonstration of a first cause; it goes on to describe the first cause as being a cause of a certain *sort*, namely, as archetype. Von Balthasar's analysis of Augustine develops this as an inference, with reference to the difference between the Augustinian and Cartesian versions of the *cogito* argument.[15] This is to some extent allowed by the fact that von Balthasar has already given a more necessary argument in his analysis of Irenaeus. It is to this Irenaean argument that we now turn.

b. Irenaeus and the Archetypal Relation between Creator and Creatures

Irenaeus begins with the logic of creation, offering us the following choice: either God used Godself as the original upon which all created reality would be based, or God must have used some other original.[16]

Built into this choice is the assumption that there must have been some model according to which God created. This is a perfectly natural Platonic assumption—however, for Irenaeus it is not established through the Platonic tradition, but rather through the Incarnation. In the Incarnation the revelation of God comes to human nature epistemologically and ontologically; but this can only happen if the nature that is to receive this weight is strong enough to bear it. Von Balthasar presents what he considers to be the Irenaean notion of *Deum portare*, to carry or bear God. His interpretation is that the God-bearing individual is one who has been prepared for this very task of carrying God, who is characterized by an ability to withstand the great burden. While it is true that this titanic task is one to which creaturely being is gradually acclimated, were creaturely being before this gracious help such as to be incapable of enduring this burden, no progress could be made toward making it capable. In other words, only that which has been crafted to be capable of enduring the divine presence can ever be made suitable and able to actually endure it. Von Balthasar refers to this as a "fundamental power" of creaturely being, and asserts that it could not have this power were there not a likeness.[17]

Here we could note that Barth, at least at a certain stage of his life, would disagree.[18] Barth's objection would be that the ability to bear the Creator is not a created potency of the creature, but is a grace conferred after creation which is in fact more like a new creation than the activation of something latent in the original creation: The creative act of redemption makes that which was formerly impossible possible.

Von Balthasar can only disagree with this. He doesn't think that it makes sense for God not to create in God's image. That is, *imago Dei* theology grounds *portare* theology as a prior, Biblically given commitment. But in fact *imago Dei* theology is not enough to separate the two: only an *imago* of a certain sort gives von Balthasar what he wants, namely an *imago Dei* that cannot see God creating in the way the Barthian position requires. This Barthian position in fact reduces, in von Balthasar view, to a version of the Pure Difference Thesis.

Returning to Irenaeus, we see that the historical fact of the Incarnation, where a human nature was made the vessel for a person who was God, requires that there be a likeness, and therefore an original (archetype). Further, since no creature would be capable of bearing the divine person if there were no likeness between God and creatures, the archetype must be like God in a significant sense, such that to be like the archetype is to be like God.

This requirement of likeness itself rests upon a Platonic causal scheme wherein causality is an action of like on like—this is the notion of mediation we have already encountered. But here there has been a subtle addition—we have seen that a mediator must partake of both realities in some way if it is to be capable of mediation; now we see that this is only possible if a gulf of infinite distance does not exist between the two terms to be mediated, for no mediator (even, apparently, a divine person) could bridge such a gap. Therefore it is on the basis of a prior *rapprochement*, determined by God in the moment of creation, that the union of God and humanity in the person of Christ is possible.

All this was intended to show the necessity of a likeness, which entails a relationship of archetypality—for every likeness is a likeness *of* something, which means there must be an original it is being compared to. But it seems to remain possible to ask whether this original need necessarily have been God, or whether some intermediary could have served as this original. After all, if the intermediary original were like God, those things that are patterned after it will be to some degree like God, and perhaps that will be enough to allow the *portare* von Balthasar sees in Irenaeus.

This brings us back to the original choice we were offered, whether God used Godself as the original upon which all created reality is based, or some other original. The argument that it must be God is based on the avoidance of an infinite regress. For the original is either identical with God, or not identical with God. If it is not identical with God, then it must either be co-eternal with God, or created by God. It can't be co-eternal with God, for nothing can be such. Therefore, it must have been created by God. But it is then asked, "what was the original on which that original was based?" and an infinite regress ensues. Therefore, the archetype cannot be other than God.[19]

Thus, the likeness required for Incarnation is a likeness to God directly. Although von Balthasar does not specify the likeness further at this point, it will be clear that it must be an ontological likeness (and not merely moral or epistemological) if it is to be strong enough to ground the Incarnation and the ensuing Christological claims. Further, the famous Irenaean *recapitulatio*, which lies at the heart of his Christology and metaphysics, is only possible on the basis of this original relationship of archetypality between the Creator and the highest of physical creatures, human nature.

c. Augustine and the Unity between Creator-as-Archetype and Created Beings

At this point, having established that von Balthasar sees the relation between Creator and creatures in terms of archetypality, the next task is to ask in more detail about how this works. How is the claim that the Creator is the archetype of creaturely beings to be understood? Is there a deistic overtone here, such that while creaturely being is made to image uncreated being, there was a final break (at the moment of creation or later) that leaves creaturely being stranded, as it were, cut off from its original? Or is there still some connection between the two, and if so, of what type?

To answer these questions, we turn back to von Balthasar's reading of Augustine. The starting point is one that is fundamental for the frame of von Balthasar's own project, the unity of being. This unity, which is an aspect of Platonism that von Balthasar feels has been too often overlooked, unites the transcendentals beauty, truth and goodness such that they may truly be interpenetrating transcendentals and not merely properties which remain extrinsic to one another. Methodologically, it is why *The Glory of the Lord*, *Theodrama*, and *Theologic* form a triptych rather than a trilogy, for trilogy implies a separation among the three parts that would deny the type of unity von Balthasar wishes to champion; rather, the dramatics is already both an aesthetics and a logic, and so on.

Thus, he says that Augustine has the two-pronged belief that "the highest existing being is understood in a Platonic sense as absolute unity, and contingency and createdness are therefore sufficiently expressed by the unity of things that is only striven for, never attained" (*H* II.117).[20] Von Balthasar has here effected a subtle shift from what we might have expected, given the general Platonic background notion of being: the claim is not that Being as such is absolute unity, but rather that the "highest existing being" is absolute unity. This specification serves to block a univocal predication of absolute unity of both uncreated being and creaturely being on the basis of the fact that they are both types of *being*. If absolute unity is not predicated of being in general, but of a particular instance of being, the highest existing being, and if we understand that it only has this absolute unity by virtue of being the highest existent, then it follows that creaturely being will not express absolute unity, but only a sort of relative unity. Absolute unity will therefore stand over and against all creaturely being as that norm by which they are judged, even while remaining a limit they can never reach. This striving is properly termed a "sufficient expression" for created things, because absolute unity is something they are naturally intended to lack.

From this, von Balthasar draws the conclusion that "if being consists in unity, then creaturely participation in being also consists in a graduated participation in unity" (ibid.).[21] It cannot be doubted that creatures participate in being, for they *have* being, they *are* created beings. But the subtle shift effected a moment ago has not been maintained—now we are once again speaking as if unity is a quality of being as such, and not a quality of the highest existing being. As previously indicated, this would seem to lead to the conclusion that creatures would only lack from unity to the extent that their participation in being is deficient.[22]

Which of these statements are we to privilege? Is it Being as such that is absolute unity, or the concrete, highest existing being? It is ultimately the question of the relationship of God to Being—are they identical, or is there some separation to be noted between them?

Either way we answer the question involves difficulties: If God and Being are not in every way the same, then Being is a class which contains within it both God and creatures, and would therefore seem to be metaphysically prior to God. It would, in fact, convert all metaphysics into ontology, and it could only be with reference to this center that Christ could be understood. This is classical metaphysics, exemplified by Plato (for whom the form of the Good was above even the Demiurge).23

On the other hand, if God and Being are entirely the same, how is one to block the inference to pantheism? In other words, if God is Being, and creatures are beings and therefore have their proper share in being, why is the whole totality of beings, taken as one whole, *not* the unity that God is?

As will become evident shortly, von Balthasar opts for the second set of difficulties, those involved with identifying God and Being. The key to the solution of the difficulties lies precisely in the notion of participation we are in the process of examining, and how it is applied to this relationship of the original unity of Being and its subsequent multiplication.

However, the fact that God and Being are to be identified renders further questioning as to whether it is Being itself or a highest existing being that is the absolute unity moot, for Being exists only *as* the highest existing being. The identification of God and Being will mean that there is no abstract concept of Being in the metaphysical system, but rather a concrete existent that is the source and plenitude of being. That is to say, where before he secured this by the assertion that only the highest being can have absolute unity, now he has done so by the assertion of something like Unity-itself. But in the identification of Unity-itself and Being-itself with the highest existent, he has also preserved the earlier way of securing this conclusion.

Returning then to von Balthasar's claim that all creaturely being is a graduated participation in unity, the claim can be seen to be more plausible. For if unity in an absolute sense is the being that God is, creaturely being can only be said to have unity to the extent that it approximates the being of the Creator, and different beings will do this to varying degrees (lowest will be those things that merely *are*, then those things that *live*, and highest are those things that *understand*). If that is granted, it remains to be seen how one gets from creaturely being "approximating" divine being to the notion of creaturely being participating in the divine being. Von Balthasar's only answer is to insist that the answer lies in the notion of unity: "Thus Augustine explains the Biblical creation with the categories of Platonic participation: that anything is able to exist outside the complete, absolute unity is only thinkable if out of the quasi-nothing of matter, 'out of which God made everything', through a creative irradiation of the essences and forms that are in the mind of God and are identical with him, the finite existing essences are formed" (*H* 117).24 But unity alone does not seem to be enough to motivate the claim that only that which participates in unity is able to exist outside of that unity. The mention of forms only adds a presupposition about the first mode of existence of the unity—it does not explain why existence outside that unity must be read in terms of participation. Only if unity is taken to mean not just a continuity and perfectly attuned harmony of substance, not even just a simplicity of substance, but also as *fullness* of substance, can this claim be motivated. To say that God is the absolute unity must mean not only that God is absolutely unified in himself, but is the fullness of unity; it is to say that God is not just the One, but the One and Only.

The essences of creatures, therefore, are formed from the forms that are in the mind of God in such a way that these forms are not other than God. This dynamic is called *participation*, based upon the very etymology of the word: both the Latin *participatio* and the German *mitteilung* contain the notion of something that is shared, something imparted. The image is not of two things meeting in a third thing, but rather of one thing opening itself to another to give to that other something of what it is in itself. Yet the question remains, what is the relationship of the created forms to the original on which they were based? If participation is not to collapse into identity, what is to secure the difference?

Nothing less than the fact of the unity of the divine essence and the multiplicity of created essence will do here for von Balthasar's reading of Augustine. This reading, which recovers an emphasis on the importance of the *De Musica* (and therefore of the entire Pythagorean component of Platonism) for Augustine's thought, understands form in a way that is closely allied with number: "Form and beauty, taken immanently, can no longer be anything other than number, for number is the multiplication of unity, which springs out of it and can only be explained through it and in it" (*HII.118*).[25]

Von Balthasar thus sees Augustine setting up an analogy between unity and its multiplication (number) on the one hand, and the divine being and its multiplication in created being on the other. Without that unity that is the Law of Identity, there can be no multiplication, for the recognition of plural identities rests upon the possibility of distinguishing one entity from another. Because we know that *a* is *a* and not *b*, we are able to take that first step without which no math is possible, the postulation of the number *1*. From this, the whole of mathematics will follow. Nevertheless, the rule that *a* is *a* and not *b* is not imperiled or altered by the addition of the whole sequence of numbers that follow upon it.

In like fashion, the divine being sits at the root of the possibility of other beings, at every moment enabling their existence and conditioning their potentialities, but it is no one of those beings, and is not altered even as it is participated in by the created realities. Von Balthasar is careful to note that this is merely an analogy, however; a pure translation of being into the realm of mathematics is not possible.[26] This can be interpreted to mean that the measure of the distance between the original Unity and the many that depend upon it cannot be described merely in terms of degree, but must also be described with reference to kind. Created being, for all that it bears a relation to the divine that involves similarity at a fundamental level, is nevertheless also a fundamentally different type of reality than the divine original on which it is based. Von Balthasar does not fail to remind us that it is the failure to pay attention to precisely this point that lands the Plotinian system in pantheism.[27]

2. THE KATALOGICAL APPROACH: FIRST CAUSE FROM ABOVE

The character of participation can be specified by turning to von Balthasar's reading of Anselm of Canterbury. With the analysis of Anselm, von Balthasar begins the desired turn away from an analogical (or bottom-up) approach to a katalogical (top-down) approach.[28] Accordingly, the relationship between creatures and Creator is no longer to be thought from the perspective of creaturely requirements, but rather from the *character* of the Creator, specifically from divine freedom. This emphasis on freedom, which von Balthasar attributes to Anselm's Benedictine heritage, is also that which gives Anselm's theology its distinctive stamp.[29] Anselm stands in the privileged place historically, where theology is seen to be the consummation of that ancient philosophy which was always truly theology because it was always concerned with the eternal and with being.[30] It is no wonder therefore that it is here that von Balthasar sees the heretofore philosophical reflection on the Creator beginning to take on its properly theological overtones.

In interpreting the *Monologion*, von Balthasar sees the first moment for Anselm as a personalization of the original causality. "What comes from God is also created by him" (*H* II.233);[31] the divine action that results in a *something* is creation, and therefore we will not be speaking of a generic "first cause" but of an intentional action of a being endowed with rationality. This is, he claims, the change from philosophical vision to theological vision. He characterizes the change as happening "as unremarkably as possible,"[32] no doubt driven by his thesis that there is in fact very little distance between the classical philosophical act and the Christian theological act in the first place. The entire weight is placed upon an equation of *ex Deo* with *per ipsum*, that what comes "from God" is also made "through him." What is involved in this choice?

What von Balthasar claims here is that every movement of the divine *ad extra* is creative. This seemingly unremarkable thesis has two very specific effects: the first is that it reduces creation, at this early moment in the philosophical reflection, to something without a specific structure to be examined. In systems where creation is seen early in the development of the system to have a specific structure, to be of *this* sort specifically, we tend to go on to question the conditions of the possibility of it being of this sort, and the process of analogical induction begins. By reducing this structure to the point where it is not visible, by in essence defining creation as that which is not God (but in such a way as to be derived from God), the investigation is firmly planted in the Creator: What must this Creator be like to be able to call something out of non-being, on the basis of nothing more than pure creative ideas?

The second effect of this thesis is a radical difference between God and everything else. That any movement outside of God whatsoever is creative emphasizes that there is no neutral, uncreated ground in which God and the creature can meet. There is only God and not-God, and so the creature, if it is to encounter God at all, will either encounter God in the multiplicity of created things, or within the divine life itself. The fact that nothing stands outside of God except that which is not God also grounds a strong identification of God with the divine perfections. No longer standing over God as conditioning categories, the infinite perfections of God take on a personal character and are found to arise from rather than condition the divine life.[33]

This principle, that every movement of the divine *ad extra* is creative, thus serves both as a safeguard against analogical approaches (by placing the center of concern on that being who is the cause of all others) *and* as an emphasis on the personal character of that cause. But if the way of shifting from philosophy to theology was by personalizing the first cause, it remains to ask what unique stamp personhood as such puts on the causal relationship of archetype.

Creatures are made either out of nothing or out of a creative idea.[34] The disjunct signaled by the word *or* seems to me to be a small one—Anselm, like Augustine, clearly allows the creative idea as a source for creaturely being. Still, in so doing, he is not denying the Christian doctrine of *creatio ex nihilo*; but adding to it. Thus, on the one hand, creatures come from nothing, which means there is no antecedent explanation for the existence of the creature. No argument or logic could be found that would compel the creation of the creature, which comes onto the stage out of nowhere. This pure spontaneity underscores the freedom of the act of creation.

On the other hand, that creatures spring from a creative idea is taken to be an indicator of the character (*Personalität*) of the Creator. If we take this in a banal sense, we are left with the notion that we learn that the Creator is the *kind of person* who creates using creative ideas. *Personalität*, however, is offered as the middle step between our recognition of divine freedom and our recognition of

God as spiritual word. There must be more to this idea if it is to take us from the one to the other; it must be the case that we are learning from the creative ideas something about who God is, which could only happen if the creative ideas in some way *express* who God is. Forefront here is not what we learn about the divine essence, but that the fact that we could learn anything at all in this way means that the creative ideas are to some extent *expressive*.

The importance of the creative ideas is immediately underscored by von Balthasar: "For that reason one of the standing titles of God now becomes creative essence (substance, nature)" (*H* II.233-4).[35] What all this amounts to is Anselm's affirmation of the archetypal relationship. Like Augustine and Irenaeus, it is wrapped in ontological terms, but the transposition von Balthasar has been tracking, from philosophy to theology, is evident here. Naked philosophical being has been dressed in the language of Christian ontological categories, an ontology that has been adjusted to account for Trinitarian and Christological claims (signaled by the reference to nature and substance), which is the necessary move for seeing the person of Christ as the central figure metaphysically.

What von Balthasar finds most interesting about Anselm's version of archetypality, however, is the fact that the divine ideas are no longer deduced analogically, but on the basis of divine freedom itself. God is free, and therefore creation is contingent; and because God creates in accordance with God's being not on account of any necessity (internal or external), but only by free choice, the fact of resemblance between Creator and creatures may be called an act of divine self-expression.[36] This idea of expression, which is other and superior to Augustine's conception for von Balthasar precisely because it begins with the freedom of God, becomes the entry into the theology of Bonaventure, which so closely approximates von Balthasar's own theology.

B. BONAVENTURE AND THE SYNTHESIS OF EXEMPLAR AND EXEMPLARITY

In Bonaventure, the metaphysical relation between the Creator and creatures undergoes a transformation. Bonaventure establishes exemplarity as the ground for an ana-logical move from the contemplation of the creature to the contemplation of the Creator.[37] As it was such an analogical move that landed Irenaeus at likeness and Augustine at archetype, Bonaventure's deduction may be seen as specifying the nature of the archetype by means of his idea of exemplarity. That von Balthasar sees this as a development of all the theologies discussed so far is clear.[38] What remains is to see the way in which this development is carried out, and what conclusions von Balthasar himself draws from it for his own system.

For von Balthasar, the starting point in Bonaventure must be reason, which is the ground of the communicability of God in the Word: "But reason is first of all the prerequisite for the communicability of God in his Word: objectively as *verbum incarnatum*, innerly-subjective as *verbum inspiratum*, and the fontal source of both as *verbum increatum*, which expresses the inner essence of God and thereby also the whole world" (*H* II.285).[39]

The notion of communicability is distinct from the notion of impartation—it references not just the ability to give something, but also the subsequent reception of what is offered. If there is not reception, then something has not been communicated, merely offered. The use of communicability rather than mere impartation to parse the meaning of participation is therefore a development that keeps in view both the active and passive dynamics involved.

The passage cited above thus argues that this communication happens objectively in the incarnate Word, and "innerly-subjective" in the in-breathed Word. In both of these cases, the active and passive sides of communication are not difficult to see: On the one hand, the flow of grace from God into creation by means of God's hypostatically uniting Godself to creation calls to mind Irenaeus's conception of a communication that is best described as *portare Deum*; on the other hand, the Word of Truth dwelling in us richly may be related to the turning of the mind from creaturely realities to the uncreated original. Both, we are told, have their roots in a fontal source, which is the uncreated Word, that Word that expresses the divine essence. At this point, the notion of *expression*, which is to be the key category in von Balthasar's read of Bonaventure, is offered as the prerequisite for communication, which might more literally be translated as *participation*.

Further, it is not only the case that expression grounds participation; the Word is said to express the divine essence "and thereby also the whole world." The "thereby" (*damit*) of this last statement must be examined more closely. What must the relationship of God and the world be like such that the Word that expresses the inner being of God *by virtue of that fact* also expresses the whole world? This claim requires the claim that the inner essence of God has a non-trivial relationship to the whole world, such that by expressing the former one could also express the latter. At the same time, however, the very ability to share oneself points to distinction; for *a* to be able to share itself with *b*, *a* must be other than *b*.[40]

At least part of what is at stake here is motivating a non-trivial likeness between God and creation. This is the participation of creation in God, grounded on this peculiar notion of expression first introduced in Anselm and now blossoming in Bonaventure. At the same time, however, it is necessary to guard against allowing all of creation to collapse, in a Plotinian way, into identity with the one (pantheism).[41]

In order to explicate Bonaventure's doctrine of expression in a way that will not lead to such theological inconveniences, von Balthasar will draw upon nothing less than the very notion of archetypality he has been at such pains to develop in this volume. He begins with an analysis of the Bonaventurean terminology.

Under discussion here is the nature of that Word which is the divine reason and communicability. This Word is called a *similitudo expressa et expressiva*.[42] Von Balthasar focuses on the fact that *expressus* is distinguished from *expressivus*. Where *expressus* ("express") indicates exactness, *expressivus* (roughly "expressing"), emphasizes the relationship of expression.[43] Thus, when "Word" is called a *similitudo expressa et expressiva,* von Balthasar understands this to mean that it is both an exact likeness and a likeness which expresses, or, to combine the two notions, that it is a perfect and complete expression. Thus, while *expressio* may be understood in an active sense as "that which expresses" (the original or archetype) or in a passive sense as that which results from this process (the copy), *expressus* is always subordinated to the expressive relationship (*expressivus*).[44] Exactness, or the perfection of the image, is judged with reference to that original on which it is based. Its fundamental character is not its perfection of representation (*expressus*), but that it is an expression or imitation *of* this original (*expressivus*).

If the *similitudo expressa et expressiva* is grounded first and foremost in the likeness which expresses and is only able to be judged exact when it has been first judged to be an expression *of* something else, then von Balthasar's conclusion follows: The copy is bound to the original, for the copy will first be recognized to be a copy and then be assessed with regard to how exact a copy it is. What is more immediate for our purposes is that this subordination of *expressus* to *expressivus* also protects the distinction between the original and the copy. In the Trinity, this means that the Son is not the Father, and so a collapse into a monistic modalism is not possible; in the God-creature relationship, it means that even the whole world taken as a totality is not the divine on which it is fashioned, and a Plotinian collapse into the One is not ultimately possible.

With this demonstration of the way in which the archetype binds the copies, protecting a space of distinction that is irreducible, the Word has been brought into view as that which is expression (*expressio* in both the active and passive sense) within the Godhead. The distinction that is a prerequisite for expression finds its first fulfillment in the procession of the Son within the Trinity. In this sense, the Son is the *expressio expressa*, the complete expression, but also the *expressio expressiva*, the expressive expression. Here von Balthasar gives us a hint of the Bonaventurean bottom line: "This means nothing less than the founding of the act of Creation on the act of generation within the Godhead" (*H* II.296).[45]

Let us first focus on the generation, in which the Father gives all that he is to the Son.[46] This means that everything the Father is and can do is fully expressed in the Son. He is the *expressio expressa* because the Father held nothing back. In the Son, all *possibilia* have taken on reality, though a reality that is still embraced by identity with the divine nature, and is not yet that external, creaturely existence we might wish to call "objective."[47] The Son has become the locus of the reality of all created possibilities, and therefore if any of those possibilities are to be actualized in an existence defined by distinction from the Godhead, in extra-divine reality, it can only be through the Son that this can happen.[48] Indeed, the act of creation appears to be more an externalizing and objectifying of the subset of *possibilia* contained in the Son. Thus, while the Son contains all possibilities, his role as archetype is deduced not primarily from the richness of his content, but rather from the Father's complete expression in the Son.

This is the Bonaventurean revolution, to von Balthasar's eyes: that he grounds the Son's role as archetype, idea and exemplar (three ways of saying the same thing for von Balthasar) not in the fact that the Son contains all possibilities, but in the fact that the Son is absolute expression.[49] This may seem like a small distinction, but to von Balthasar it is a pure theological insight of the highest order. For if the Son's role as archetype is grounded on the richness of possibilities contained within the archetype, then the question will be asked: On the basis of what is the Son archetype? The answer will have to be that it is because he contains all *possibilia*; but this is to say that the Son is the archetype for creaturely realities on the basis of something other than the divine nature. Followed through to its conclusion, it is to claim that the Son may count as the exemplar because he satisfies the job title—this ultimately posits some standard outside of God by which God is measured. However, if it is as the expression of the complete divine power that the Son is the archetype, then it is not through some external standard, but through the being of God that the Son stands at the head of creation.

If therefore the full creative power of the Father was poured into the Son such that all creation is to be accomplished through and in the Son, the Son could rightly be described as the means by which the Father carried out creation, or as the medium of the Father's expression of himself outside the Godhead. Here von Balthasar arrives at an idea in Bonaventure that will be of enormous importance, the idea that it is the generation of the Logos that enables all other generations.[50] Just as there can be no Holy Spirit without the Son, there can be no creation without the Son. The full work this idea does in the Balthasarian system will not be examined until chapter 6; for the moment, we will only mark its first appearance.

This leads von Balthasar to note that the Word of God is the "archetypal world" in three ways: (1) as the complete expression of the origin (the Father), (2) as the Father's medium of expression, and (3) as expressing in the Incarnation that which was originally intended for creation.[51] There is, therefore, a first image (this is what it means to be the complete expression of the Father), and this image is the means of expression. If the Son is the means of expression, then the Son is not the one expressing, but only that through which expression is made (just as the language by which I express myself is not the one expressing—rather it is *I* who express, using the language as a medium). That which is expressed, creatures, will therefore be an image of the one expressing, the Father. But because the Father expresses himself in the "language" of the Son, the creaturely expressions will be modulated by this mode of expression. The creature will therefore be an image of the first image.

Furthermore, it is necessary that the creaturely imitation of God be multiple, for creatures lack that highest perfection which is required to express in themselves the divine perfection in singularity of number. For creatures, the highest perfection they can hope to attain to is to express through a harmonious hierarchy the undifferentiated unity of the original image.[52] This is what motivates Bonaventure's famous hierarchy of created being, which ascends from traces to images and thence to likenesses, in which he sees the Trinity imaged.[53]

This trinitarian image in humanity becomes the vehicle for the proper interpretation of everything else: the human spirit can only understand its fundamental image character as trinitarian when it has been elevated to a likeness by grace, and this elevation to likeness is required for the human spirit to be able to truly understand the meaning of the fact that even the least of created things are a trace.[54] The meaning of the trace-character of all created being is that all created being points to the archetype; or, to say the same thing differently, that the self-realization of creaturely being is to become an inner-worldly sign of the indwelling of the archetype.[55]

This referential character of created being, in which it points beyond itself to the archetype both by pointing outside of itself and by pointing within itself (in such a way that a denial of the beauty and dignity of creaturely being is not possible), is nothing other than the expression of the possibility and even necessity of an analogical move from created being to uncreated being. Along with Augustine, Bonaventure can speak of a "flight to the immortal and eternal;"[56] however, Augustine fails to motivate the one-sided necessity of creaturely reference to uncreated being:[57] for him, the necessity to turn creation into a path to the eternal is an ethical, not a metaphysical necessity. Like Anselm, Bonaventure can speak of a divine self-expression which is evident in and through the resemblances of created things and their archetype. However, while Anselm could only motivate the category of expression on the basis of the divine freedom such that it rests almost at the level of implication and remains a paradox (necessity founded in freedom), Bonaventure has motivated it on the basis of the trinitarian processions, binding the copies to the original with the necessity of the trinitarian first being.[58]

The union of the archetype and the notion of expression results in a characteristically Bonaventurean outlook on the God-world relationship. Bonaventure's own idea for noting this unique understanding is the notion of exemplarity, with which he is able to signal the archetypal character of the relationship as well as its expressive dimension. This expressive dimension brings with it a notion of causality, which then becomes the basis for a re-thinking of the Aristotelian categories of causality in Bonaventure's academic works.[59]

With the notion of exemplarity, we have arrived at the height of the theological reflections on the relation between the first principle and every dependent reality. It has been established through von Balthasar's historical researches that God and the world have a profound relationship to one another in their being. It is clear that the relationship between God and world is not best described in terms of pure difference for von Balthasar, but rather by means of the notions of archetypality and participation. It remains to face this assertion of likeness directly, to question in what ways it is able to be understood and in what ways it must not be understood. This will be the task of the next chapter.

III. IDEAL FORM OF THE REJECTION OF THE PURE DIFFERENCE THESIS

These historical researches leave no doubt that von Balthasar thinks that major theologians of the Christian tradition have rejected the Pure Difference Thesis, and that he approves of theologies that do. However, questions remain as to the exact reasons why von Balthasar feels this is so important. The arguments developed through the figures considered in *The Glory of the Lord* volume II are certainly reasonable, but hardly force us to necessarily concede their conclusion. At several key moments in the exposition it is clear that what is involved is not so much rational demonstration as aesthetic preference: that is, the consonance of the ideas in their place within a larger framework. While such aesthetic considerations are a necessary and even salutary part of theological reasoning, their presence is worth noting because they themselves indicate that we are in the presence of a preference which perhaps has more to do with what von Balthasar would call "theological style" than with what could be properly said to be a logical conclusion.

The concern is heightened by the fact that it would be just as easy to construct a different theological story that made the Pure Difference Thesis appear as central to the development of Christian doctrine. Indeed, not only could theologians of equal reputation be named, but in fact many of the same theologians could be named. Augustine's flight to the immortal could be interpreted in a strongly apophatic direction, in which created things are the occasion for our contemplation of the uncreated not because of any resemblance, but because of their inherent deficiency; Denys above all could be and usually is interpreted in a much more apophatic way than von Balthasar here allows. Even Bonaventure is often read, in light of the closing passages of the *Itinerarium*, as a theologian of the negative tradition who believes all intellectual activity must cease when it arrives at its goal of union with God.[60]

The possibility of such an alternate reading of even the theologies von Balthasar makes central to his own historical argument brings to focus the importance of the prior commitments von Balthasar utilizes in interpreting these texts. I do not intend to claim that von Balthasar has, at the end of the day, misinterpreted these texts; but if he has interpreted them properly, he has done so against a counter tradition of interpretation, and has done so with the help of an understanding of the right path for a Christian notion of the Creator-creature relationship whose evidence must be deeper than these texts.

It is therefore worth considering what the desiderata are which are for von Balthasar touchstones of whether a theology correctly answers Q (our question about the relation of Creator and creation). In effect, there is here something von Balthasar wants to affirm, which as a consequence excludes the

Pure Difference Thesis, and there is something he feels that any theology based on the Pure Difference Thesis would itself not be able to account for, and this serves as a second reason against such an understanding of the Creator-creature relation.

A. THE NECESSITY OF IMAGO

The first reason, the affirmation that rules out the Pure Difference Thesis, is von Balthasar's claim that God *must* be manifest in any world that God creates. This is a bold idea, but one which von Balthasar is able to affirm with surprising seriousness. Consider the following text: "the manifestness of God's being is immediately traced back to his primordial freedom to manifest himself (which is only a hypothetical necessity: assuming, that is, that God has in fact willed to create a world)" (*TL* I. 230). What, in this passage, is "hypothetically necessary," and what would it mean for necessity to be hypothetical? It is the manifestness of the divine being that is necessary: given any world created by God, it is necessary that God be manifest in that world. What makes this necessity only hypothetical is precisely the presence of that word *given*. Because God does not have to create, God is not necessarily manifest; but on the hypothesis that God creates, it is necessary that God be manifest. Thus God is necessarily manifest, but the necessity is itself contingent upon a prior free decision to create; and this is what von Balthasar calls a "hypothetical necessity."

Now, this does not prove that it is the case that for God to be manifest there must be *imago*. But if the requirement for God to be manifest were able to be satisfied apart from *imago*, then the Pure Difference Thesis could still be a live theological option. A separate argument is required, or else it must simply be assumed that the only proper form of the manifestness of God is through imaging.

Von Balthasar has obviously already approved of the Irenaean logic that asks us to consider what sort of original God could use in creating: Godself or something else. However, this will hardly do as an actual argument that the manifestation of God in any created world must be in the mode of imaging. For why should we concede that God must "use" an original or model to create at all? There *is* a certain force to Irenaeus's claim (shared by Bonaventure) that to act without a model is to act without a plan, and this is to act inordinately and randomly, like a bad artisan. However, it wouldn't take too much imagination to suppose that this seems so compelling to us because of the particular nature of *our* reasoning faculties, which are such that they must work in such and such a way. A Balthasarian might reply that it is because our reason is in the image of God that they work this way, and therefore God's way of thinking would be somehow analogous. But this is not to prove *imago* theology; it is to assume it. And I think it is in fact true that the Irenaean argument must assume *imago* theology to get off the ground, and so it cannot be offered as proof of it.

There is a deeper and better argument, one that does rise to the level of an argument, which is also to be found in the discussion of Irenaeus we have cited. It is in fact the second reason against the Pure Difference Thesis, the need to be able to ground the possibility of Incarnation. We will discuss that argument in the next section. It is sufficient to say at this juncture that the current argument seems to require the second argument to complete it.

Before leaving this question of the relation of the manifestness of God and the necessity of *imago*, let us look at it one more time from a different angle. If God is manifest, God is manifest either in Godself or in another. If in another, it seems that von Balthasar will be able to have what he needs for *imago*. Therefore if the premise of the hypothetically necessary manifestation of God is not to automatically issue in the establishment of a concomitant necessity of *imago*, we would have to be able to give an account for how God could be manifest in the requisite way through Godself.

Fortunately that "in the requisite way" causes little problem, because the range of possibilities for what would count as sufficient manifestness has not been specified.[61] Nevertheless, the possibility of God being manifest in or through Godself is still a challenge. A vast variety of considerations could be brought in here that would send any possible discussion down numerous, divergent pathways. But all we need to do is to remember that we are considering this position insofar as it is a positive claim that rules out the Pure Difference Thesis. That means that any account of how God could be manifest in or through Godself that is not *itself* compatible with the Pure Difference Thesis can be eliminated from discussion out of hand: such accounts may produce challenges to which von Balthasar will need to respond when considering the Identity Thesis, but they do not help the attempt to motivate the Pure Difference Thesis, because in effect they already deny it.

Given this provision, it becomes very difficult to see what kind of answer could be given. For if the Pure Difference Thesis is correct, the very otherness of the divine being would shroud it in inaccessible light, or the depths of darkness, or a cloud of unknowing, or a supersubstantial *more* that would make it exceed not only our words but also our concepts. But how is that which exceeds our concepts to be clear in itself? The majority of the apophatic tradition encourages some sort of engagement with creaturely realities and concepts, in spite of the fact that they are woefully and decisively inadequate to the divine reality, because without them we could have *no* thoughts of God at all. My concept of God may be idolatrous, and certainly does not make God clear: but it at least makes clear that there is something that is *not clear*, and therefore it is useful. The claim is that God cannot be known adequately or clearly, and *for this reason* we can only begin to approximate knowledge of God by a (very careful) reflection focused by creaturely reality. If God were knowable in Godself, such theology would typically be happy to do away with creatures in reflecting on God.

Thus it seems that the history of the use of the Pure Difference Thesis in theology contains a claim, implicit or explicit (varying from case to case), that radical transcendence rules out the possibility of God being manifest in Godself. But if that is true, then the only way for God to be manifest that would not destroy the Pure Difference Thesis would be through some reality that was not God.

Perhaps a step still remains before von Balthasar wins *imago*. For while it is undoubted that an image represents that of which it is an image, and therefore counts as a form of manifestation, we may perhaps still question whether it would be possible for x to make y known without having to be the image of y. It seems that a positive answer could be given: for something can be made clear through that which resembles it, but also through that which in no way resembles it, that is, its opposite. It is at least logically possible that the clear vision of x may be such that it leads one to conclude that not-x is what must be desired, is what is in fact true.

This situation would cause von Balthasar little trouble. For y is not known *as* y in the affirmation of not-x. Thus, if this were how God were made known through the creature, we would not know "God," but "the uncreated, the infinite," and so on. This is, in fact, a favorite claim of proponents of the Pure Difference Thesis, namely that all we can know about God is the negation of created concepts. But all von Balthasar need do is deny that any such compilation of negations of creaturely concepts could count as an adequate concept of God to be able to deny that such a strategy could satisfy the requirement of the manifestation of God in any created world. He will in fact make just such an argument when detailing his disagreements with the classical understanding of the doctrine of God and progressing his own account of the Trinity.[62]

Thus, at worst, von Balthasar can fill out this concern with the one to follow. But even apart from that possibility, there seems to be a decent argument here for the denial of the Pure Difference Thesis: that is, assuming one grants von Balthasar his rather unusual starting point in the claim that

God must be manifest in any possible created world.[63] While the latter is a big concession for many, our discussion underscores the depth of von Balthasar's commitment to *imago*theology.

B. PURE DIFFERENCE AND CHRISTOLOGY

The second reason von Balthasar has for rejecting the Pure Difference Thesis is, as I have already mentioned, contained in the same passage of Irenaeus that was examined earlier. Irenaeus's understanding of *portare*, as von Balthasar reads it, means that a likeness between Creator and creature is the necessary presupposition for Incarnation. Thus, if this likeness is denied as it is in the Pure Difference Thesis, then Incarnation becomes logically impossible, and Christology is destroyed.

This is, significantly, the exact criticism von Balthasar had of his mentor and friend, Erich Przywara, the great twentieth-century champion of the analogy of being. Nicholas Healy makes this point nicely: "It is here that Balthasar notes his reservation regarding Przywara's doctrine of analogy. By emphasizing the 'in *tanta* similitudine maior dissimilitudo' to the 'point of exaggeration,' Przywara's account of analogy undermines the possibility of a Christological union that is able to bridge the distance between man and God without abrogating the abiding distance. 'It is no accident,' suggests Balthasar, 'that Przywara never produced a Christology,' *TD* III.220-1 n.51."[64] Steffen Lösel, who has much to say about analogy in relation to Protestantism, further underscores the point: "With this distinctive negative theology of revelation Balthasar distinguishes himself from those radical interpretations of the analogy of being that extend the *maior dissimilitudo* between God and the world beyond the created order to the hypostatic union. Balthasar is well aware of the pitfalls that Eberhard Jüngel identified in the *theologia negativa*. In an important footnote in the second volume of his *Theologik* he concedes to Jüngel that the tradition of negative theology creates severe problems for a theology of revelation based on the Christ event. He is even more candid a few pages earlier, when he criticizes his former teacher Erich Przywara. According to the latter's Aristotelian interpretation of the formulation of the Fourth Lateran council, Balthasar claims, God and humankind relate to one another *allo pros allo* [different against different]. In Balthasar's view, such an interpretation falsely applies the proviso of the ever-greater dissimilarity of Creator and creation toward the supernatural similarity between God and humankind in the hypostatic union. As Balthasar comments, 'It seems difficult to comprehend, how it should be possible to come up with a Christology given such an understanding of analogy.'"65

This is von Balthasar's abiding and continual critique against the Pure Difference Thesis, that it cannot provide an adequate grounding for the Incarnation. What he means is that it is incapable of explaining how Incarnation is *logically possible*. Thus, his worry is that a consistent adherence to the Pure Difference Thesis would require us to claim that Incarnation is *a priori* impossible. In response to this, it must be said that, as for Barth, the fact of the Incarnation is not a commitment von Balthasar is interested in revisiting: it is a given and not questionable. Therefore, if the Pure Difference Thesis says that Incarnation is impossible, then the fact of Incarnation disproves the Pure Difference Thesis.

The challenge we might pose to von Balthasar here is whether it is necessary to accept that a likeness is a necessary condition for Incarnation. Why could we not say that the divine omnipotence is able to take even the total otherness of the creature and make use of it as the vehicle of the divine expression, precisely because, as omnipotent, no barrier exists to its will? This would not require us to revisit the question whether Incarnation is logically possible, because von Balthasar has resources to answer the charge that God cannot do the logically impossible, both as a voluntarist of sorts and given his understanding of the relation of logic to divine freedom (two sides of the same coin).

Von Balthasar will respond with a theological intuition which is absolutely foundational to his thought. That intuition is expressed repeatedly in the words of Thomas Aquinas: "grace perfects rather than destroys nature." This marks out a characteristic mode of divine action toward the creature that is a point not to be transgressed.

Now, if it were true that the divine omnipotence took that which was in no way like unto itself and made it the vehicle of its self-revelation, this would entail violence: the creature is being put to a use to which it is, by supposition, in no way suitable, in no way directed, and which is necessarily foreign to its nature. (The denial of any of these ways of describing the creature's usability would also constitute the denial of the Pure Difference Thesis.) Such a violent use of the creature could in no way be seen as perfecting its nature, precisely because the concept of perfection requires that there be something present, minimally in a latent form, which is to be brought to completion or fulfillment. But the presence of any such thing is also the denial of the Pure Difference Thesis.

Thus, while it may be possible for divine omnipotence to act in this way, it would not be fitting, and is ruled out by supposition of the necessary mode of interaction between grace and nature.[66] So it seems that von Balthasar would say that to accept the Pure Difference Thesis he would have to deny the Thomistic understanding of the relation of nature and grace. Pure difference would be conceived dualistically, as an ongoing standing over against one another of God and all that is not-God. A Creator who was entirely and radically other than the creation in this way could only fling it into being, could only address it from the outside as a foreigner. The ongoing works of such a Creator would perhaps rightly be seen as meddling, and any advent would be interpreted as an invasion, as a violation of the fundamental and self-contained principles of the creation as such.

This is a scenario von Balthasar finds contradicted by every moment of the Christian revelation. Further, it is likely he would find it to be logically contradictory: for how could a universe be entirely for itself if it were not entirely from itself? If its origin lies in God, if only in a first moment in which it is "thrown," it cannot have the necessary self-sufficiency to stand apart from God in pure difference.[67]

There is a concern that motivates Jean-Luc Marion and to which one might still think von Balthasar owes a response. That concern is that God's sufficiency and transcendence are imperiled if the distance between God and the world are measurable.[68] If God and the world are alike (in the fact that they are beings, or in any other way), then does it not follow that the difference between them is one of degree and not kind? But transcendence requires a qualitative and not merely quantitative distance.

von Balthasar is disallowing the mechanism by which Marion and others are attempting to safeguard the qualitative difference between God and creatures, which is sometimes referred to as the "ontological gap."[69] He has, however, another possible response to the type of concern that motivates Marion (and, before him, Heidegger), expressed in the following lines written about Barth: "this mention of the concept of God is crucial, because it highlights that God does not possess his absoluteness primarily in his relation with the world but first and actually in himself. This absoluteness and freedom, therefore, cannot be at all threatened by the existence of a world" (*Barth* 111). In other words, God possesses absoluteness in actuality (and not merely potency) before the creation of the world, and if God creates in freedom, then God's absoluteness can in no way be thought to be imperiled by the addition of a world.

This is a difficult concept, but I think von Balthasar is thinking that what Marion is conceiving is a *potential* absoluteness in God. God *could* be the absolute, but the jury is out because all the data isn't in yet. One piece of that data is the existence of other things. So God runs the risk in creating of giving up the chance to be the absolute, the self-sufficient, the all-in-all. At one level, this seems very commonsensical: if God does not create, then the set of all beings contains one member (or three-in-one): God. But once God creates, that set contains God and all the other created beings, so God is hardly the sole and all-encompassing definition of the set any longer. Marion's solution is to remove God from the set, such that the set is empty before creation, and populated by only created things afterward.

Von Balthasar's solution is different: he will point out that the analogy is flawed because it assumes that the set (Being) and God are something different to begin with. In that case, God would be the *only* being, but not *absolute* being. Solitariness is not absoluteness. If God *is* being, then creation does not entail shunting God aside to make room for fellow members of the class of being; rather, it means that God makes room *within Godself* for the existence of other beings.

This of course raises the question about the distinction between God and these other beings: we could become suspicious that they are not going to be really different at the end of the day, and that the system will collapse into some kind of pantheism. That is of course the question of the Identity Thesis, and it will be considered in detail in the next chapter.

C. AMBIGUA CONCERNING THE PURE DIFFERENCE THESIS

Before leaving our analysis of the Pure Difference Thesis, there are three objections that are worth considering, derived from texts in the Balthasarian corpus. Each of these objections derive from a moment when it could seem that von Balthasar is *not* denying the Pure Difference Thesis, but in fact endorsing it. Each of these texts can be explained from within their own contexts as in fact not constitutive of such an endorsement. To explain them from their immediate context is important, because it shows that von Balthasar is to some extent aware that he must give an account of what he means with these cryptic sayings. It is perhaps too characteristic of von Balthasar that this awareness of our need for help isn't exactly commensurate with the depth of our need.

1. OBJECTION 1: NEGATIVE THEOLOGY

In *Cosmic Liturgy*, von Balthasar is generally kinder to negative theology than he will be later in his life (in *Theologic*II). He even uses the phrase *tout autre* approvingly. Is this not an acceptance of the Pure Difference Thesis, or does it not at least imply that it is possible to make room for this thesis?

Everything hangs on what von Balthasar means by *tout autre*. If we read carefully, we see that he actually interprets it in a way that makes it more like analogy than is customary. For example: "The point of all this dialectic is first and foremost to make clear that no neutral, common 'concept' of being can span the realities of both God and creature; the analogy of an ever-greater dissimilarity stands in the way, preventing all conceptualization of the fact and the way they are" (*CL* 89). On the face of it, this is the denial of any common concept, which for von Balthasar is going to mean the denial of any commonality at all. What is this if not a clear statement of the Pure Difference Thesis? But note what follows: he interprets this not as totally other, but as "ever-greater dissimilarity." The comparative of "ever-greater" prompts us to ask than what this dissimilarity is ever-greater, and the only answer can be a similarity which is in fact affirmed. Lest we think that we are importing the Lateran IV conception of analogy into what might merely be an infelicitous turn of phrase, von Balthasar in fact uses the word "analogy." What is meant here is not a dissimilarity that does not *also* include some similarity. And with the assertion of similarity we have the denial of Pure Difference.

It is in fact only this analogical interpretation of negative theology that accounts for his seeming praise of Maximus's removal of God from the realm of being here *and* his disdain of Marion's similar project. Otherwise, we would have to leave these two judgments as irresolvable contradictories, perhaps the result of a development in his mature thought whereby he realized that he had been too easy on Maximus, or worse, flat out wrong about him. It is true that ultimately von Balthasar decides not to speak as Maximus does, and the Triptych has much less room for a positive appraisal of negative theology (the most von Balthasar can manage is to say that it is a necessary corrective).[70] Perhaps this is precisely because the idea, still only a nugget in *Cosmic Liturgy*, of what the greater difference between God and creation is explodes into something finally and ultimately inimitable in the later period. This is, to anticipate, the divine aseity.[71]

But surely the fact that von Balthasar ultimately eschews this way of speaking has at least as much to do with the fact that the radical negative nature of Maximus's thought cannot ground Christology in the way von Balthasar needs. I suspect that he feels that Maximus can at best provide a structural account of the meaning of Incarnation (as the analogical transposition of the Chalcedonian themes of existence [hypostasis] and essence [ousia] into metaphysics), and is unable to ground the concrete Christocentrism of von Balthasar's *Theology of History*.[72]

2. OBJECTION 2: GOD AND THE SUBJECT-OBJECT SCHEME

There is a lengthy discussion in *Theologic* volume 1 about the relations of subject to object and vice versa. Drawing upon phenomenology (and especially Heidegger), von Balthasar attempts to motivate a mutual interdependence of subject and object. Both need each other to be what they are, and both have responsibilities and opportunities relative to the other.[73]

Now if this discussion were to be applied to God as divine subject, with creation as the object, the consequences could be theologically disastrous. Most notably, it would seem to imply that God is in need of the world in order to be God, an idea that von Balthasar consistently condemns (often in the person of Hegel, with whom von Balthasar has such a complicated relationship).

This conclusion (and others like it) is blocked by the section in this volume on the object: God's subjectivity stands to objects as causing their existence rather than caused by them.[74] This means that God's subjectivity has a different relationship, not only to objects, but to the whole subject-object scheme as presented in this text. God's subjectivity is the grounding condition of this scheme, and therefore it is no part of it.[75] Is this not a statement of the Pure Difference Thesis in the key of Marion?

Once again, everything hinges on what von Balthasar means by God's subjectivity being "no part" of the subject-object scheme. Where this "no part" differs from projects like Marion's is that such projects believe they must secure the "no part" by means of a *tout autre*; von Balthasar does not share this intuition. In fact, the language of *tout autre*, which we saw that he could use so comfortably when speaking of Maximus, has dropped out by *Theologic*, and is not appealed to here at all. Rather, God is not inherently part of the dynamic by virtue of the *maior dissimilitudo* of aseity.

The advantage of the Balthasarian position is that, unlike in Pure Difference systems, God is not forbidden to enter into certain kinds of relational dynamics with creatures. Should God wish it, God could in fact enter into these dynamics and expose Godself to their vicissitudes. von Balthasar's claim will be that God in fact wills to do this because of love.

3. OBJECTION 3: REVISITING THE WHOLLY OTHER

Although we have dealt with the use of *tout autre* in the *Cosmic Liturgy*, it remains the case that the use of this concept survives fairly late into the Balthasarian corpus. Most notably, it plays an important role in *Love Alone Is Credible*, where the "wholly other" shows up early and often. If it does not mean what it would mean in the Pure Difference Thesis, how are we to understand this?

The "wholly other" for von Balthasar in this text is not that which is ontologically totally different, but rather that which is surprising. This surprise is expressed by the important word *unvordenkbar*, that which cannot be anticipated or foreseen. The "wholly other," which is the farthest distance of God in the dynamics of love (the subject of *Love Alone*), is not that which communes in no likeness with us but that which so far surpasses our expectations and imagination that we could never see it coming. In this way, it is best expressed by the same gloss von Balthasar gave on *tout autre* in the *Cosmic Liturgy*: ever-greater dissimilarity.

One could add here a discussion of *Theologic* II.68ff, where Jesus is paradoxically presented as possessing "a human nature that is complete in every respect, and yet he appears before his fellowmen as wholly other" (*TL* 68). After some discussion (and some reference to Maximus), von Balthasar concludes: "We see, then, that the total otherness of the man Jesus with respect to all other human beings (whom he calls brothers only on the day of Easter [Jn 20:17]) must be interpreted as a total otherness *within* a perfect equality of human nature [. . .] The most obvious point here is that the Jesus of the Gospels does not simply absorb the total otherness of God, whom he exposits in truth, into the difference between divinity and humanity within himself. Rather, this very difference has in truth passed entirely into the 'language' of his humanity. This difference does not at all make him into a human monster or a superman. He reveals that he is wholly other precisely in his abasement, his humility, his service of all" (*TL* II.70). The wholly other is not ultimately referenced here to the divine nature, but to the human nature: it begins as a way of describing not the ontological relation of divinity to humanity in Christ, but as the distinction between the one who in his *person* is the fullness of both natures, and so distinct from us. But in the end, it is the acts of love (abasement, humility, service) that are the locus of the wholly other, and in this way they also can be imitated.

This shows how deeply rooted von Balthasar is in the theology of image: the furthest he can imagine difference going is the radical freedom of divine sovereignty, which surprises us by doing that which we could never have anticipated: "In the Old Testament, this glory (*kabod*) is the presence of Yahweh's radiant majesty in his Covenant (and through this Covenant it is communicated to the rest of the world); in the New Testament, this sublime glory presents itself as the love of God that descends 'to the end' of the night of death in Christ. This extremity (the true the true eschato-logy)—which could never have been anticipated from what we know of the world or man—can be welcomed and perceived in its truth only as the 'Wholly-Other' (*LA* 10-11)."

Notes

1. Aristotle, *Politics* V.4 (1303b28–30).

2. *ST* 1a q. 13

3. Barth's famous insistence on holding our focus to God in Christ (for example, the hiddenness of God in *CD* II/1:179 *et plures*) comes to mind here. I think it would be hasty to transfer this to von Balthasar's system. A better statement of his fundamental ground would be "God *as* Christ."

4. *GL* II.13

5. On von Balthasar's use of Biblical texts, see W. T. Dickens, *Hans Urs von Balthasar's Theological Aesthetics: A Model for Post-Critical Biblical Interpretation* (Notre Dame: Notre Dame University Press, 2003) and John Riches, "The Biblical Basis for Glory" in McGregor, Bede and Norris, Thomas, eds. *The Beauty of Christ: An Introduction to the Theology of Hans Urs von Balthasar* (Edinburgh: T&T Clark, 1994).

6. Following von Balthasar's practice, I omit the customary *Pseudo* from the name of the author of the *Corpus Areopagiticum* as unnecessarily polemical. The use of "Denys" over "Dionysius" should alleviate any confusion that might arise from this practice.

7. *The Gift of Death* (University of Chicago Press: Chicago, 1996), 71.

8. Such as the one offered by Jean-Luc Marion in *God without Being*, Thomas A. Carlson, trans. (Chicago: Chicago University Press, 1991). For Marion's discussion of Heidegger's version of the critique, see 61ff.

9. It is of course an interpretive claim that negative theology falls under the heading of the Pure Difference Thesis. The only careful way to proceed would be to treat each instance of negative theology on its own. Von Balthasar himself interprets the apophatic tradition in this direction. That this is his claim and what sorts of conclusions follow from this will be examined in the second half of this chapter.

10. Von Balthasar himself followed this same approximating approach in *TL* II, treating analogical aspects of the divine logic before turning to katalogical aspects.

11. It must be emphasized that von Balthasar is reading Augustine in a Platonic way here. The contemplation of beauty is not an epistemological exercise, according to this read, but a communing with being. Thus, although it may seem that the idea referenced is one about the creature coming to knowledge of God through recognition of beauty in the world, what is actually meant here is that the quality of being which strikes us as beautiful leads the creature to the "vision" of the beauty that belongs to the being of God. If we take "vision" literally, it will reinforce an epistemological read—but taken as a metaphor for that faculty that "sees" into the natures of things, an ontological understanding is restored. Von Balthasar references this: "Ist Gott als die transzendente Einfachheit das Licht, dann wird die Seele ihn nicht mit einem einzelnen ‚Vermögen', sondern nur mit ihrer zur Ganzheit gesammelten und gemittelten Substanz schauen können" (*H* II.101). [If God, as transcendent unity, is light, then the soul will be able to see him not with a particular "faculty" but only with its substance, collected and centered into a whole.]

12. "Gewiß kennt Augustin die Betrachtung der Weltschönheit, aber sie ist ihm, schon lange vor der Ostiavision—viel stärker als den griechischen Vätern die theoria physikê—Mittel und Weg: 'Nicht fruchtlos und nicht umsonst muß man anschauen (intueri) die Schönheit des Himmels . . . Solche Betrachtung darf allerdings keiner eiteln und vergänglichen Neugier frönen, sondern muß zur Staffel zum Unsterblichen und Immerwährenden gemacht werden'" (H II.1.102). [Certainly Augustine knows the contemplation of the beauty of the world, but long before the vision at Ostia it is for him (much stronger than the *theoria physikê* for the Greek Fathers) a means and a way: "It is not fruitless and in vain to contemplate (*intueri*) the beauty of the heavens [. . .] In no way is such contemplation permitted to indulge in vain and passing curiosity; rather it must be made into a flight to the immortal and eternal."]

13. It is worth noting that both Plato and Plotinus are being interpreted to understand this contemplation as no mere intellectual exercise, but as in some fashion unitive. What accounts for this is the notion, equally Platonic and Neo-Platonic, that the highest realities, and Being itself, are intellectual in character. This keeps the discourse squarely in the realm of ontology, but it also to some extent refuses to admit the customary distinctions of epistemological and ontological realms. All true knowledge is had not merely in adequation to but in communion with the Ideas (Platonic) or the One (Neo-Platonic), and so they are a real participation of intellectual substance in intellectual substance.

14. Causality is, in other words, analytic to the notion of creation. Not all causation is creation, but all creation is cause, which is all that is required for the current argument.

15. H II.108ff.

16. "Die Forderung, daß das geschaffene 'Bild' dem schaffenden Urbild gleiche, ist für Irenäus eine elementare Forderung an den erschaffenden Künstler Gott, 'denn wenn der Weltenschöpfer die Dinge nicht nach sich selber schuf, sondern wie ein schlechter Handwerker oder ein eben erst lernender Knabe nach andern Archetypen abzeichnete, woher soll dann ihr "Urgrund" das Urbild haben?'" (ibid., 71). [The demand that the created "image" resemble the creating archetype is for Irenaeus an elementary demand on the creating artist, God, "for if the Creator of the world did not create things after himself, but, like a bad artisan or an apprentice just starting out, copied another archetype, whence is their 'source' to have gotten this archetype?"]

17. "'Portare' dehnt sich zwischen der Würde und Eignung, eine Last, die Last Gottes, aufgebürdet zu erhalten, der Verantwortung, sie mit sich zu tragen, durchzutragen, auszuhalten, der Kraft, sie in sich zu hegen wie eine Mutter ihr Kind, und jeder Art von sorgender und mittragender Hilfe. Die Mitte des Begriffs bildet bei Irenäus der Gott tragende Mensch: Er hat die Eignung, die Belastbarkeit, die Fassungskraft dazu: portante homine et capiente et complectente Filium Dei. Und Gott gewöhnt den Menschen daran, 'Gottes Geist zu tragen', ja capere et portare Deum. Das ist mehr als das biblische, zugrundeliegende portare imaginem ejus; nämlich das grundsätzliche Vermögen des geschaffenen Wesens, den Schöpfer auszuhalten, was freilich 'Bild und Gleichnis' zur Voraussetzung hat" (ibid., 56–57). ["Portare" ranges between the dignity and suitability to receive a burden, the burden of God, the responsibility to carry it with oneself, to carry it through, to endure; the power to care for it in oneself as a mother cares for her child, and every kind of nurturing and supporting help. The center of the concept for Irenaeus forms around the man who bears God: He has the suitability, the resilience, the mental capacity for it: carrying and understanding and embracing the Son of God. And God accustoms humanity to "bear God's Spirit," indeed to understand and carry God. This is more than the Biblical underlying idea of bearing his image: namely the fundamental power of the created essence to endure the Creator, which of course has the "image and likeness" as a prerequisite.]

18. For a discussion, see Edward Oakes, *The Pattern of Redemption: The Theology of Hans Urs von Balthasar* (New York: Continuum, 1994), 45ff. The degree to which the final version of the *analogia fidei* in its most developed form in the *Church Dogmatics* holds to this point is a matter that cannot be settled here. Von Balthasar seems to think that Barth's mature position acknowledges this in its use of obediential potency (*Barth* 165).

19. See H II.71, quoted in note 21 above.

20. "Weil für ihn das höchste existierende Sein platonisch verstanden wird als die absolute Einheit, und die Kontingenz und Geschaffenheit deshalb hinreichend ausgedrückt wird mit der nur erstrebten, nie erreichten Einheit der Dinge."

21. "Wenn das Sein in der Einheit besteht, dann besteht auch die geschöpfliche Teilnahme am Sein in einer abgestuften Teilnahme an der Einheit."

22. The notion of participation remains vague. All that we are discussing here is the process of clarifying what von Balthasar means by it.

23. "In seiner Tragweite wird dies ermeßbar beim Timaiosmythos, wo mythischem Vorstellen entsprechend ein persönlicher Gott über die Weltgötter gesetzt und dennoch im philosophischen Denken der Idee des Guten untergeordnet wird" (*H* III.1.179). [This becomes measurable in its consequences in the *Timaeus* myth, where, in accordance with mythical imagination, a personal God is set above the worldly gods and nevertheless is subordinated in philosophical thinking to the Idea of the Good.]

24. "Augustin erklärt also die biblische Schöpfung mit den Kategorien der platonischen Partizipation: daß etwas außerhalb der vollendeten absoluten Einheit existieren kann, ist nur denkbar, wenn aus dem quasi-Nichts der Materie, „woraus Gott alles gemacht hat", durch schöpferische Einstrahlung der in Gottes Geist wesenden und mit ihm identischen Formen, die endlichen existierenden Wesenheiten gebildet werden."

25. "Gestalt und Schönheit können, immanent betrachtet, nunmehr nichts anderes sein als Zahl, denn Zahl ist die aus der Einheit entsprungene, nur durch die Einheit und in ihr erklärbare Vervielheitlichung der Einheit." Though we may question this account of the relation of unity to number on the basis of mathematics (1 being itself a number), if the starting point is a philosophical doctrine of identity, which is understood as the content of the notion of both unity and, to some extent, simplicity, the objection is seen to have much less force. See also the following note.

26. "Daß das Wesen Zahl sei [. . .] kann man deshalb nicht als eine reine Quantifizierung und Mathematisierung des Seins ansehen, weil die Einheit, die diese Zahlen und Zahlenverhältnisse spiegeln, jenseits aller Quantität das Qualitative schlechthin ist" (*H* II.118). [That essence is number can nevertheless not be considered a pure quantification and translation into mathematics of being, since the unity that these numbers and numerical relations mirror is most properly the qualitative, beyond all quantity.] This also helps to explain why unity is not to be equated with the *number* one.

27. Von Balthasar's strategies for avoiding pantheism and the pitfalls of identity will be examined in detail in the next chapter.

28. Even the Irenaean approach, which began with the Incarnation, can be seen to be analogical insofar as it began with the conditions of the possibility of the Incarnation within creatures, and only then ascended to the necessary conditions in the godhead.

29. *H* II.217

30. *H* II.220

31. "Was von Gott herkommt, ist von ihm auch geschaffen."

32. "Die Wende wird so unmerklich wie möglich vollzogen" (*H* II.233).

33. "auch die philosophischen Kategorien der Unendlichkeit, der Überlegenheit Gottes über Raum und Zeit, seiner Leidlosigkeit (apatheia) und gerade deswegen seiner Immanenz in allem Endlichen werden personal gefüllt: die Impassibilität muß eins sein mit Gottes Erbarmen, seine Immanenz wird sogleich zu seinem persönlichen Anwesen" (*H* II.234). [also the philosophical categories of infinity, of God's transcendence over space and time, of his impassibility (*apatheia*) and therefore his immanence in all finite things is filled out personally: impassibility must be one with God's mercy, his immanence becomes equivalent to his personal presence.]

34. The full passage concerning the logic of the *Monologion* is relevant here: "Was von Gott herkommt, ist von ihm auch geschaffen, und zwar, wie die Folge zeigt, notwendig aus Nichts oder aus seiner schöpferischen Idee, woraus Gottes Freiheit und Personalität und schließlich sein Geistwortsein folgt" (*H* II.233). [What comes from God is also created by him, and as it clearly

follows, necessarily out of nothing or out of his creative idea, whence God's freedom and character and finally his being as spiritual word follow.]The German word *Personalität* presents us with problems for translation. "Personality" would be misleading, for it would encourage us to interpret this passage with psychological categories, which von Balthasar does not intend. "Personhood" is not exactly correct either, for it does not seem that the personal distinctions in the Trinity follow either from *creatio ex nihilo* or from the creative ideas.

35. "Deshalb wird einer der stehenden Titel Gottes nunmehr creatrix essentia (substantia, natura)"

36. "Die 'Ideen' werden nicht primär von unten aus der Kontingenz und den Stufen der Weltqualitäten erschlossen, die in ihren Steigerungen Grade der Vollkommenheit, ja der Wirklichkeit sind, die auf ein Vollkommenstes und Wirklichstes in ihrem Bereich verweisen (persuadet), vielmehr von oben: aus der freien Selbstaussprache Gottes, der plant und sich 'vorstellt', was er will. Damit erhält die Kategorie des Ausdrucks (exprimere) ihre Stelle, die bei Bonaventura so wichtig werden wird" (*H* II.234). [. . .the 'Ideas' are deduced not primarily from below, from the contingency and grades of worldly qualities, which exist in their increasing degrees of perfection, indeed of reality, and which point to a most perfect and most real thing within their own realm; rather, they are deduced from above, from the free self-pronouncement of God, who plans and 'imagines' what he will. And with that the category of expression, which will become so important in Bonaventure, receives its place.]

37. "pro eo quod illius primi principii potentissimi, sapientissimi et optimi, illius aeternae originis, lucis et plenitudinis, illius, inquam, artis efficientis, exemplantis et ordinantis sunt *umbrae, resonantiae* et *picturae*, sunt *vestigia, simulacra* et *spectacula* nobis ad contuendum Deum proposita et *signa* divinitus data; quae, inquam, sunt *exemplaria* vel potius *exemplata*, proposita mentibus adhuc rudibus et sensibilibus, ut per sensibilia, quae vident, transferantur ad intelligibilia, quae non vident, tanquam per signa ad signata" (*Itinerarium* 3.11). [Because they are *shadows, resonances* and *pictures* of that most powerful, most wise and best first principle, of that eternal origin, light, and fullness; of, I say, that effectual, exemplating and ordering art—for this reason they are traces, images and demonstrations given to us in order that we may contuit God and they are signs divinely given to us.] All references to Bonaventure are from *Opera Omnia*, edited by PP Collegii a S. Bonaventurae (Roma: Quaracchi, 1882–1902). The concept of "art" in connection with exemplarity is an important idea worthy of its own study. We can afford only to pass over it with the most cursory mention here in quoting a few texts: "Pater enim ab aeterno genuit Filium similem sibi et dixit se et similitudinem suam similem sibi et cum hoc totum *posse* suum; dixit quae posse facere, et maxime quae voluit facere, et omnia in eo expressit, scilicet in Filio seu in isto *medio* tanquam in sua arte" (*Hexaemeron* 1.12) [Therefore the Father eternally begot a Son similar to himself and spoke himself and the likeness similar to himself, and with this his total power; he said those things that he was able to do, and most importantly those things that he willed to make and expressed everything in him, namely, in the Son or in that medium as if in his art]; "Rather, the divine ideas are themselves *expressive* and give rise to the created world, and do not arise from the created world. Hence the eternal reasons are called the Eternal Art, *ars aeterna*" (Leonard J. Bowman "The Cosmic Exemplarism of St. Bonaventure," *Journal of Religion* 55 [1975], 82); "Der Begriff der Ars findet seine eigentliche Erklärung im theologischen Begriff des Verbum (Ars Patris)" (Romano Guardini, *Systembildende Elemente in der Theologie Bonaventuras* [Leiden: Brill, 1964], 12).

38. "Der Hauptzustrom käme dann immer noch von Augustinus her: Philosophie der Liebe, des Trinitätsbilds im geschaffenen Geist, der Stufen des Seins und entsprechend der Schönheit, erleuchtende Einstrahlung und Einwohnung der ewigen Wahrheit als des personalen magister interior im geschöpflichen Geistakt; aber fast ebensostark wäre der Zustrom von Dionysius her, unmittelbar, sowie durch die Chartresschule und Richard von Sankt Viktor vermittelt: göttliche Transzendenz und mystische Ekstasis zu ihr hin, Schöpfung als Ausströmung Gottes, und zwar nunmehr in Kombination mit der augustinischen Trinitätslehre, wodurch sogleich eine neue Figur entsteht: die Zurückhaltung sowohl Augustins wie Dionysius', was die Offenbarung und

weltliche Mitteilung der Trinität angeht, fällt dahin, weder ist die Trinität, wie bei Dionysius, das schlechthin Entrückte, Unerkennbare, noch bleibt, wie bei Augustin, jeder weltliche Verweis auf die göttlichen Personen bloße Appropriation, vielmehr wird die Trinität in ihrer Ergießung in die Welt (in Schöpfung und Menschwerdung Christi) wahrhaft eröffnet und erweist sich so als Grund und Apriori alles weltlichen Seins. Als dritter Zustrom wäre Anselm zu nennen, in dem, was er Eigenstes hat: dem 'ontologischen Beweis', den Bonaventura übernimmt und der auch bei ihm nur der Höchstfall einer ästhetisch-theologischen Schau ist, wie denn an entscheidenden Orten gerade auch die hymnischen Stellen Anselms und seine Gebete angeführt werden: ihm wird das letzte Wort gelassen, wo es geht um die Überwältigung der von Gott beseligten Kreatur, die ihr Glück nicht faßt, sondern von ihm gefaßt wird" (*H* II.267–69). [The principle influence would always come from Augustine: philosophy of love, of the image of the Trinity in created spirit, of the hierarchy of being and accordingly of beauty, of an illuminating irradiation and indwelling of the eternal Truth as the personal *inner teacher* in the intellectual act of the creature; but almost as strong would be the influence of Dionysius, directly as well as mediated through the School of Chartres and Richard of St. Victor: divine transcendence and mystical ecstasy toward it, creation as a radiation of God, and even now in combination with the Augustinian doctrine of the Trinity, through which a new figure immediately arises: the restraint, as much of Augustine as of Dionysius, which concerns the revelation and worldly participation in the Trinity, is lacking; neither is the Trinity, as for Dionysius, the removed and unknowable being *par excellence*, nor does it remain, as for Augustine, the mere appropriation of every worldly reference to the divine persons; rather, the Trinity is, in its pouring into the world (in creation and in the Incarnation of Christ), truly revealed and shows itself thus as the ground and *a priori* of all worldly being. Anselm would be taken as a third influence, in that which is most uniquely his: the "ontological proof," which Bonaventure adopts and which is also for him only the highest instance of an aesthetic-theological display, as in the decisive passages also precisely the hymnic loci of Anselm and his prayers get cited: to him is the last word reserved, when the overpowering of the creature made blessed by God is in view; the creature that does not grasp its happiness, but rather is grasped by it.]

39. "Aber sie [die Vernunft] ist erst die Voraussetzung für die Mitteilbarkeit Gottes in seinem Wort: objektiv-gegenständlich als Verbum incarnatum, subjektiv-innerlich als Verbum inspiratum, und für beide fontal als Verbum increatum, das das innere Wesen Gottes und damit auch die ganze Welt ausdrückt."

40. Von Balthasar makes the point explicitly in the *Epilog*: "Darum hat jedes Wesen die Gabe, sich andern gegenüber 'äußern' zu können, was ein 'innern' voraussetzt, sich mit-teilen zu können, was ein geheimnisvolles 'teilen' 'mit' den andern besagt, indem das sich Mitteilende zugleich sich gibt und—um sich geben zu können—sich wahrt" (*Epilog*, 41). [Therefore every being has the gift to be able to externalize itself to another, which presupposes an inner ability to share oneself, which indicates a secret "division" "with" the other in which the one sharing oneself at the same time gives oneself and, in order to be able to give oneself, maintains oneself.] This idea of the necessity of distinction for participation will be discussed at more length in chapter 3, II.A.

41. Interpretations of Bonaventure that drive the system in the direction of pantheism are certainly extant—Paul Tillich's self-declared pan-en-theism counts Bonaventure among its spiritual predecessors. Von Balthasar's reading of Bonaventure flatly contradicts any such reading.

42. "'Nun ist aber das Wort nichts anderes als eine ausdrückliche und ausdrückende Ähnlichkeit. . .'" (*H* II.291). [Now Word is nothing other than an exact and expressing likeness.]

43. "'Expressus' wird mehrfach 'expressivus' entgegensetzt: das erste Wort entspräche ungefähr dem deutschen 'ausdrücklich' im Sinn von 'genau', ex-akt in der Wiedergabe, das zweite dagegen entspräche dem deutschen 'ausdrückend', wobei alles Gewicht auf die Ausdrucksrelation selbst gelegt wird" (*H* II.291-2). [*Expressus* is often opposed to *expressivus*: the first word corresponds roughly with the German *ausdrücklich* [Eng. "express"] in the sense of "precise," exact in the reproduction; but the second corresponds to the German *ausdrückend* [Eng. "expressing,"

but better translated with the Latin-based "expressive"], by which all of the importance is laid on the relationship of expression itself.]

44. "Kennzeichnend ist aber, daß jene mit 'expressus' bezeichnete Genauigkeit doch immer sozusagen im Schatten der Expressivbeziehung gelesen und gedeutet, auf keinen Fall aber diese auf jene zurückgeführt wird, womit schon gesagt ist, daß der bonaventurianische Schönheitsbegriff (auch als 'Exaktheit', als 'aequalitas numerosa') sich immer im Rahmen einer Ontologie des Ausdrucks (als Fruchtbarkeit, Hingabe, Liebe im Sein selbst) bewegen wird. So wird auch das (Ab-) Bild innerlich an das Urbild gebunden: 'Wo Bild ist, dort ist Nachahmung' (Imago wird von imitago hergeleitet)" (H II.292). [But it is characteristic that that exactness termed *expressus* is always, so to speak, read and interpreted in the shadow of the expressive relationship, but in no case does the latter get reduced to the former; whence it was said earlier that the Bonaventurean concept of beauty (even as "exactness", as "numerical equality") always gets deployed in the framework of an ontology of expression (as fruitfulness, giving-over, love within being itself). So the (reflected) image becomes bound inwardly to the archetype: "Where there is an image, there is imitation" (*imago* gets derived from *imitago*).]

45. "Das besagt nichts weniger als die Fundierung des Schöpfungsaktes im innergöttlichen Zeugungsakt."

46. "Aber in der Zeugung des Sohnes drückt sich Gott (der Vater) einmalig und endgültig aus: sich selbst und damit auch seine ganze Macht und sein ganzes Können: dixit similitudinem suam, et per consequens expressit omnia quae potuit" (H II.296). [But in the generation of the Son, God (the Father) expressed himself uniquely and definitively: himself and therefore his entire power and his entire ability: "he said his likeness and consequently he expressed everything that he was able to."]

47. "Hat aber der Vater im Sohn all sein Sein und Können wirklich ausgedrückt, dann ist im Sohn alles durch Gott Mögliche wirklich" (H II.297). [If the Father expressed his entire Being and ability in the Son, then everything possible through God is real in the Son.]

48. "Und was außer Gott durch Gott noch verwirklicht wird, kann nur durch den Sohn und im Sohn sowohl Möglichkeit wie Wirklichkeit haben" (ibid.). [...and whatever else is realized outside of God through God can only have both possibility and reality through the Son and in the Son.]

49. "So kehrt das schon Gesagte hier wieder: nicht vor allem weil er absoluter Inhalt, sondern weil er absoluter Ausdruck ist, ist der Sohn Urbild, Idee, Exemplar aller Dinge außer Gott; Bonaventura ist in dieser Aussage unerschöpflich" (ibid.). [Thus the aforementioned returns here: the Son is the archetype, the idea, the exemplar of all things outside of God not because he is above all absolute content, but because he is absolute expression; Bonaventure never tires of this statement.]

50. Von Balthasar produces a string of quotes to substantiate this in Bonaventure: "Alles Geschaffene ist also im Vorgang des Logos fundiert: 'Niemals wäre Gott fähig gewesen, auf Grund seines Willens ein Geschöpf hervorzubringen, wenn er nicht auch den Sohn auf Grund der Natur hervorgebracht hätte.' 'Jeder Hervorgang ist entweder Zeugung oder Folge dieser Zeugung.' 'Im Hervorgang des Wortes ist alles gesagt, im Hervorgang der Gabe (des Heiligen Geistes) ist jede Gabe gegeben.' 'Gibt es die Erzeugung von etwas Ungleichem, so setzt sie begrifflich die Erzeugung des Gleichen voraus. Das läßt sich so beweisen: das Gleiche verhält sich zum Ungleichen wie das Selbige zum Verschiedenen, das Eine zum Vielen; aber notwendig geht das Selbige dem Verschiedenen, das Eine dem Vielen voraus. . . . So geht von der ewigen Substanz das Unterschiedene solange nicht aus, als nicht das Selbige erzeugt worden ist'" (H II.300). [Every created thing is therefore founded in the procession of the Word: "God would never have been capable of producing a creature on the basis of his will if he had not also produced the Son on the basis of his nature." "Every procession is either generation or the result of this generation." "In the procession of the Word everything is said; in the procession of the Gift (the Holy Spirit) every gift is given." "If there is a production of something dissimilar, it thus presupposes conceptually the production of something similar. This is proven thus: the similar is to the dissimilar as the same is to the different, the one to the many; but the same necessarily goes before the different, the one

before the many . . . thus the different does not procede from the eternal substance unless the same has first been produced."]

51. "Ist das Wort Gottes als totaler Ausdruck Gottes die 'archetypische Welt' in der dreifachen Hinsicht, daß es 1. zum Ursprung hin gesehen diesen vollkommen ausdrückt, 2. dem Ursprung als Ausdrucksmedium dient (wie dem Denkenden der innere Begriff) und 3. vom Ursprung auch—ohne seine Geistimmanenz zu verlieren—bei der Menschwerdung in äußere Gestalt (also Inbegriff des in der Schöpfung Gemeinten) ausgedrückt wird, so kann alle Kreatur nur, im Abstand des Andersseins, eine „defiziente" und deshalb notwendig vielfache Nachahmung der ursprünglichen identischen Bildgestalt in Gott selber sein" (H II.303). [If the Word of God as complete expression of God is the "archetypal world" in a threefold respect, namely in that (1) seen with respect to the origin, it expresses it completely; (2) it serves the origin as a medium of expression (as the inner concept serves the one thinking), and (3) it is also expressed by the origin—without losing its spiritual immanence—in the Incarnation in outer form (thus the quintessence of that which was intended in the creation), then every creature can only, in the distinction of otherness, be a "deficient" and therefore necessarily multiple imitation of the primal, identical form of the image in God himself.] See Andrew Louth: "We are in fact reaching back behind Augustine to the doctrine of the Trinity found in the Greek Fathers. The crucial difference between Augustine and the Greeks […] is that for the Greeks the Image of God is the Son, who is also God, whereas for Augustine the image of God is something other than God, indeed the highest created spiritual substance, man's soul (and indeed the angels), which is a trinitarian image of the Trinitarian God. God is over against us as Trinity: therefore we are not God. For the Greeks God is over against us as God (the Father), revealed to us as God (the Son) and present in us as God (the Holy Spirit). This characterisation of the Greek patristic doctrine of the Trinity […] is presupposed here by Balthasar" ("The Place of *Heart of the World* in the Theology of Hans Urs von Balthasar" in *The Analogy of Beauty*, edited by John Riches, [Edinburgh: T&T Clark, 1986], 152). Von Balthasar explicitly acknowledges this (cf. H II.295–96).

52. "Weil aber in der engelischen Hierarchie die zusammengeordneten Geister je als einzelne nicht die höchste Vollendung besitzen, muß notwendig aus einer angemessenen Verschiedenheit in einer verhältnismäßigen Stufung eine gewisse Ordnungsharmonie und Schönheit erreicht werden, die auf der kreatürlichen Seite die höchstmögliche Vollkommenheit ist" (H II.304). [But because in the angelic hierarchy the spirits, ordered one to another, do not as individuals possess the highest perfection, a certain harmonious ordering and beauty must be reached on the basis of an appropriate differentiation in a relative gradation, which is the highest possible perfection for creatures.]

53. "Diese Annäherung durch Abstand hat, nach Augustinus, drei Stufen: Spur (vestigium), Bild (imago) und Angleichung (similitudo); in der 'Spur' drückt sich das dreifaltige Ursprungsgeheimnis nur objektiv aus, im 'Bild' wird es ausdrücklich in der Struktur des Subjekts, das durch die Gestalt seines Geistseins in die Beziehung zum dreieinigen Ursprungsgeist tritt, in der 'Angleichung' wird durch die heiligmachende Gnade das Urbild im Nachbild einwohnend" (H II.304). [This drawing near through distance has, following Augustine, three grades: trace (*vestigium*), image (*imago*) and likeness (*similitudo*). In the "trace," the trinitarian primal secret expresses itself only objectively; in the "image," it becomes explicit [*ausdrücklich*] in the structure of the subject, which through the wholeness of its spiritual being steps into relationship with the trinitarian primal being; in the "likeness," the archetype living in the copy through sanctiying grace comes into being.]

54. "Aber nur im Licht der Glaubens-'Angleichung', der das trinitarische Geheimnis sich erschließen wird, kann das Geist-'Bild' sich selbst als trinitarisch verstehen, und nur von dieser Realisation her kann in allen Dingen die 'Spur' als das gelesen werden, was sie aussagt" (H II.304–5). [But only in the light of the believing likeness, to which the trinitarian secret will reveal itself, can the spiritual image understand itself as trinitarian, and only on the basis of this realization can the trace in all things be read as to what it expresses.]

---

55. "Wodurch man erst lernt, den Verweis als Darstellung recht zu lesen, den Selbstvollzug des geschöpflichen Wesens als immanentes Zeichen der Einwohnung seines Ursprungs in ihm" (*H* II. 305). [Through which one first learns to correctly read the reference as representation, the self-fulfillment of created being as immanent sign of the indwelling of its origin in itself.]

56. "Staffel zum Unsterblichen und Immerwährenden" (*H* II.102).

57. I say "one-sided" because it is a necessity on the creature, but not on the Creator.

58. Von Balthasar really seems to mean this: There can be no expession outside of God unless there has first been an expression within God. Because of this, that which binds creatures to the Creator is the procession of the Son. It follows that the necessity of this connection is as strong as the necessity of the procession of the Son. This must be understood in the light of the freedom of the divine processions, however. It cannot be understood to mean that it was as necessary for God to create as for God to be Trinity. It only means that should the free decision to create be made, the creatures will be bound with the strongest necessity to their origin.

59. The Bonaventurean schema of causality, with its complicated relation to Aristotle's understanding, is not a subject of direct discussion for von Balthasar. He is only interested in Bonaventure's category of exemplary causality, with its relations to the Platonic understanding of mediation. This relationship will be examined in the next chapter.

60. Though this is the most common reading of Bonaventure, in my opinion von Balthasar is right to reject it. It is in fact to interpret Bonaventure through Thomas Gallus, which, while not implausible, forces one to ignore many important passages in Bonaventure's own writings. For a thorough argument against this reading of Bonaventure, see my upcoming *Seraphic Grace: Participation and Ontology in the Theology of Saint Bonaventure.*

61. Von Balthasar cannot, in fact, specify it for systemic reasons. To do so would be to impinge upon the divine freedom, which must be able to determine the form of its actions in a way that we cannot foresee. This concept of unforeseeability (*unvordenkbar*) will be considered later in the chapter, and at more length in the Excursus on supralapsarianism.

62. See *TD* V.66

63. I am not using "possible world" in its more technical philosophical sense. What I mean by it is what was stated earlier: if God creates a world, God must be manifest in that world. A possible world is a world such that God could have created it. The more philosophical concept would allow the conception of possible worlds that did not come about by divine creation, and even worlds in which no God existed.

64. Nicholas Healy, *The Eschatology of Hans Urs von Balthasar* (Oxford: Oxford University Press, 2005), 94 n8

65. Steffan Lösel, "Love Divine, All Loves Excelling: Balthasar's Negative Theology of Revelation," *Journal of Religion* 82, no. 4 (October 2002): 586–616).

66. Necessary because God wills that the interaction be this way: thus, looked at from the side of the creature, it is necessary; looked at from God's side, it is characteristic.

67. Heidegger's notion of "fallenness" and "thrownness" may be understood as an attempt to think through the possibilities of precisely this situation. That any ontological Being-itself which could underlie the givenness of Being-there (*Dasein*) is bracketed by his discussion only serves to support the interpretation of the project as an attempt to think creation as ultimately from and for itself, without primary (and ultimately any) reference to an external whence. See *Being and Time* §38.

68. This is ultimate a Heideggerian critique. Von Balthasar acknowledges this, saying that Marion "seems [. . .] to concede too much to the critique of Heidegger and others" (*TL* II.134–35, n10).

69. Though to call it such in this context is misleading. Von Balthasar does have such a gap in the *maior dissimilitudo* of aseity; it is simply not a gap with no bridge across it.

70. *TL* II.87 ff.

71. We will discuss this in more length in chapter 6.

72. This will be discussed more fully in chapter 5.

73. *TL* I.61 ff.

74. *TL* I.56 This idea is to be found in Augustine's *Eighty-Three Different Questions*, David L. Mosher, trans. (Washington, DC: Catholic University of America Press, 1982), but it is Bonaventure who fleshes it out most thoroughly and is likely the proximate source for von Balthasar (I *Sent.* d. 35, a. un., q. 1 and *Disputed Questions on the Knowledge of Christ*, qq. 1–3).

75. Text from *TL* I.71 ff., especially the conclusion that "the creative side of human knowledge is therefore the creature's analogical participation in the act by which God's archetypal, productive knowledge creatively metes out truth" (*TL* I.78).

3

The Positivity of the Other
Rejection of the Identity Thesis

Our reconstruction of von Balthasar's metaphysics has so far been concerned with answering the question (Q): "What is the nature or character of the God-creature relation?" So far, we have seen that the relationship is not to be construed according to the Pure Difference Thesis—rather, the language of *archetype, exemplar,* and *participation* in the analogical, katalogical, and ideal investigations have driven the analysis in the direction of the Identity Thesis. Even so, we have already seen that von Balthasar must shy away from asserting *pure* identity for fear of landing the system in pantheism. There is therefore already a tension between considerations that on the one hand seem to be driving towards the strongest type of identity (driven by the notion of unification with the metaphysical ground) and the need to respect a distinction between the first principle and the dependent realities. The prejudice within the Balthasarian system is in the direction of identity: to err on the side of the Identity Thesis at least allows one to construct a Christology, which is the central point of von Balthasar's own system, and therefore is of central concern. Von Balthasar is in fact after a principle that will allow him to steer a course between these two extremes, but he is not after a median, equidistant from both dangers. Rather, he wishes to affirm the intuition behind identity without valorizing the systemic consequences of identity. The principle he seeks is one that can drive the relationship as far as possible in the direction of the Identity Thesis while at the same time blocking the collapse into it.

The line is thus to be drawn between identity and analogy. This distinction defines a battle against compromise, which follows when analogy is allowed to slide over into identity.[1] In fact, von Balthasar credits Aquinas with a major victory in this battle, arguing that, on the basis of Aquinas's revolutionary doctrine of being, a safeguard is established against the dialectic of identity.[2] It is for this reason that Aquinas occupies so conspicuous a place in the *Theologic*, though he is hardly discussed in *The Glory of the Lord*, and seems to be held in little esteem when he is.[3]

I. HISTORICAL FORM OF THE REJECTION OF THE IDENTITY THESIS

The Identity Thesis, it will be remembered, is the claim that God and creatures turn out, in the end, to be identical. Now, this thesis, even more so than the Pure Difference Thesis, comes in many forms. Aside from a distinction between pantheism (the whole is God) and panentheism (the whole is in God, to whom it is identical but who exceeds it), there is a great difference in whether this identity is considered to be actual right now, or in a temporary state of alienation which will be overcome at some eschatological re-absorption. Further, this re-absorption may be seen as a simple return to the primal state of things, or as an enrichment whereby the One becomes more than what it was before the journey of estrangement and reconciliation. In spite of this diversity, all versions of the Identity Thesis are founded on a fundamental affirmation of the identity of God and creatures, and it is the implications of this that are of interest for von Balthasar's dismissal of these styles of theology.

Here we have to look at von Balthasar's reflections on Plotinus and the Neo-Platonic tradition that follows him. This will clarify the historical version of the rejection of these sorts of views.

A. PLOTINUS

In the beginning of the metaphysical investigations which occupy the first half of the third volume of *The Glory of the Lord*, von Balthasar admits that there is a great danger that his work will be misunderstood and dismissed as Neo-Platonic; at the same time, he believes that he must be willing to run this risk in order to articulate the theological vision he is after.[4] This fact alone announces a complicated relationship with the entire Neo-Platonic tradition; for on the one hand von Balthasar believes it is critical that he not be associated with it, while on the other he recognizes that the things he must say will invariably remind many readers of Plotinus and his followers.

As the great patriarch of Neo-Platonism, Plotinus is mentioned no fewer than twenty times in the second volume of *The Glory of the Lord*, largely in connection with Augustine and Denys. He is someone Augustine goes beyond,[5] a storm in theology which has passed,[6] and an example of the way in which the theology of Denys is *not* to be understood,[7] to name a few. Yet in spite of this, when von Balthasar treats Plotinus directly in *The Glory of the Lord*,[8] the overall treatment is very sympathetic. Plotinus is discussed with regard to his contributions to a theology permeated by beauty; therefore, if one comes to these pages seeking a polemical treatise against all that is wrong with theology under the transcendental of beauty (an expectation which might have been developed from the reading of *The Glory of the Lord* to this point), one will be disappointed. What we find instead is an extended reflection on why Plotinian theology is so attractive in the first place, without much thought given to the danger that attractiveness empowers.

In order to accomplish this, it is necessary for von Balthasar to rescue Plotinus from being read in light of the doctrines that trace their lineage back to him. Thus, after concluding that the intellect or *nous* eternally finds itself in its unceasing activity (*energeia*), von Balthasar asks: "Why ought one not interpret Plotinus definitively towards Hegel, by belittling and removing every other aspect of his doctrine as relics of a by-gone era?"[9] The answer, which doesn't come for several pages, proves to be surprising.

To understand the answer, we must back up slightly. The Plotinian cosmic picture, it will be remembered, bases itself upon the One, which is the eternal existent, and the emanations which flow from it. The first emanation is *Nous*, the pure act of thinking and the condition of the possibility of any thinking whatsoever.[10] The object of *Nous* (that is, the object of thought) is not external to *Nous*; rather *Nous* is its own object. *Nous* is thus always driven by yearning, *eros*, insofar as it is driven to seek its object (as all acts of intellectual striving are), but insofar as it eternally possesses its object (itself), it is at rest (*stasis*). The object of thought, however, exists only as it is in fact being thought; thus, its reality (*energeia*) is to be found in thought. Therefore the subject (whose *energeia*, conceived of as activity, consists in the activity of thought) and the object (whose *energeia*, conceived of as reality, consists in the fact of being thought) are said to have an identical *energeia*, as it is the common space that they inhabit.[11]

Pure reason, von Balthasar continues, is always in act, and pure being (the One) is always actual. All of this leads him to conclude that there is a complete reciprocity between thinking and being, between the One and *Nous*. Thus, von Balthasar concludes, because the One thinks, it is two, but because what it thinks is itself, it is One.[12] Von Balthasar considers this an attempt to sum up the entire history of Greek philosophy. It is, he says, an objective idealism or ideal realism.[13]

This leads to the question of the relationship of the two-in-oneness of thought-being to the pure unity of the One.[14] As it is a Plotinian doctrine that the proper object of *Nous* is the One, and what the *Nous* finds in its striving is itself, it seems clear that a collapse into the One is not really to be avoided. This is the point at which it makes sense to ask why this is not to be understood in a Hegelian sense as the journey of the One into alienation through *Nous* and its ultimate return to itself in a final sublation.

Before answering the question, von Balthasar admits that there is much in Plotinus to support such a reading.[15] Owing to the fact that *Nous* encompasses all in its synthetic identity, no revelation can come to *Nous* except from the very depths of *Nous*.[16] "But then there remains nothing other than to turn the One into the element of identity in the stretching out of the mind: God is nothing other than the 'inner depth' of things, the center of that circle whose periphery they are."[17]

This is, however, as far in this direction (at the end of which lies Hegel) as we are able to go, according to von Balthasar. For while it is true that Soul, *Nous* and the One coincide in their centers, the hierarchy between them is not demolished.[18] The One cannot be reduced to *Nous*, for it is that theological reality which stands above and beyond being and thought, though it breaks through from the depth of being. In so doing, it bestows on being its transcendental beauty, allows it to be an epiphany of glory.

Now, it is crucial here to observe the way in which the defense of Plotinus was achieved. von Balthasar in effect argues that Plotinus is not to be read in a Hegelian fashion because, unlike Hegel, in Plotinus all of reality cannot be reduced to identity. The Hegelian mistake, he claims, is that while noticing the close coincidence of the One, *Nous*, and soul, Hegel fails to attend to their differences. In short, von Balthasar defends Plotinus against the synthetic reduction to identity in Hegel on the basis of something approximating *analogy* in Plotinus. This putative Plotinian analogy consists in whatever conceptual space is to be allowed between the One on the one hand and being, thought, and *Nous* on the other.

This very generous reading of Plotinus is not sustained throughout *The Glory of the Lord*, as has already been mentioned; apart from this one privileged moment, Plotinus will continue to be the prime example of a philosophical theology that rushes down the road to identity. This defense is necessary here in order to avoid losing the substantive theological achievement of Plotinus in the great cloud of error that threatens to loom at every stage: He has integrated beauty (which consists in the harmonious correspondence between the various aspects of reality) into the theological system, even though his tendency to exalt identity over everything else will ultimately dissolve this correspondence, thereby stripping theology of its beautiful dimension. Nearly everywhere else Plotinus is mentioned in the Triptych, he is frowned upon as the source of a most pernicious misstep in the development of a proper theological metaphysics. But if the explication of the nature of that misstep is not to be found here, where Plotinus is directly treated, we must turn to the treatment of the intellectual heirs to this tradition, the German Idealists.

B. FICHTE

Von Balthasar briefly discusses the Idealists in the "Prolegomena" of *Theodrama*. He is concerned with their notions of individuality, and whether these notions will be strong enough to allow a robust analysis of the actors in the drama between God and humanity. The tyranny of identity therefore presents itself here as the disappearance of individuality into the impersonal whole of the universal Spirit. Plotinus is mentioned at this point in the text: his *monos pros monon* becomes, in the hands of the Idealists, the expectation that one's own uniqueness can only be found when one is face to face with the uniquely One. This leads to the paradoxical notion that in the discovery of one's own uniqueness, one also loses one's individuality.[19]

Of the Idealists considered (Fichte, Schelling and Hegel), it is Fichte in whom this is most clear for von Balthasar. It is Fichte who, "discovering the *ethos* of the Neo-Platonic upward gaze," considers the One to be the "tomb of concepts."[20] Therefore, it is to von Balthasar's discussion of Fichte that we shall turn for an explication of the dangers of the Neo-Platonic descent into identity.

At the beginning of Fichte's ethics, founded as they are on a radical freedom wherein we shape ourselves and are a law unto ourselves, von Balthasar finds that Fichte has already made a place within his logic for the dissolution of the individual. There exists what von Balthasar calls a "sheer demand" to sacrifice the individual to the universal, the person to the idea.[21] Thus, the ethical duty of human persons is to dissolve into spiritual fullness[22] with self-forgetfulness (*Selbstvergessenheit*), always concerned only for the totality. The totality or ideal here is humanity, which is set over against individuals as a species.[23] Thus, when the One manifests itself in an individual, the resultant concretivity is purely expressive of the eternal realities of the One—the distinctiveness of the individual is not taken up *as distinct* into the One.[24] Thus, the particularity of the individuals is extraneous.[25]

What is *theologically* dangerous about such an idea becomes explicit when a theological transformation is attempted. According to von Balthasar, Fichte's system takes a turn towards pantheism at this juncture.[26] The identity of subject and object within the *I* is taken as the first step in the relativizing of the *I*.[27] This process of reduction of the *I* continues when one comes to contemplate the ground of the *I*; originally parsed as "life," it becomes the Absolute, "pure being."[28] This entails a transformation of the type of ethical surrender required of the *I*; for where it was originally called on to submit to *I-ness* in general, to lose the specificity of being this *I* for the sake of the general concept and ideal of *I*, it is now to surrender to the ground of *I-ness*. This amounts to a sublation [*aufheben*] of the *I* and *I-ness* as such.[29]

Such a metaphysics of identity is unable, in von Balthasar's view, to support the claims of Christology. It will ultimately "erase, as it were, the 'two wills' in Christ, in such a way that God and humanity coincide in a way that is monotheletist (and therefore in the final analysis also monophysite)" (*TDg*I.531).[30]

This conclusion underscores that what is at stake for von Balthasar in the rejection of the Identity Thesis, as it was in the rejection of the Pure Difference Thesis, is Christology. It is thus clear that claims about the person of Christ serve as both the motivation and the measuring stick for metaphysical claims about the relation of God and the world. Christ, though he will be viewed in a very traditional way as the point of closest *rapprochement* between God and creatures, also carries within his metaphysical make-up the demand that a final difference between God and creatures be respected.

II. Ideal Form of the Rejection of the Identity Thesis

The rejection of the Identity Thesis is perhaps the metaphysical topic von Balthasar takes up most frequently in his writings. So many other statements are reducible to this one, and it is dismissed out of hand or argued against in a sustained way so often that it is challenging to set forth the full force of the polemic. The following examples will be taken as representative of the generally sustained negative evaluation; other examples will follow in the succeeding discussion.

In *Theologic* volume 1, von Balthasar disapproves of "every kind of pantheist-idealist or immediate or dynamic-progressive equation of the finite and the divine subjects" as "a failure to grasp the most basic laws of truth" (*TL* I.228). He goes on to say: "But if there is an absolute self-consciousness, it must by nature possess in itself the measure of all being and, therefore, must have no need of any natural, unfree relation of expression or passive receptivity. The infinite freedom that comes with infinite self-consciousness guarantees the infinite subject an infinite interiority and, therefore, an absolute transcendence vis-à-vis all subjects and objects in the world" (*TL* I.228–29). What this means is that an identity between God and God's creation is *ruled out* by the proper understanding of just what type of being God is. That is to say, when we have grasped that God is not just the *supreme* being but *absolute* being (which means that anything else can only be a being by participating in God's own being), we should also see that God's infinite interiority is something that could never be transposed out of itself in a way that would be sufficient to identify the external expression with that interiority of which it is the expression. Were this to be the case, that interiority would be in a sense *repeatable*; but von Balthasar has said earlier in this text that interiority is the result of this unrepeatability (*TL* I.81).

However, the above logic only rules out pantheism, not also panentheism. For one could argue that the divine interiority is not transferrable to the outside *in toto*, but nevertheless some part of it may be so transferred, such that the created world is in fact identical with the divine interiority, but not in such a way as to be co-extensive with it. This is certainly allowable on the basis of the second quotation above; but it still fails, in von Balthasar's scheme, to "grasp the most basic laws of truth," because truth requires a real positivity of the other *as* other.

In considering the range of Balthasarian texts, there are two main concerns that must be satisfied in the rejection of the Identity Thesis: a) the positivity of the world,[31] and b) the possibility of union with God. It is noteworthy that the positivity of God is *not* one of the primary concerns. This is a recognition that in identity schemes everything collapses back into God; therefore not even proponents of the Identity Thesis endanger the positivity of God.

A. THE POSITIVITY OF THE WORLD

In *Cosmic Liturgy*, von Balthasar says that: "A certain ineradicable mistrust for an autonomous, objective nature, which exists prior to all participation in grace and which is not only spiritual but corporeal—a mistrust, in fact, for the fundamental analogy between God and the creature—has always characterized Eastern thought and his led it to feel primordially related to all forms of self-transcendence, absorption, release of the finite into the infinite" (*CL* 190). The correlation between a "mistrust for an autonomous, objective nature" and "self-transcendence, absorption, release of the finite into the infinite" is for von Balthasar a very tight correlation. How justified is this?

Von Balthasar phrases the correlation very judiciously: precisely because what he is talking about is "mistrust," he cannot say that it leads necessarily to the stated conclusions. Rather, this mistrust grounds what he calls a feeling of "primordial relation;" one is tempted to say merely "attraction." As such it may be resisted or overcome, but to the degree that the mistrust is present, this fundamental intuition or orientation will also be present. Let us call this claim [T]: "a mistrust of the notion of an autonomous, objective nature increases the likelihood of the acceptance of some form of self-transcendence, absorption, release of the finite into the infinite."

To test this, it is perhaps necessary to absolutize von Balthasar's laudably restrained phrase. So, what if the claim were [Ta]: "A rejection of the notion of an autonomous, objective nature leads to some form of self-transcendence, absorption, release of the finite into the infinite?" This stronger version of the claim allows us to test the intuition that guides the plausibility of von Balthasar's weaker version. For if we approve of [Ta], we are likely to grant [T]; if we do not approve of [Ta], [T] is likely to feel under-motivated to us as well.

To evaluate [Ta], it is necessary to pay attention to the clarification of terms as von Balthasar presents them in the original text. For he specifies that the type of autonomous, objective nature he means is one that "exists prior to all participation in grace and which is not only spiritual but corporeal." These are, in fact, two possible evasions that might enable one to claim that creation is good, but in so doing, uphold the intuition of suspicion about its character. Thus, we are not allowed to affirm the goodness of creation 1) purely on the grounds that it has received grace: to do so would be to say that it is not *in itself* good, but is only good because God has added something on after the fact. Likewise, we cannot say that it is good because 2) it is spiritual; this would leave us still having to deny the goodness of the physicality of creation. This last is ruled out by the Christian doctrine of the bodily resurrection. To accept (1) or (2) is not really to say that creation is good: it is to say only that it has been made good (1) or that only part of it is good (2).

At this point, we might suppose that the way to proceed would be to ask whether, given that the acceptance of either (1) or (2) is the definition of the first half of [Ta], the acceptance of either (1) or (2) necessarily leads to the second half of [Ta]. However, it is not clear to me that von Balthasar thinks that (1) and (2) are the only ways of fulfilling the first half of [Ta]: it is not necessarily true that the denial of the goodness of ungraced creation (1) or the denial that part of creation is good (2) entails the rejection of an autonomous, objective nature: it would only entail the rejection of a positive value judgment of that nature. To connect the two ideas in von Balthasar's thought requires another assumption, namely that "autonomous and objective" are a sort of crib for "good in their positive existence." The missing material is supplied by von Balthasar with a phrase that replaces the entire notion of autonomous and objective, namely "the fundamental analogy between God and the creature." The fact that what he means when he says "autonomous and objective" is something whose denial would count as a denial of "the fundamental analogy between God and the creature" shows us that autonomy and objectivity are not considered in themselves, as quasi-scientific terms, but are pointed at participation in the divine being. They therefore mean a certain gift of participation in the divine being which is itself a positive good. Augustine's understanding that it is better to exist than not to exist is all that is required here, but we may safely surmise that for the future author of the Triptych, more is at stake. It is not merely that being or existence is *a* good, but rather, Good is a transcendental property of being, which means it inheres necessarily and properly in everything that participates in being.

At this point, an adjustment to [Ta] is probably in order to clarify just what two things are being correlated. Perhaps we ought to say: [Tb] "A rejection of the fundamental analogy between God and the creature leads to some form of self-transcendence, absorption, release of the finite into the infinite." In this form, it is clear that the thesis is false, because it could, as we have seen, just as easily lead to the Pure Difference Thesis. It is only when coupled with the Identity Thesis that [Tb] has any chance of being true.

Very well, but we still have to test this thesis: [Tb^1] "Given the rejection of Pure Difference, a rejection of the fundamental analogy between God and the creature leads to some form of self-transcendence, absorption, release of the finite into the infinite." Since von Balthasar only admits of three possible theses governing Divine-creaturely relations, the rejection of the Pure Difference and Analogy Theses necessarily entails the acceptance of the Identity Thesis.[32] This brings us to one final thesis: [Tc] "The Identity Thesis leads to some form of self-transcendence, absorption, release of the finite into the infinite." And this form of the thesis seems true, unless one holds out the possibility of an eternal estrangement within the greater God-world identity. But even in that case, it could be argued that some form of self-transcendence is still in play, at least at the level of the subjective consciousness that recognizes that it is part of this greater whole that is all things.

What is clearly at stake in this whole discussion is the affirmation of the goodness of the world, of its character as an intrinsically good positive thing.

It is in light of the preceding reduction that von Balthasar interprets all those committed to the Identity Thesis. We have already seen this in his treatments of Plotinus and Fichte; one would necessarily have to add Hegel to the list, who von Balthasar says is "the final conclusion to that interpretation of the world which understands the universe to be the self manifestation of God" (*GL* V.574).[33] A detailed description of von Balthasar's problems with Hegelian theology is not necessary here: the outlines are present in what has already been said in this chapter.[34] We will turn instead to a name that one perhaps finds surprisingly listed in a consideration of the problems of Identity: Karl Barth.

The reason Barth must be mentioned here is because in von Balthasar's read, Barth's struggle to come to the concept of analogy was a struggle to free himself from an allegiance to some form of the Identity Thesis. This is stated explicitly in the chapter on Barth's dialectical period: "What goes unchallenged is this whole notion of 'Being in the Idea,' that original existence, the only true and authentic existence, is 'Being in God.' In this first edition we read that this Being is 'immediacy' (15, 73, and so forth), 'immediate, direct relation' (106), 'immediate union' (202). [. . .] The 'divine in me' (207), 'the original divine nature and humanity' (61), empowers humanity to become 'a divine race of beings' (18) that 'sees things as God sees them' (94) and creates an ultimate *identity*: humanity is thus a 'particle of God's universal power' (237), for 'it is not we who are at work, but it is God who is working in and through us'" (194) (*Barth* 65; the emphasis is von Balthasar's). Thus, the dialectical starting point from which Barth would struggle through so much of the *Church Dogmatics* to free himself was one that was committed to some form of the Identity Thesis. von Balthasar characterizes Barth's understanding on the eve of the *Church Dogmatics* in the following way: "The best way of characterizing this ideology is by describing it as a dynamic and actualist *theopanism*, which we define as a monism of beginning and end (protology and eschatology): God stands at the beginning and the end, surrounding a world-reality understood in dualistic and dialectical terms, ultimately overcoming it in the mathematical point of the miracle of transformation. . . . As we have seen, this monism of the Word of God, which invades the hostile world and is expressed in such idealist categories as mediacy and immediacy, object and objectlessness, threatens time and again to swallow up the reality of the world" (*Barth* 94). Von Balthasar then points out that Barth would eventually come to "feel the deeply unchristian tenor of such a panorama" and strive "with all his might to overcome it" (ibid.). The precise task von Balthasar finds Barth engaged in during this period is the attempt to save the world from being absorbed into God while holding on to his original principles.

There can be no negotiating with the Identity Thesis for von Balthasar, because it will constantly eclipse the world's positivity as an other in relation to the divine Other who does not need it in order to be or in order to be God, but nevertheless freely willed to make an other with whom to enter into relationship and covenant.[35] But why fight for such otherness at all? Even granted the Christian story, which posits that we were created for God, what grounds the necessity of an abiding creaturely otherness? Why not, for example, say that our destiny in God is precisely to be re-absorbed into the most intimate of relations, the relation of unity? The answers to these questions give von Balthasar's fundamental ground for distinction, and therefore his fundamental ground for the rejection of the Identity Thesis. It is the necessity of distinction to the possibility of union.

B. THE PRESUPPOSITION OF UNITY

It is axiomatic for von Balthasar that there can be no union if the terms involved were a) not really distinct in the first place and b) do not remain distinct even in union. This is a somewhat controversial claim, and rather than trying to prove or defend it with complicated articles, let us instead notice what this really amounts to: it is a fundamental choice of one philosophical intuition over another.

When it comes to thinking about something in relation to itself, one has an option. One might think that self-identity is a relation whose two terms are identical: "$a = a$" is thus "a has a relationship of identity to a," and is structurally analogous to "a has a relationship of similarity to b." Alternately, one could interpret "$a = a$" as "a is a" in such a way that one denies that there is a relation involved. One in fact denies that "$a = a$" is analogous to "a has a relationship of similarity to b." In this second instance, likeness goes right up to but stops short of identity: once numerical identity has been attained, a is no longer *like* b, it *is* b.

We needn't be distracted by the intricacies of the debate among philosophers: we already have what we need for understanding von Balthasar. For in choosing the second intuition about identity and relations, von Balthasar is in effect affirming that likeness necessarily presupposes unlikeness: when all unlikeness disappears (and the last bit of unlikeness to go is numerical), likeness also disappears, and one is left with identity. The terms used here are significant and decisive: a principle of analogy is at work here whereby likeness and unlikeness are united in one. It is not the ever-greater unlikeness of the analogy of being; but it is nevertheless the logic of analogy. Once we have seen this, we see that von Balthasar could not have opted for the other account of identity and relations.

This philosophical intuition, that something is not *like* itself, it *is* itself, is an important part of von Balthasar's insistence on the positivity of otherness. But this alone does not account for the valuation of difference over sameness. It may be true that distinction is required for union, but it does not follow that union is to be preferred to identity. Would it not be better to *be* God than to be *united* to God?

Von Balthasar disapproves. At an obvious level, this is the first temptation and sin of humanity, to seek identity with God rather than union with God. But there is a deeper reason, transcending the order of creation and the contingencies of its subsequent history, why von Balthasar wishes to affirm union over identity: because union requires that both terms remain in their own proper natures, it affirms the fundamental goodness of both terms. A choice for union over identity is thus a choice for the inherent good of otherness and difference as opposed to a choice for the inherent good of univocal sameness. It is not just that the *other* is good, but *otherness as such* is good. This von Balthasar finds grounded in the Trinity, where otherness is elevated to an eternal and necessary principle in the life of God.

All of this is summed up well in von Balthasar's words from *Cosmic Liturgy*: "This mutual ontological presence (περιχώρησις) not only preserves the being particular to each element, to the divine and the human natures, but also brings each of them to its perfection in their very difference, even enhancing the difference. Love, which is the highest level of union, only takes root in the growing independence of the lover; the union between God and the world reveals, in the very nearness it creates between these two poles of being, the ever-greater difference between created being and the essentially incomparable God" (*CL* 63–64).

So also Barth, when, according to von Balthasar, he had emerged from the confusion of the Identity Thesis, correctly cognized the issues: "The relation between God and creature can in no way be one of identity. 'Identity would either mean that God had ceased to be God or conversely that man had himself become God.' But the relation cannot be one utterly lacking in any resemblance either. 'Such total dissimilarity would then mean that we could not in fact recognize God. For if we *re*-cognize God, this must mean that we see God using our prior views, concepts and words; thus we see God not as something totally Other. But in and with these human means of images, concept and words (the only ones we have), we truly do see God'" (*Barth* 109). In this we see the rejection both of the Identity Thesis and the Pure Difference Thesis.

This is the triumphant conclusion of Barth's journey to analogy, and von Balthasar expresses it in words that describe his own doctrine of analogy equally well: "Thus the relation must be described as a *middle ground* lying somewhere *between* two extremes, and this we call analogy. This middle term cannot for its part be transposed to another level or reduced to a 'partial identity' and a 'partial dissimilarity' (3, 264f). [. . .] Analogy is an ultimate relational term: it cannot be explained by any more fundamental identity or nonidentity" (*Barth* 109). And so the reasons for the rejection of the Pure Difference and Identity Theses are clear, as are the basic reasons for the acceptance of the Analogy Thesis. It remains to see what the structure of the acceptance of the Analogy Thesis is.

Notes

1. "Kompromisse werden vor dem Hintergrund falscher Gleichsetzungen geschlossen: vermeintlicher Univozitäten, dort wo allenfalls unübersteigbare Analogien herrschen" (*H.* III.I.1.36). [Compromises are reached against the background of false equations: supposed univocities, where, at most, untranscendable analogies rule.]

2. "Und gewiß wird diese Dialektik alsbald nach Thomas wieder einsetzen (Cusanus) und nicht ruhen, bis sie bei Hegel anlangen wird; aber sie wird sich seit Thomas dennoch—und immer klarer und bewußter—als Gegensatz zu einer Philosophie der Seinsanalogie (im angedeuteten Sinn) als eine solche der Identität deklarieren müssen" (*H* III.I.1.355-6). [And certainly this Dialectic will begin again soon after Thomas (Nicholas of Cusa) and not rest until it reaches Hegel; but nevertheless since Thomas it must declare itself ever more clearly and explicitly as the antithesis of a philosophy of analogy of being (in the indicated sense), as a philosophy of identity.]

3. Cf. *H* III.1.354.

4. *H* III.I.1.17, footnote 4: "Ich mußte darauf gefaßt sein, ehe man mich auch nur ausreden ließ, zum alten neuplatonischen Eisen geworfen zu werden." [I had to be prepared to be thrown out as an outdated Neo-Platonist before anyone let me finish speaking.] He goes on to quote H.-E. Bahr, who does just that, saying that von Balthasar is in pursuit of a Neo-Platonic Christian mysticism.

5. *H* II.110

6. *H* II.155

7. *H* II.189

8. *GL* IV.280 ff.

9. "Warum man also Plotin nicht entschlossen zu Hegel hin interpretieren dürfte, indem man alle übrigen Aspekte seiner Lehre als Relikte einer vergangenen Epoche abwertet und ausschaltet?" (*H* III.I.1.266)

10. *H* III.I.1.262

11. *H* III.I.1.262-3

12. *H* III.I.1.263

13. "Gemeint ist ein objektiver Idealismus oder Idealrealismus, der alles Sein in seiner Logizität, seinem ursprünglichen Gedachtsein im archetypischen Intellekt begründet" (*H* III.I.1.263). [What is meant is an objective Idealism or ideal-realism, which grounds all being in its logicality, its primal thought-nature in the archetypal intellect.]

14. *H* III.I.1.263

15. *H* III.I.1.267

16. Ibid.

17. "Dann aber bleibt nichts übrig, als das Eine zum Moment der Identität in der Zerspannung des Geistes zu stempeln: Gott ist nichts anderes als 'die innere Tiefe' der Dinge, der Mittelpunkt jenes Kreises, dessen Peripherie sie sind" (*H* III.I.1.269).

18. *H* III.I.1.269

19. "Das Schlußwort der Enneaden *Plotins*: monos pros monon, 'der Einzige hin zum Einzigen, Aug in Auge mit ihm' meint nicht sosehr ein Ideal der Abgeschiedenheit als zentral die Erwartung, in der Konfrontation mit dem einmalig-Einen die eigene Einmaligkeit zu finden. Das 'Gnothi Sauton' fände so für jeden, der seiner Forderung entsprechen will, eine unverhoffte, wenn auch paradoxe Antwort. Jeder entdecke im Einmal-Einen seine unverwechselbare Einmaligkeit, ein Fund, der nur zusammenfallen kann mit einem Verlust des individuellen Selbstseins" (*TDg* I.512). [The conclusion of Plotinus' *Enneads*, *monos pros monon*, "the unique before the unique, face to face with it," means not so much an ideal of seclusion as most importantly the expectation, in the confrontation with the uniquely-One, of finding one's own uniqueness. The *gnothi sauton* thus finds an unexpected, if also paradoxical, answer for everyone who wants to respond to its demand: Each one discovers in the unique-One his distinctive uniqueness; a discovery which can only collapse into a loss of individual selfhood.]

20. "*Fichte* wird, das Ethos des neuplatonischen Aufblicks treffend, das Eine als die Grabstätte des Begriffs bezeichnen" (Ibid.).

21. "von hieraus die schroffen Forderungen [...] 'daß die Person der Idee zum Opfer gebracht werden solle, und daß ... das Individuum gar nicht existiere, da es nichts gelten, sondern zugrunde gehen solle'" (*TDg* I.526). [Hence the sheer demand "that the person is to be sacrificed to the idea and that ... the individual does not at all to exist, because it is to be of no importance, but ought to perish."]

22. "In ihrer geistigen Fülle" (*TDg* I.526), that is to say, a fullness controlled by the Idea, and thus the realm of the ideal. The *Geist* of the German Idealists is like nothing so much as Plotinus' *Nous*.

23. *TDg* I.526–27

24. "Dann ist *Fichte* bereit zuzugestehen, 'daß die Eine ewige Idee in jedem besonderen Individuum, in welchem sie zum Leben durchdringt, sich durchaus in einer neuen, vorher nie dagewesenen Gestalt zeige': was näherhin aber nur heißt, daß die Idee, in die Realisierung absteigend, in einem bestimmten Menschen einen 'Durchbruch' zu neuer Konkretheit vollzieht, nicht aber, daß die personale Individualität dieses Menschen in ihrer Bestimmtheit in die Idee aufsteige" (*TDg* I.527). [Then Fichte is ready to admit "that the One eternal Idea, appears definitively in a new, never before existing form in each specific individual through whom it penetrates into life": which on closer inspection, however, means only that the Idea, descending into realization, realizes a "breakthrough" into a new concretivity in a particular person; not, however, that the personal individuality of this person in its particularity ascends into the Idea.]

25. "Die Besonderheit dieses Werkzeugs ist letzlich belanglos" (ibid)

26. "*Fichte* verwandelt nach dem Atheismusstreit sein System stufenweise auf einen religiösen Pantheismus hin" (*TDg* I.528).

27. "Schon der 'Versuch einer neuen Darstellung' (1798) stellt an die ursprüngliche Ich-Anschauung die Frage, wie eine solche möglich sein kann, ohne daß das Ich sich in Subjekt und Objekt spalte; die Antwort verweist auf die ursprüngliche Einheit beider, womit der erste Schritt auf eine das Ich (als Subjekt) relativierende Identität hin getan ist" (*TDg* I.528). [The *Versuch einer neuen Darstellung* (1798) already posed to the primal perspective of the "I" the question how such a thing is possible without the "I" splitting itself into subject and object. The answer points to the primal unity of both, wherewith the first step toward an identity that relativizes the "I" (as subject) is taken.]

28. "Dieser Begriff des Lebens wird nun im weitern zu dem dem Ur-ich als Grund und Wurzel vorausliegenden, begrifflich unfaßbaren Absoluten (*interior intimo*), dem 'reinen Sein' (*Wissenschaftslehre* 1801), das bewußtloses Ineinanderfallen von Leben und Licht ist—vergleichbar

dem plotinischen 'Einen'—und dem gegenüber das ganze Reich des Ich und der Reflexion (Subjekt-Objekt) als Nichtabsolutes, (seiendes) Nichtsein zum bloßen Schema und Abbild des unbegreiflichen Einzig-Wirklichen absinkt" (*TDg* I.528). [This notion of life is expanded into that which precedes the primal "I" as ground and root, the conceptually inconceivable absolute ("deep interior"), pure Being (*Wissenschaftslehre* 1801); it is the senseless coincidence of life and light—comparable to the Plotinian "One"—and that in contrast to which the whole realm of the "I" and of reflection (subject-object), as the not-absolute, (existing) non-being, falls to the level of mere pattern and image of the inconceivable Uniquely-Real.]

29. *TDg* I.528

30. "Löscht gleichsam die 'zwei Willen' in Christus aus, so daß monotheletisch (und damit im letzten auch monophysitisch) der Mensch und Gott zusammenfallen."

31. Which is to say, its evaluation as an existent thing whose existence is of itself affirmed to be good.

32. Or the rejection of theism, but that is not relevant to von Balthasar.

33. Von Balthasar lists as the great members of this tradition the Stoics, Plotinus, Denys, Scotus Erigena, Nicolas of Cusa, Ficino, Spinoza, Herder, and Goethe. This list relativizes the accolades heaped on some of the figures in the list elsewhere in *The Glory of the Lord*, most notably Plotinus (as we have discussed), Denys, and Cusa.

34. Von Balthasar's major discussions of Hegel in the Triptych can be found in *GL* V.572–90 and *TL* III.40-47.

35. The place in this discussion of the question of otherness *within* God, that is to say, of the fundamental face-to-face of trinitarian relations, will perhaps have occurred to the reader. This otherness, and its relation to the external otherness of the creature, will be discussed in chapter 6.

4

Analogy

A Theological and Philosophical via Media

We turn now to the Analogy Thesis, which has survived as the only possible option for cognizing the relationship between God and the world. However, our explication to this point has shown that it is not von Balthasar's position by mere process of elimination: its logic has been invoked to deny both the other competing theses. Therefore some examination of the historical arguments for accepting this thesis is in order, along with a consideration of the ideal reasons for accepting it. Unlike in the previous two chapters, however, the examination of the ideal reasons will be less about the underlying commitments (which have in fact already been cited in our discussion of the previous two theses) and more about specifying the form this doctrine of analogy takes.

I. Historical Form of the Analogy Thesis

To detail the historical arguments in favor of the Analogy Thesis, we return to *GL* II, in fact resuming the argument as von Balthasar develops it there. Our study of this text in chapter 2 concluded with the assertion of exemplarity as the most advanced form of the explication of creaturely participation in the divine. We will now turn to the discussion of Denys the Areopagite to further complete that picture before returning to Bonaventure to fill in the final contours of von Balthasar's historical understanding of analogy.

A. The Ontology of Participation

It falls upon Denys, the great synthesizer of Christianity and Neo-Platonism, to give a robust account of the ontological implications of participation. In the

Dionysian vision, in which God's self-impartation plays such a decisive role, von Balthasar sees both a development in the articulation of the participatory character of the God-world relationship and an anticipation of the kenotic theme that will be so integral to von Balthasar's own theology.[1]

Although the logic of participation to be found here is consonant with that of Augustine, it will nevertheless be of benefit to examine it in some detail because the strategies von Balthasar sees Denys employ to avoid the adverse cosmology of Plotinus parallel those von Balthasar himself will employ. The articulation of participation in what has become a Neo-Platonic context (as opposed to the more purely Platonic context of Augustine's thinking) will therefore serve to underscore the narrow path von Balthasar himself is trying to follow with his emphasis on analogy.

Von Balthasar sees in the Dionysian theology of creation a fundamental act of sharing, a first action which originates and constitutes creaturely being. This act of sharing is also God's very self; therefore every creature, by virtue of having been called into existence by means of an act of sharing, participates in God. To unpack this, von Balthasar presents two analogies: a radius and the center of a circle, and a stamp and the imprint that makes it, adding that the act of sharing that grounds creation is identical with Godself.[2] What does this really amount to?

1) *creation:God's act of sharing::a radius:the center of a circle*
2) *creation:God's act of sharing::an imprint:the stamp that makes it*

The problem with these analogies is that on the one side, the second term is an activity (God's act of sharing), but on the other side, the second terms are existents (a mathematical point or a material object). This is not enough to invalidate the analogies, but it does make them more difficult to understand. For this reason, the claim that the act of sharing is identical with God (which is the main point of the sentence quoted) does significant work. This identity of God with God's act of sharing, easily motivated from a doctrine of divine simplicity, allows one to substitute the problematic "God's act of sharing" in the above analogies with "God," yielding:

1a) *creation:God::a radius:the center of a circle* and
2a) *creation:God::an imprint:the stamp that makes it*

The consequence is that a distinction is made between the agent and the product (an imprint is not the stamp that makes it), but the very existence of the product is grounded in an act of the agent which can only be to some extent the surrender of part of itself, a surrender which implies no diminution or giving away of what is one's own.[3] Unless the stamp shares its form with the wax, there will be no imprint, and yet the stamp does not give away its form, it in no sense loses its shape in the process of imprinting.

The equivalence of God and God's action does more than simply smooth out the analogies, however. Without it, if God's act of sharing is distinct from God, it will ultimately be the case that the creatures are made after the image of God's activity rather than after the image of God properly speaking. This is an important moment for von Balthasar to note, because it amounts to a choice *not* to validate a Neo-Platonic system of hypostasized intermediaries such as characterized the type of Gnosticism against which Irenaeus writes, but to re-affirm the Augustinian view in which God is the direct archetype of created being.

The same choice for an unmediated archetype is also the first articulation of participation. By expressing the divine archetypality with the notion of an "act of sharing," participation has been offered as the content of the notion of archetype.

Notably, it is at this point that Denys, having avoided the first danger of Neo-Platonism— that of hypostasizing the causal intermediaries (thereby creating a cosmic hierarchy that is necessary rather than contingent)—could run the danger of its other problem, that of parsing the participation of created being in the highest being with the notion of identity, reducing the entire system to pantheism. Therefore we are reminded that a radius is not the center, an impression is not the stamp that makes it, and that therefore there is "participation in non-participation."[4] This rather dense locution is really just a statement of the necessity of distinction for unity (explicated in the last chapter), which is itself the compound of the rejection of both the Pure Difference and Identity Theses.

Returning to the notion of participation thus far developed, if the act of sharing by which creation is called into existence is viewed as identical with God, creation itself will appear less as an event in the list of deeds accomplished by God and more as a fundamental ontological relation between God and the world that is nevertheless grounded in the will of God.

The myriad of existing beings are now situated in a fundamental ontological relationship to their source; that relationship can be described using the notions of multiplication and differentiation, for though they participate in the One, they are not the One. It follows that once something exists which is not the One and which is numerically distinct from the One, there has been multiplication (for now there is the One *and* something else) and there is differentiation. This means in the first instance that with the existence of creation it becomes necessary for the first time to speak of nearness to God and distance from God.[5]

Comparing these two pairs of notions, differentiation and multiplication on the one hand and nearness and distance on the other, differentiation and distance naturally ally themselves. Creatures, in so far as they are differentiated from God, are distant from God. If we wish to speak of nearness to God, we are left with "multiplication" as our rubric. While this might at first seem counter-intuitive, von Balthasar can comfortably stand by the equivalence. For multiplication is to be understood as a creative irradiation of the primal unity issuing in the creation of the many derivative beings. It therefore follows that "multiplication" is a crib for "participation," and is an apt if surprising means of understanding nearness to God.

Von Balthasar admits that all this sounds very similar to both Origen and Plotinus, but it is to be understood quite differently. The difference hinges upon, on the one hand, remembering that all creatures, however noble, are deficient with respect to the being of God (this against Plotinus), and on the other hand remembering that it is God who determines the level of a creature in the hierarchy (this against Origen).[6]

These precautionary points introduce a shift in the conceptuality, however. When we attend to the fact that all creatures are necessarily deficient, which follows from their derivative nature and the fact of being multiplied copies of an all-sufficient original, we begin to feel that multiplication is a way of speaking of distance, not nearness, with relation to God. But if we then consider the tender attentions described in the divine predestination, differentiation now not just establishes the basis for the distinction of this creature from that, but rather the thoughtful and wise ordering of every creature to its proper place in the cosmos. The particularity of the attention represented here, which constitutes the paradigmatic idea of the creature in God, is just another way of expressing the tender love of God that makes everything according to its proper measure. Differentiation has come to be allied with nearness.

We are to understand from all of this that both multiplication and differentiation are *both* distance and nearness. Every ontological aspect of the creature declares both that it is conceived in the image of God and that it is not the ultimate reality, is in fact only derived from it. Thus, the creature carries within its very being the ontological marker of distinction from that being which is its source and in which it participates.[7] The full explication of this idea will only be possible in light of the Trinitarian dimensions of analogy of being, and so will not be undertaken until chapter 6. Its presence at this early stage in the development of the metaphysical system serves to underscore the importance of the analogy of being, especially at those points where the system seems most open to misinterpretation in a Neo-Platonic direction.

B. BONAVENTURE—EXEMPLARITY AND MEDIATION

Our historical survey thus brings us once again to the analysis of Bonaventure.[8] We ended our earlier analysis of Bonaventure at the point where the notions of archetype and expression were coming together to form the relationship of exemplarity. What we earlier referred to as the "Bonaventurean revolution," the notion that the Son is exemplar, not on the basis of containing all possibilities, but on the basis of being a complete expression of the Father,[9] becomes the foundation for the Bonaventurean doctrine of analogy.[10] von Balthasar claims that this is the reason that Bonaventure can agree with the Platonic axiom that things are more truly what they are meant to be in the eternal mind than they are here below.[11] But what does the Son's nature as complete expression of the Father have to do with a doctrine of similarity between the divine being and created being?

As von Balthasar begins to answer this question, the reader who has been following the argument carefully to this point experiences a moment of conceptual disorientation. He begins by denying that there is a "likeness of participation" on the grounds that there is nothing common between God and creatures; indeed, even a "likeness of imitation" is "quite slight."[12] In order to underline this point, he cites Bonaventure's understanding of *proportionalitas*, which is not a proportion, but a proportional relation between two proportions. The operative difference here is that in a proportion, two things of the same type are being compared; but in proportionality, the things compared are of different types.[13] Put more clearly, proportionality is able to compare two proportions that needn't themselves be of the same type.

What is happening here is the development of a defense against the Identity Thesis—any assertion of participation will miss the point if it fails to attend to the fundamental disjunct between God and the world, and any doctrine of imitation must always remain aware that it is attending to something very slight, to that which is not the fundamental rule in describing the God-world relationship.

Yet the disjunct is not absolute, and although the distance between God and the world is "highest" (*summe distantia*), it remains a *distance*, and therefore there is some communication. Von Balthasar immediately reminds us that the above prohibitions must be balanced by the fact that the likeness of expression does hold between God and creatures—that is to say, that creatures are an expression of God. And of all the types of likeness in the Bonaventurean scheme (here, in 1 *Sent.* d.35, which is the text von Balthasar is analyzing), this *similitudo expressionis* is the highest because it is caused by the divine truth, which is itself expression.[14]

Here at last we arrive at the revolution, the fact that it is as expression of God the Father that the Son is the archetype. This means that the analogy is not to be read from the bottom up (the way Augustine does with his "flight to the immortal"),[15] but from the top down.[16] This means that the first moment is the recognition of difference, and only subsequently do we come to see the deep, abiding similarities.

This is in fact a mild criticism of the method we have been pursuing here—for the sake of the systemic analysis, we have started from the fact that the relationship between the first principle and the dependent realities, between God and creatures, is not characterized by pure difference, and only then gone on to assert that neither is it mere identity. *Theologically* speaking, however, von Balthasar will hold that the analogy must be controlled completely from the side of the Creator, and therefore that the meaningful part of analogy is the act of divine expression which causes us to be expressions of the divine (katalogy). This is the upshot of the fact that Christ's archetypal character is deduced from his being the first expression, rather than from a claim that all that is down here is expressed in him.[17]

This principle is to be expressed in the words of the great pronouncement of Lateran IV, alluded to by Bonaventure in I *Sent* d. 35 a. u. q. 1, that "A likeness is not able to be noted between Creator and creature unless a greater unlikeness is to be noted between them" (DS 806).[18] It is the downward thrust of analogy that assures that we will not lose sight of the dimension of greater dissimilarity and end in Plotinian indistinctness. So central is this to von Balthasar's construal that he will give it a surprising and fundamental place in the life of God by means of the notion of *kenosis*, which will elevate the downward direction to the highest place in existence while at the same time safeguarding the freedom of the Creator.[19]

It is here that our analysis of von Balthasar's metaphysics takes its leave of Bonaventure. Although much remains to be said about the influence of Bonaventure, von Balthasar's reading of him to this point has led us to the place where we are able to focus the inquiry still tighter. We have moved from the analysis of the general relationship between the metaphysical first principle and the dependent realities to the relationship conceived of more concretely as that between God and creatures; now we are able to become more concrete still, and examine the person of Christ itself, standing at the center of all reality. Before turning to this analysis, however, we will look in von Balthasar's constructive works for further specification on just what it is he thinks he has arrived at in terms of a doctrine of analogy.

II. Ideal Form of the Analogy Thesis

The Analogy Thesis is, as I have mentioned, a middle way between the Pure Difference and Identity Theses. As such, it has something of a compound nature, which may be expressed negatively as the denials of both theses, or positively (von Balthasar's clear preference)[20] as the affirmation of those things that the other two theses artificially and monstrously exclude. Following this positive expression, the Analogy Thesis is made up of the affirmation of both (a) likeness and (b) greater unlikeness between God and creatures. We will examine each of these in turn.

A. ANALOGY UNDER THE SIGN OF LIKENESS

The likeness asserted by the Analogy Thesis returns us to a theme already discussed under the rejection of the Pure Difference Thesis: the necessity that any world created by God image God.[21] But, understood through Bonaventurean exemplarity and the fact that it is *as expression* that the Son is the archetype, we understand that the Son is the exemplar, not just of our world, but of any possible world.[22] Any world that could be created would image God, and specifically would image the Son, whom it would have as exemplary cause of its being. This "hypothetical necessity" is true because of a free decision on the part of God. Again, what was hypothetical was that God create. It now becomes clear that the necessity of imaging is grounded in the trinitarian processions themselves, in the fact that the Son proceeds as an image of the Father.

Likeness is therefore coded into the very logic of creatureliness. In fact, von Balthasar will go so far as to say, with Bonaventure, that the procession of the Son is the necessary pre-condition for the possibility of creation.[23] Only when there has been an expression within the Godhead may God dare to attempt an expression outside the Godhead.[24] Thus, returning to the claim cited earlier (from *TL* I.232) that if God should create, that world will image God in some way, we see that von Balthasar can put this same idea even more strongly: "The very idea that God's essence is imitable presupposes at least a hypothetical will to a possible, free creation" (*TL* I.241). This last statement is true only because the procession of the Son is the precondition for the imitability of the Father in that which is not God. Von Balthasar's claim is that God, in choosing to be such as to be imitable (that is, in choosing to be Trinity), has at least already considered the possibility of going further and carrying out the creation that is made possible by this way of being. This creation would be the second expression of the divine essence, following the Son as first expression.[25] This assertion of a double expression (first in the consubstantial image, with a view to nothing but this image, and secondly in the non-consubstantial image, with a view to dependent reality) creates an analogy between the processions of the divine persons and the creation of the world.

The recognition of such an analogy opens exciting possibilities for the speculative imagination: perhaps we can, in fact, say a lot more than we thought about not only the dynamics of the world, but about God, if we read this analogy back up to its source. And while it will turn out to be true that von Balthasar does in fact believe we can say a lot more about God than has typically been thought to be the case,[26] von Balthasar also sounds a strong warning against excessive exuberance in this realm: "It is impossible to subsume the relation of participation and manifestation that obtains between God and the creature under some (univocal) category, as if it were a 'case', one distinctive form of participation and revelation among many. The analogy between God and creature established by creation is congruent with every other analogy only in an analogous way. Now, the fact that such an analogy of analogies nonetheless exists is a consequence of the analogy of God's revelation at the level of creation, which is the ground of every inner-worldly analogy" (*TL* I. 232). This rather densely packed passage is worthy of some attention. The basic goal of this passage is to keep us from interpreting the analogy of being in light of our worldly understandings of analogy. These worldly understandings may be used to help us understand the analogy of being, but not in a univocal way: they must be applied *analogically*. Thus, when we look to specify in what ways the fundamental analogy of being is like and unlike our worldly understanding of analogy, we must start from the analogy of being. It is the ground of the possibility of analogy at all.

One response to this situation would be to turn from that in the world that is merely analogous and to give up on worldly analogy as a possible means of understanding the fundamental analogy. Von Balthasar doesn't see this as warranted; instead, he thinks the fact of these worldly analogies is sufficient to ground their use as a possible means for understanding the true analogy, even though we are approaching the prior reality from the posterior: "The inner-worldly analogies, then, have their ultimate measure in the analogy of creation, yet this very fact grounds the legitimacy of using the former to illustrate the essence of the latter—especially since it is precisely in this process that the inner-worldly receives its definitive interpretation in the light of the God-world relation" (*TL* I. 232). To read backwards from inner-worldly analogy to the analogy of being is not to project finite realities into the infinite, but rather to for the first time interpret finite realities in their proper relation to the infinite. Of course this only works as long as we remember that the relation between God and the world is not itself God.[27]

At this moment in the system, von Balthasar is in fact very consistent, because he rejects in the realm of analogy what he rejected in the realm of being. When speaking of being, he rejected, along with Marion, that it is right to say that God is one being alongside others under the heading of a general concept of being; here, speaking of analogy, he rejects the idea that this analogy is one analogy among others under the heading of a general concept of analogy. Likewise, in the realm of being, the solution was not, with Marion, the disallowal of the predicate; so also here. Rather, he says in both cases that there is a *concrete particular* that stands at the top of the class, and all others of the class only belong to the class by graduated participation in the one true *exemplar* of that class.

Thus, God and God's relations are unique, but not incommunicable: they communicate (*mitteilt*) something (*teil*) of themselves to be participated in (*teilgenommen*). But they do not do this in such a way as to suffer loss. This is essential to the proper understanding, not only of the God-world relationship in creation, but to the account of *kenosis*, with which we will be concerned in chapter 7. This picture of communication cannot be interpreted to be giving *away*; this would not lead to participation, but transference. Transference ultimately leads to a form of the Identity Thesis, for God would then be thought to portion God's being out to the world. At the end of the day, this view lands in either pantheism or panentheism. The claim here is that God communicates Godself *to be participated in*, not to be possessed.

But this communicability is not communicability *simpliciter*. God is not communicable as God is in Godself, but only *in some way*. To participate in being is not to *be* Being-itself. This is not because to be Being-itself is incommunicable; it is in fact communicable, but only within the confines of consubstantiality (and in this way it is communicated to the Son and the Holy Spirit). But participation includes in its concept non-consubstantiality, and so it rules out this type of total communication. In so doing, it marks out a hierarchical relationship between the reality itself and those beings which participate in that reality. In this way we see that even within likeness, we cannot totally bracket the awareness of unlikeness.

What really controls this discussion, very much deep in the background, textually speaking, is von Balthasar's understanding of the problem of universals: that is, his belief about the ontological status of universals. While this may seem a rather arcane philosophical point to raise, it is a question of central concern for a system like von Balthasar's precisely because of its Platonist roots. For the version of the disagreement over the problem of universals that first really captured the Western mind was Aristotle's disagreement with Plato's theory of forms. As a Platonist of sorts, von Balthasar's understanding of universals is surprisingly non-Platonic. As it turns out, Platonic forms interpreted in any sense other than an Augustinian one (and, in fact, not even Augustine's but Bonaventure's version of this) are the most consistently critiqued of Plato's ideas.

The relevance of this to the current discussion is confirmed by the presence, a few pages on from the passage we are examining, of an argument against an ideal world (a world of forms) between God and creatures (*TL* I.239). Von Balthasar is against the postulation of any such world, and rules it out on compound grounds: on the one hand, the divine sovereignty; on the other, the assertion of the infinite imitability of the divine. The latter makes the hypothesis of a separate ideal world unnecessary, because the divine nature itself is able to be imitated in all the ways required for exemplary causality, and so additional, created forms are superfluous. The former makes such an ideal world impossible, insofar as it constricts the possible range of the expression of the divine freedom.

But why would the presence of an ideal world constrain the divine freedom? Wouldn't it be sufficient to secure the divine sovereignty that the ideas be themselves created by God? The problem is that an ideal world is, by hypothesis, a world that exists between God and the creature. Thus, these ides could not have been created by God, or they would be themselves creatures and would not therefore be a middle ground. The ideas must either be not other than God (Bonaventure's view, taken over by von Balthasar), or they are pre-existing matter from which God creates. What the supposition of an ideal world outside of God endangers is therefore the doctrine of *creatio ex nihilo*. But for von Balthasar, the *ex nihilo* is what guarantees that God is completely free in the act of creating: God has no conditions or provisions God has to satisfy in creating.[28] This is why the ideal world would compromise the divine freedom.

By contrast to this Platonic approach, von Balthasar affirms with Aristotle that universals are only real in particulars, while at the same time stringently resisting the nominalist conclusion that they are only mental constructs.[29] "Nominalism" comes in for critique at several points in the system;[30] it is not always clear, however, in what sense von Balthasar intends the term. In *TL* II.138, for example, what he means by nominalism is not the denial that universals are positively existing extra-mental things, but a doctrine of God that privileges nature over persons.[31] It is likely this slippage in usage (which either is or borders on equivocation) is as much responsible as anything else for the negative evaluation of such "nominalists" as Ockham and Gabriel of Biel (with whom von Balthasar does not seem to have spent much time). The general Platonic tenor of his thought might also be at work here: while he rejects the strong realism of Plato's forms, a Platonic intuition may remain which makes "nominalism" seem especially unsatisfactory. Given this confusion, it is hard to give a compelling account for what would drive a rejection of "nominalism" in von Balthasar's system.

We are discussing participation and communicability; given von Balthasar's Aristotelian take on the problem of universals (that they are real only in particulars), there can be no Being–itself at the top of the order of being unless it is a particular being. But once that is true, and it is no longer a universal concept *except* as concretely existing, then the only way there could be anything else in the category is by means of participation. Thus, it is necessarily true that any highest member of a category must make room for other members of the category, not by self-limitation, as if God has to become less existent so that there might be other beings, but by self-giving, by offering themselves to be participated in.

All of this has been delving into some very dense material about the nature of analogy, and the way in which worldly understandings of analogy, by participating in the fundamental analogy of being themselves, may open the way to a deeper understanding of the analogy of being. What can we then say we concretely learn about this more fundamental analogy? "Looked at humanly, this world of ideas is in dynamic movement; for us, it is the constantly new apportionment of unchangeable divine truth to the world's creaturely truth and the constant readjustment of the latter to the former. For this reason, it can even be described as the formal pattern of the analogy between God and the creature, inasmuch as it implies both that the truth begins in God and ends in the world and that there is a movement of expression that goes from God to the world" (*TL* I.239–40).

The formal pattern of the analogy of being is therefore a) a truth that begins in God and ends in the world, and b) a movement of expression that goes from the direction of God to the world. And what is the relation of *a* and *b*? Given the Bonaventurean commitments, we may safely say that they are two different ways of saying the same thing, depending on whether Christ is conceived as the Truth or as the Exemplar. The downward, katalogical motion of self-giving in order to allow for participation is the formal pattern of the analogy of being. Thus the analogy of being "represents the measure of truth. For this measure is not an independent measure standing over against the measure of the self-revealing God. It is not a measure in the sense of a perfectly balanced proportion between the two terms. On the contrary, anything resembling a proportion between two terms is rigorously reduced to God's sovereignly free apportionment of truth. In a word, any self-contained world of ideas is dissolved into a measure that we can no longer inspect from above but is hidden in the mystery of the Creator" (*TL* I.240).

With the mention of measure, we are prepared for the next step in the clarification of analogy, the role of Christ as the concrete analogy of being. However, to move to that discussion without first considering analogy under the sing of greater unlikeness would be to violate the primary directive of analogy. As Lateran IV has it, no likeness is to be noted *unless* a greater unlikeness is also noted.

B. ANALOGY UNDER THE SIGN OF GREATER UNLIKENESS

Although this section is structurally necessary in order to keep our exposition balanced according to von Balthasar's own rules, most of what belongs here will need to be discussed in chapter 6. This is because once we have entered the tabernacle of greater unlikeness, we have already made the transition from philosophy to theology, from talking about the world to talking about God, and specifically that in God which remains inimitable even in the midst of the infinite imitability of divinity. There is then a sense in which chapter 6 is the real content of this section. However, two comments that can be safely made this side of the boundary between metaphysics and theology will be offered here as a sort of forecourt.

In a preliminary way, the greater unlikeness of analogy is often invoked by von Balthasar as a limit to his generally quite cataphatic approach to talk about God. Thus he warns us at the beginning of the *Theodrama* that "[The conceptual categories of secular drama] remain at the level of image and metaphor, as is clear from their ultimate ambiguity; here too, the greater dissimilarity in the analogy prevents us from using any terms univocally" (*TD* I.18). So no matter how clear he thinks we can be in our correlation of worldly realities to their divine originals, it remains vital that we not slip into univocal predication. If we are to talk of a "pain of God," we will certainly speak truly of that in God that is the ground of pain in this world (vulnerability). But we must be careful not to conceptualize it under the same concept: as the ground of pain, it is not itself what we experience as pain. But neither is it incorrect to speak of it with the same word, for the connection between the vulnerability of God and the pain we experience is real and inner, controlled from the top down by the dynamics of analogy. The fact of likeness keeps this from becoming the negative theology of *The Divine Names*; but dissimilarity is what guards against idolatrous projection from the created to the uncreated realm.

The other major moment in this early stage of the ever greater unlikeness is its positive utterance as the infinite transcendence of God, which not only infinitely surpasses all the realities of this world, but is even constantly surpassing itself: "this plenitude itself is infinite and is therefore always richer than itself" (*TL* I.197). This is the *Deus semper maior* that is also for von Balthasar a statement of the analogy of being, but here it is converted into a positive principle in the immanent life of God. *Deus semper maior* is in fact that in God which is the ground of the analogy of being. What does it look like for God to be always richer than Godself? It is the constant surprise of personal encounter within the dynamics of the trinitarian life, the constant wonder with which the persons encounter one another and give new gifts from their depth to one another. The fuller explication of this theme, especially in its relations to divine foreknowledge, is properly theological to such an extent that it exceeds even the scope of the theological transformations of chapter 6.

We have already seen, when discussing likeness, how the greater unlikeness could not be entirely bracketed from view. Likewise, it is the case here that while likeness recedes quite far into the background, it is never fully lost. This is the polarity of the analogy of being that von Balthasar affirms as a fundamental relationship; if it were possible to thoroughly bracket the one or the other, then it would be possible to reduce analogy to either identity or difference, and it would not be an ultimate relation. The deeper one looks into this question in von Balthasar, the more the ideas of likeness and unlikeness begin to merge. The horizon of analogy is not merely the tension of likeness and unlikeness, but their union.

Notes

1. On von Balthasar and *kenosis*, see chapter 7.

2. "Der Teilgabeakt, durch den Welt entsteht und besteht, ist Gott selber, an dem jedes Geschöpf ganz Anteil hat, wie jeder Radius am Kreismittelpunkt, wie jeder Siegelabdruck am Original" (*H* II.189). [The act of sharing through which the world originates and consists is God himself, in whom every creature participates, as every radius participates in the center of the circle, as every impression made by a seal participates in the original.]

3. This claim, which would seem to require further grounding, has already been grounded in our exposition by the claim that God is not the highest member of the class of being, but is being itself (see Ch. 2, I.C). In other words, because participation has already been established, it is superfluous to seek the grounds of this assertion at this point in the argument.

4. "Der Teilgabeakt, durch den Welt entsteht und besteht, ist Gott selber, an dem jedes Geschöpf ganz Anteil hat, wie jeder Radius am Kreismittelpunkt, wie jeder Siegelabdruck am Original; besteht aber ein Radius nur durch den Mittelpunkt, ein Abdruck nur durch das Siegel, so ist doch kein Radius der Mittelpunkt und kein Abdruck das Siegel selbst, so daß von 'Teilname in Nichtteilnahme' die Rede sein muß: Gottes Urgründe werden 'unteilnehmbar teilgenommen (amethektôs metechomena)'" (*H* II.189). [The act of sharing through which the world originates and consists is God himself, in whom every creature participates, as every radius participates in the center of the circle, as every impression made by a seal participates in the original. But although a radius only exists through the center and an impression through the seal, nevertheless a radius is not the center and an impression is not the seal itself, so that we must speak of a "participation in non-participation": God's fundamental grounds are "unshareably shared."]

5. "Die Vervielfältigung und Verschiedenheit der Teilnehmenden ist primär Sache von ‚Nahe' und ‚Abstand' zu Gott" (*H* II.189). [The multiplication and differentiation of the ones participating concerns in the first place 'nearness' and 'distance' to God.]

6. "Das ist freilich ein Bild, das sowohl an Origenes wie an Plotin erinnert und doch im Sinne keines der beiden gemeint ist—sie ist, die notwendige Defizienz alles nichtgöttlichen Seins einmal vorausgesetzt, auch Bestimmung und Setzung von Gott her, der jedem Seienden das Sein und Wesen 'analog' zumißt. Das, woran teilgenommen wird (der mitgeteilte Gott), und was die Warheit des Geschöpfs ist, ist somit zugleich die willentliche Zuwendung Gottes zur Kreatur, die Ideen oder Paradigmen sind zugleich die Prädestinationen" (*H* II.189–90). [this is, of course, an image that calls to mind both Origen and Plotinus, and that nevertheless is intended in the sense of neither. [The multiplication and differentiation of the ones participating] is, the necessary deficiency of all non-divine beings once assumed, the determining and positioning by God, who allocates being and essence to every being 'analogously.' That which gets participated in (the imparted God) and which is the truth of the creature is therefore at the same time the deliberate devotion of God to the creature; the ideas or paradigms are at the same time the predestinations.]

7. "Da aber das Geschöpf am 'Unteilnehmbaren' teilnimmt und nicht etwa spinozistisch wie ein Akzidens an einer Substanz, hat es an der *Teilgabe* teil und besitzt als geschöpfliches Sein notwendig die ontologische Differenz in sich zwischen Sein und Seiendem, allgemein gesagt, zwischen dem, woran teilgenommen wird, und dem, was teilnimmt (metocha und metachonta)" (ibid.). [But because the creation participates in the unparticipable and not in a Spinozistic way, as an accident in a substance, it has a part in the act of giving and necessarily possesses in itself as creaturely being the ontological difference between being and existence, generally speaking, between the one who gets particpated in and the one who participates (metocha and metachonta).]

8. Von Balthasar will interpret the Bonaventurean doctrine of analogy to be a precursor to his own, as will become clear.

9. Chapter 2, I.E.

10. "In den Dienst dieses zentralen Satzes stellt Bonaventura seine ganze Lehre von der *Seinsanalogie*, die sehr anders lautet als bei Thomas" (*H* II.297). [Bonaventure places his entire

doctrine of the analogy of being, which runs very different than in Thomas, in the service of this central statement.]

11. "Und nur deshalb übernimmt er das platonische Axiom, daß die Geschöpfe 'dann wahr sind, wenn sie so sind, wie sie in arte aeterna sind oder wie sie dort ausgedrückt werden; weil sie aber dem sie ausdrückenden oder darstellenden Inbegriff nicht vollkommen angeglichen sind, darum ist nach Augustinus jedes Geschöpf "Lüge"'; daß 'ich mich in Gott besser sehen werde als in mir selbst', daß die Dinge in Gott lebendiger sind als in sich selbst. Die genaue Begründung lautet: similitudo quae est ipsa veritas expressiva . . . melius exprimit rem quam ipsa res seipsam, quia res ipsa accipit rationem expressionis ab illa" (*H* II.297). [And for that reason alone he adopts the Platonic axiom that creatures "are true when they are as they are in the eternal art or as they get expressed there; but because they are not completely conformed to the idea expressing or representing them, therefore, according to Augustine, every creature is a 'lie'"; that "I see myself better in God than in myself," that things are more vivid in God than in themselves. The exact logic runs: the likeness which is the very expressive truth . . . expresses the thing better than the thing itself expresses itself, because the thing itself receives its logic of expression from [the expressive truth].]

12. "Eine similitudo participationis zwischen Gott und Kreatur ,ist überhaupt nicht vorhanden, weil nichts gemeinsam ist. Die similitudo imitationis ist ganz gering (modica), denn das Endliche kann das Unendliche nur ganz unerheblich nachahmen, so daß immer die Unähnlichkeit größer bleibt als die Ähnlichkeit: semper maior est dissimilitudo quam similitudo'" (*H* II.297–98). [A *similitudo participationis* between God and creature "is not at all not extant, because nothing is common. The *similitudo imitationis* is quite slight (*modica*), for the finite can only slightly imitate the infinite, in such a way that the dissimilarity always remains greater than the similarity: *semper maior est dissimilitudo quam similitudo*."]

13. "Hierher gehört, was über proportionalitas gesagt wird: im Gegensatz zur proportio, die ein analoges Verhalten (a:b = c:d) von Dingen gleicher Gattung ist, ist proportionalitas ein ähnliches Verhalten von Dingen, die keinem gemeinsamen Gattungsbegriff unterstehen und nichts Gemeinsames haben (non communicantium): Diese 'setzt keine Gemeinsamkeit, denn sie vergleicht nur das Verhalten zweier zu zweien, und so kann sie bestehen und besteht tatsächlich zwischen äußerst Verschiedenen (summe distantia)'" (*H*. II.298). [Here belongs what is said about *proportionalitas*: in contrast to *proportio*, which is an analogous relationship (a:b = c:d) between things of the same genus, *proportionalitas* is a similar relation between things which are subordinated to no common genus and have nothing common (*non communicantium*). This "posits no commonality, for it compares only the relation between two and two and so it can and does hold between exceedingly different things (*summe distantia*)."]

14. "Demgegenübern un aber die Feststellung: 'Similitudo vero expressionis est summa, quia causatur ab intentione veritatis. . ., quae est ipsa expressio'" (*H* II.298). [But in contrast to this is the statement: "But a likeness of expression is the highest, because it is caused by the effort of truth . . . which is itself expression."] *Intentio* here ought to have both its classical sense of "striving" or "effort" and its later sense of "intention" in the sense of the final cause of a thing. These two meanings meet in its meaning as the premise of an argument, which makes it very apt as a metaphor for the divine idea which is the expressing expression.

15. Chapter 2, I.A.

16. "Neben der kaum in Betracht fallenden aufsteigenden analogia entis steht eine stärkste, absteigende: das ewige Ausdruckswort weiß besser und sagt besser, was jedes Ding sagan will, als dieses es selbst weiß" (*H* II.298). [In addition to the scarcely considered, upward reaching analogy of being stands a most strong downward reaching one: the eternal expressing Word knows better and says better what each thing wants to say than that thing itself knows.]

17. Chapter 2, I.E.

18. "inter creatorem et creaturam non potest similitudo notari, quin inter eos maior sit dissimilitudo notanda."

19. This will be developed in chapter 7.

20. See the quote about Barth at the end of the last chapter (118), where analogy is said to be a fundamental relation and not reducible to the other two.

21. Chapter 2, II, A.

22. "For, in bringing forth the Son, the Father not only utters his own infinitely powerful essence but also, in that essence, everything the divine power could create. Thus the Son, the eternal Word, directly becomes the exemplary cause of all possible worlds and of the world that is actually to be created" (*TL* III.222). He attributes this insight to Bonaventure in the next sentence.

23. See chapter 2, I, E.

24. *GL* II.296

25. The Holy Spirit is not an expression of the Father, but the exposition of the expression which the Son is (this is really the theme of *Theologic* III; specific instances are many, but consider *TL* III.18 and 73 ff). There is therefore only one expression of the Father in the Trinity.

26. See the analysis in *TD* V p. 242 ff., where von Balthasar is engaged in the task of identifying what the aspects of God are which ground the various experiences of pain, suffering, and so on here below.

27. We will see in chapter 6 that Christ as the concrete analogy of being is the *measure* of this relation, and its embodiment. But this is still not the same as to *be* this relation, which could only be possible by some application of the Identity Thesis: for either (a) the two terms of the analogy are the same, such that the relation could collapse into a statement of identity, or (b) God would have to be identical with the relation itself. But the relation does not exist apart from the two terms of which it is the relation, otherwise there are not two things to put into relation. In this way it is posterior to God (and contemporaneous with the existence of creation), and so is itself a creature. But now (b) has identified God with a creature.

28. "The only preexistent 'matter' out of which God creates the world is his free will and his eternal idea" (*TL* I.234).

29. This is, technically speaking, conceptualism and not nominalism: von Balthasar does not seem to speak of conceptualism, and I believe that he has fallen prey to the all-too-common practice of conflating conceptualism and nominalism. I have retained his language in order to make it easy to key this discussion to the primary texts, but put it in scare quotes. It must be noted, however, that the difference between conceptualism and nominalism would not materially change von Balthasar's position, and so he could quite reasonably say it is not important for his purposes.

30. For example, *TL* II.138

31. This usage is one he seems to take over from Barth. It is possible that a connection between an anti-realist stance on the problem of universals (a more traditional notion of nominalism) and this notion of nominalism could be found in von Balthasar's works.

5

Personhood and von Balthasar's Two Metaphysics

Before we can approach the point of union between likeness and unlikeness, we should pause and realize that we have reached the point in the development of the system where it is possible at last to bring Christ fully into view as the first principle of the metaphysics. In doing so, we also bring in the question of the Incarnation, the fact that this divine person became human, and that it is as incarnate that he stands at the center of metaphysical speculation. We pointed out in the introduction how the grounding of metaphysics on a person (and a historical person) is unique in the history of metaphysics:[1] the entire realm of problems and issues that go forward are colored by this. This makes the fact that the person we are discussing (Christ) has undergone a significant personal change (Incarnation) tremendously important. It will mean, in fact, that there are *two* metaphysical systems in von Balthasar; one based on the pre-Incarnate Christ, and one based on the Incarnate Christ.

In order to explicate this point, it will be necessary to follow in some detail von Balthasar's arguments in *Theology of History*, where he establishes the importance of a robust philosophical valuation of the concrete individual for the coherence of the theological story. His arguments for the importance of concrete historical individuals, for the place of Christ in history, and ultimately for Christ's role as the concrete analogy of being, will illuminate the larger claim that it is the person of Christ that stands at the center of the metaphysic, and will open the way at last to the specifics of the Balthasarian view of analogy.

I. The Importance of the Unique

Von Balthasar begins with the conflict in the history of thought between rationalism (an upward-tending focus on the realm of the universal, the necessary and the abstract) and empiricism (a focus that remains focused on facticity, on the unique and concrete).[2] He has in mind here more than the Western philosophical tradition in which Plato is taken as the first champion of rationalism, Aristotle of empiricism; rather, there is a basic tension in all human thinking of the reflective sort which fractures along these lines.[3] He contends that rationalism has won the day in "high philosophy," sacred as well as secular.[4]

We would expect a Platonist to whole-heartedly endorse this position; since we now know that von Balthasar distances himself from Plato on just these types of questions, it should come as no surprise that he will reject this position, although he finds it deeply appealing.[5] Ultimately the reason for its rejection as a guiding principle for metaphysics is the Christian story itself—both original sin and redemption in Christ (that is to say, the first and second Adams) require a fundamental commitment to history if they are to make philosophical sense.

Von Balthasar states that "whoever undertakes to interpret the historical in its totality must, if he does not wish to fall into Gnostic myth, posit an overarching subject operating in it and revealing itself in it, which is at the same time a universally norm-giving being."[6] He is indicating at the outset that the problematic he is developing is the problematic which faces the one who wants to interpret history. Thus, what he is about to develop here is an argument about the interpretation of history. The obvious and controversial assumption is that history may only be interpreted in its totality with reference to subjectivity, to some *person* who operates in history and reveals itself through history. The alternative, he posits, is Gnostic myth; one may rightly ask, on the one hand, whether even this is offering the possibility of an interpretation of history which is other than personal, and on the other, whether there might not be more possibilities than a personal or Gnostic reading. Either way misses the point, however. The point is that the choice has been made that an interpretation of history that is *theologically* acceptable must be made in terms of person.

This subject that is acting in and revealing itself through history can therefore only be God or humanity.[7] If we answer that God is the locus of this subjectivity, we are told that God does not require the medium of history to communicate Godself.[8] This might seem an unexpected denial, for the earlier description of this "collective subject" is one that operates and reveals itself in history, which would seem to be the claim of Christian salvation history. Such a God, working in history and revealing Godself through the nation of Israel and then finally in Christ would also be, as God, the norm for all things.

If we note, however, that the reason God is a bad choice for the locus of this subjectivity is because God "does not require history to communicate himself to himself,"[9] we can perhaps glimpse what von Balthasar is trying to rule out here. If the subjectivity involved is the divine subjectivity, eternal and immutable, then it must always have been whatever it is. Thus, if it is of the sort that uses history as the means of its self-communication, this will apply not only to the divine relationship with the world and dependent human subjectivity, but it will also apply to the intra-divine relations, that is to say, to the Trinitarian processions. Taken in this way, history would be the process of God's coming to Godself as Trinity, and a modalism of the Hegelian variety would be motivated.[10]

That leaves humanity as that which is to be the subject of history; however, as free and acting subject, humanity is always some particular individual who cannot be the norm for all of history.[11] There is a dialectic in human nature between the concreteness of the human person and the universality of human nature.[12] This dialectic leads to a historical realization of the essence of humanity that "must unfold in a common destiny of the constitutive persons."[13] And it is precisely this that is the problem, for such a common destiny must, von Balthasar says, be philosophically interpreted in a democratic sense: everyone has the same share in the essence, and so, while it follows that no individual's actions can be seen as without ramifications for the big picture, it also follows that no human person can be assigned a position of special distinction as a historical agent among other human persons.[14] This rules out the traditional doctrine of original sin whereby the entire race fell in Adam's transgression, who was acting as the head of all humanity. It also rules out the possibility of the second Adam, Christ: if there is to be such a redeemer, he could at best be one who was a religious genius, discovering the path that all humans must walk, that all humans have in fact walked just insofar as it is a possibility for the essence in which they all share equally.[15]

The problem of a theology of history is in his view the fundamental problem that faces any attempt to read history theologically. The answer to this problem will therefore control the direction and possibilities of the subsequent theology of history.

This problem is only surmountable by means of a miracle—the hypostatic, that is to say, personal, union of divine and human natures in Christ.[16] In Christ as Incarnate, God can be the subject of history without endangering the nature of the Trinitarian processions, because the Incarnation doesn't condition the Trinitarian processions, but presupposes them. In Christ, who is human and divine, a human nature is able to be the subject of history, and is able to achieve the uniqueness required to be raised above any competing claims of other human natures because it has been assumed into the dignity and worth of divinity via personal union. This is the formula that von Balthasar calls "as hard as mysterious": hard because it subordinates all worldly norms to the norm of

Christ, mysterious because it bases its claim on a fact that cannot be verified by any scientific standpoint, the fact of the hypostatic union.[17]

The problem of the interpretation of history and its subsequent solution in the person of Christ has the effect of establishing the importance of the unique, and therefore of the concrete. The struggle between the factual and the normative has been overcome, and now the factual and the normative are seen to coincide.[18] The opposition has been overcome because now the ideal world is not a non-historical world which imposes meaning from outside, but is a world which arises within and is embraced by history itself, is in fact the "living center" of history.[19] The historical Logos is the center of history, and as such is the source and goal of all of history.[20]

This notion of center is important, and rightly brings the discussion back to our larger project, the explication of the Balthasarian metaphysic. The first principle of the metaphysic is center; what we have added here is that it is not merely the Logos as such, but the Logos as incarnate that is decisive. However, the Logos was not always incarnate. This is as true of the history of the second divine person (who pre-existed creation) as it is true of the historical world—we live in a world where it has not always been true that the Logos came and dwelt among us as one of us. It is the latter of these two facts that enables his historical coming to be the center of history at all—history longed for this fact, stretching forward to meet it in anticipations and precursors, and now history reels with the accomplished fact, casting numerous reflective and interpretive glances back to it.

Now the fact that the historical life of the Logos has a historical starting point means that Christ has now become the measure, not just of the irreducible difference between the uncreated being of God and all creaturely being, but of *every* distance and nearness between God and humanity. This is a point of great systemic importance, for it allows a shortcut from the arguments made here about the importance of the person of Christ to the interpretation of history; now we apply those arguments to all of reality, to every imaginable relation between God and creation: Christ will measure them all, because he is more than *a* man, he is the God-man.[21] All room for complaint or suspicion of unfairness is left out in this measuring, for he applies no external measure, but rather the measure of his humanity itself.[22]

This is the basis for what Nicholas Healy calls "the most original aspect of Balthasar's understanding of analogy": the notion that Christ is the concrete analogy of being.[23] The theoretical question about what types of intervals are possible between God and creation, whether it be posed in terms of nearness or distance, is overcome in the concrete reality of the person of Christ. No one can know the love of God like he can, and no one can know abandonment like he can.[24] In the unity of his person, he demonstrates the greatest possible nearness of God and creatures while at the same time, in the distinction of the natures, he demonstrates the inviolable and irreducible difference between them.[25]

This is the person who is so central that we cannot even begin to think without him;[26] this therefore is the metaphysical first principle in all the specificity of Christian revelation. Decisively and in the first moment, the system is not founded upon the divine nature (God with personhood abstracted), nor upon a generic personal deity (such that many faiths might claim this being as the object of their worship), nor upon the revealed trinitarian God of Christianity, nor on one person of that Trinity—none of this is specific enough. It is founded first and foremost upon the one person of the Christian Trinity who assumed a human nature and took humanity in its widest range of created possibilities into real and unalterable union with himself (with such specificity that we must say "himself" in spite of our gender politics).

With this incarnate Christ firmly in view, we may at last begin the real task of analyzing the ramifications for the system itself. Having worked our way down to the starting point (backing into it through historical analyses and deductions), we are at last enabled to reason forward, to follow the logic of a Christian metaphysics founded on the incarnate Word of God.

II. The Two Metaphysics of Hans Urs von Balthasar: Ideal and Historical

The path we have taken to this point, through the necessity of the concrete specificity of the Christ, entails that the historical Logos has a starting point within history, as was mentioned.[27] This in turn entails a change in the person of the Logos—before the Incarnation, the Logos is a divine person only, but after and forever more, the Logos is now a divine and human person. While this obviously does not imply any change in the divine nature, it certainly requires a change in the person who is assuming human nature in such a way as to count as a human person as well as a divine person.

This point, obvious as it may seem, is of no small importance for a system of the type von Balthasar is developing. For it is a system which takes as its first principle a person, understood neither as a placeholder for personality generally (a more modern tendency) nor as a single personal life abstracted from its particularities (which von Balthasar contends to be the Neo-Platonic tendency);[28] rather, it is a person in all the concretivity of a lived life (first divine, then divine-human). It follows that a fundamental change in the nature of that person must also entail a fundamental change in the nature of any reality founded upon that person. And the hypostatic union is by definition such a change in the person of Christ.

We have in fact seen the emergence of two different grounding reasons for the metaphysical primacy of Christ: (1) On the one hand, Christ's primacy has been grounded through the order of creation. This line of thinking, that which began with Augustine and found fulfillment in Bonaventure's exemplarity, proceeded from the notion of Christ as image within the Trinity, and thus as the image on which all created images are based. The resulting metaphysics of the created order will be controlled by the dynamics of the divinity of Christ and his place within the Trinity, and as such defines the realm of possible and actual relationships between the created world based on him and the trinitarian world he represents. (2) On the other hand, Christ's primacy was also grounded in the historical problem of human salvation, in the necessity of a God-human who alone could solve the paradox of a historical existence which is nevertheless universally conditioned: from above by the archetypal divine reality, but also from within, by the fact of original sin and the universal human need for salvation. The metaphysics that follow upon this must think the center as a divine-human reality, as an analogy which is no longer able to be thought in classical Platonic terms as a downward conditioning reality, but which must now be taken to be the dynamics of concrete existence in the union of the uncreated and created worlds (a union that nevertheless remains controlled from above).

It is therefore necessary to speak not of one but of two metaphysical systems in von Balthasar, defined (and therefore distinguished from one another) by the constitution of the person who is the metaphysical center. We may refer to the metaphysic preceding the Incarnation as an Ideal Metaphysic, insofar as it has to do with the original and determinative relations of uncreated to created reality, with all questions of the actualities of created beings at least subsumed, if not in fact bracketed. The metaphysic following the Incarnation may be referred to as a Historical Metaphysic, insofar as it necessarily and in its first moment makes reference to the historical conditions of the created realities.[29]

A. THE IDEAL METAPHYSIC

Our exposition to this point has been necessarily focused on the Ideal Metaphysic; necessarily, because the project has been to reconstruct the metaphysical system from the ground up. Therefore, as far as possible, we started with generalities and worked our way back toward the specific claims of a revealed metaphysics. Rather than recapitulate what has already been said, the task of this section is to say a few synthetic words about the nature of this system.

First, as to terminology, I have named this the Ideal Metaphysic, in the same sense in which we spoke in the last chapter of an ideal world, that is to say, a world of ideas that exists between God and creation. Von Balthasar rejected the notion of an intermediary ideal world; what he did not reject were the ideas themselves, according to which God creates. He is simply unwilling that the ideas be separated out from God, "hypostatized," as it were.[30] With Bonaventure he will insist that they are not other than the divine, and in fact that the Son as such is the Idea that is able to be the ideas for all created things.[31] The Ideal Metaphysic is therefore the relationship of the world to its source and the consequent dynamics of worldly relations as that source is considered as the exemplary cause of the being and shape of the world (and every individual thing in it). In other words, it is the Son as source, beginning, or *alpha* that is the controlling idea for this metaphysic.

Now, in order to avoid making too much out of the fact that there are two distinct metaphysical systems to be found in this one author, we must not lose sight of the fact that each is a distinct and theoretically self-sufficient account of the relationship of things to their first principle. Therefore, the task of analysis cannot include a division of labor, so to speak, whereby the fundamental questions why there is something rather than nothing, and why there is a diversity of things rather than only one thing, are assigned to the Ideal Metaphysic, while questions about teleology, modes of action, and causation are assigned to the Historical. Rather, each metaphysic will have a specific way of addressing every necessary metaphysical question.

This means that all questions have in effect two answers. At one level, this seems to double motivate the solutions to metaphysical problems in von Balthasar, and this could be seen as a very infelicitous result. However, we must keep in mind the fundamental principle, already affirmed in the Ideal Metaphysic, that grace fulfills rather than destroys nature. Thus, even before we examine the relation of these two metaphysics to each other (in the final part of this chapter), we can say that the desired relation will be one of development, of the deeper clarification of what was latent, or merely possible, in the earlier system.

In effect, insofar as a metaphysical system describes the fundamental causal and relational dynamics of a world, what we see in von Balthasar is the claim that the Incarnation entailed a fundamental shift in these fundamental dynamics.

In a way perhaps deeper than any other theologian, he has implied that the Incarnation is an event after which the world can literally never be the same again, all the way to the core metaphysical principles that run it. It is no doubt due to the continuity affirmed by the denial that grace does violence to the creature that accounts for the fact that we could miss this monumental event, and convince ourselves that the world goes on as usual.

So, what have been the salient features of the Ideal Metaphysic? As a sacred metaphysics, the Ideal Metaphysic has assumed the answer to the first question of being, why there is something rather than nothing: because God exists necessarily. The derivative question, why is there something other than God, is answered with reference to God's will. This metaphysic, as our analysis has shown, has emphasized participation as the concept that enables us to account for the multiplicity of created things. Exemplarity is the first causality, as it is the expressive power of the Word that accounts for both the possibility and the existence of things outside of God. This required an affirmation of analogy, which enables us to correlate truths about the world to truths about God, though not in a simplistic, univocal way. Because analogy is the sign under which the entire God-world relation stands, the polarities of likeness and unlikeness become central in the interpretation and analysis of the creature.

All of this is a true description of the original character of the relation of creation to God. And yet, von Balthasar is extremely hesitant, when speaking in an explicitly theological vein, to talk about the creation apart from Incarnation. It is clear that for him, all things are thought not just through Christ, but specifically the Incarnate Christ. It is for this reason that we have required such a complicated analysis to deduce the outlines of the ideal metaphysic in the previous chapters: it is at best considered as a presupposition or antecedent condition of the Historical Metaphysics, and only in certain privileged moments (which I have attempted to highlight) does it come into the light in its own right. There is something preliminary about it, because it is pointed to the Incarnation. This is not because von Balthasar thinks the Incarnation was an original, creative purpose of God; it is because von Balthasar's starting point for reflection includes the Incarnation.

B. THE HISTORICAL METAPHYSIC

Having arrived at the realization of the depth of the change that Incarnation introduces into the metaphysical picture, it remains to fill in the content of the new metaphysic thus opened, the Historical. If the Ideal described creation in its relation to its origin, Christ as the Alpha, the Historical will describe creation in relation to its goal, Christ as the Omega. One will still ask the same questions about the grounding of creaturely reality, and so on; but they will now have an ultimate dimension that places them in the context of the full actuality of God's plan in Christ (as opposed to the Ideal Metaphysic, when the form of God's ongoing work of grace was still undetermined and determinable in many possible directions).

Much of the specific content of the Historical Metaphysic is material still to be discussed in the remaining chapters of this study: for just as the first chapters were focused on the Ideal Metaphysic, the remaining chapters will be focused on the Historical.[32] However, there are some general aspects of the Historical Metaphysic that it is important to discuss at this stage.

The importance of the historical as a category of human existence for von Balthasar is difficult to overstate. This is readily seen in his method, which is almost lamentably embedded in historical specificities: one is at times struck by the language or conceptuality used, which cannot help but feel dated, to carry with it the sense of academic buzz words and fads. Now it is certainly true that every product of human genius has a necessary historical situation, and it is foolishness to think that one can extricate oneself from this. But do not the best works achieve a sort of transcendent dimension relative to their time, which gives them a looser dependence on their historical milieu, enabling them to achieve a broader scope to which one is attempted to apply the adjective *universal*?

Von Balthasar does not even strive after such a view: his understanding of history and its value forces him to tie much of what he is saying to the forms of thought and expression that were most prevalent at his time, with little thought for critiquing them from outside their historical perspective (with say, a critique from a past era). For all his researches into the early Church, what he praises is their *modernity*, not the way in which they can *criticize* modernity.

The point is that this is no accidental feature of his thought. He has built historicity into the metaphysics at a fundamental level: only that which /yes is unmistakably marked by its temporal setting can be truly individual, and thus truly unique, and thus the focus of divine love (because only persons can encounter one another, and the person is above all unique and unrepeatable and unpredictable). Therefore essentializing of a certain sort is out; but more importantly, the project is too quickly dated, too deeply tied to the structures of its own historical appearance. It is precisely this that is lamentable about it: because the project, which has for a brief moment raised its head above the secular philosophical forces that would take it captive, immediately turns and bows its head to them again in the form of *Zeitgeist*, their tacit but iron grip on the general modes of perceiving and judging characteristic of a given historical moment.

I will offer no further criticism of this feature of von Balthasar's thought than this; even what has been said so far has been for the purpose of introducing the central importance for von Balthasar of a certain dynamic, which we also saw at work to some extent in the Ideal Metaphysic, namely the question of the problem of universals, and von Balthasar's rejection of a strong form of realism (Plato). We saw that von Balthasar opted instead for a more Aristotelian scheme by which universals were real, but only in the particulars. Here in the Historical Metaphysic, particularity comes to the fore with a relentless intensity. Our concern, therefore, is to analyze the dynamics of universality and particularity or concretivity. This is von Balthasar's answer to my critique about the need for great works to acquire a transcendent dimension with respect to their time: historical transcendence, he will argue, is a function of deeper, not looser, embeddedness.

The question of the concrete and the universal is treated in many places in von Balthasar's work. He himself gathers up the references in the last of the great treatments, *Theologic* III.196ff (a section entitled "Concrete and Universal"). This last treatment is very incomplete, however, focused as it is on the necessarily trinitarian dimensions of the dynamic. It can therefore at best only introduce the problem, which von Balthasar thinks has been sufficiently treated elsewhere.

Von Balthasar describes this topic as "the point where we feel most tangibly both Christianity's unique opportunity at its abiding stumbling block" (*TL* III.196). As he goes on to explain, the opportunity is to embrace the full historicity of human existence, without which a religion must either "bypass the real human being" or "actually question his whole existence or (like the doctrines of rebirth) dissolve it" (ibid.). The stumbling block is how to account for the universal validity of that which is historically specific without discounting bodiliness on the one hand (which would just be to deny historicity) or relativizing this appearance in a human life to one among many, which in its own way also denies the historicity (von Balthasar says "concrete historicity") of the person.

To analyze this further, we return to the *A Theology of History*, the clearest discussion of this theme. Von Balthasar points us in *Theologic* to the third chapter of *A Theology of History*, entitled "Christ the Norm of History." The discussion there points to the importance of the role of the Holy Spirit in applying the norm of Christ to history, and in this way it anticipates the Spirit-Christology of the *Theologic* III that in its turn will point back to it. But the role of the

Holy Spirit, as expositor of the Christ-form, is the *application* of Christ's unique historical life to the rest of history, to all human subjects. The Spirit "exposes the full depth of what has been completed, giving it a dimension which is new for the world: a total relevance to every moment of history" (*TH* 82). The central importance of the Spirit in the *dynamic* of Christ's universality for von Balthasar is unmistakable. However, in the explication of the *logic* of Christ's universality, it need play no great role. This surprising conclusion is borne out by the fact that the Spirit, although foregrounded in the title to this section of *A Theology of History*, recedes into the background for the first two moments of the exposition.

The application of the historical life of Christ as the norm for all of history, that is to say, its acquisition of universal validity, requires a change in his existence: "his existence needs to be modified in further ways if it is to be the immediate and inward norm of every life, and these modifications will apply primarily to the being of Christ [. . .] and then go on to affect the rest of history" (*TH* 81). This modification consists in three moments, which are really one, and which are the work of "carving out of a section of history in order to make it relevant to the whole of history" (*TH* 82): 1) the forty days between resurrection and ascension, 2) the sacraments, and 3) the application of the life of Christ to create the missions of the Church and of individual Christians. These moments are "one and belong together" (*TH* 83), but are distinct: their unity comes from the fact that the first moment (the historical last days of Christ on Earth) and the third moment (the life form of Christ as the norm for my life) meet in the second, the sacraments, and above all, the Eucharist. Thus the "one" von Balthasar predicates of these moments is a oneness of unity and not of identity.

Given this, it is clear *a priori* that the forty days have a privileged place among these three moments. For (3) comes from and is dependent on (1), and (2) is but the medium that allows (3) and (1) to encounter one another. It is the first moment that really conditions the other two and controls them (even the Eucharist, which is, as it were, confected again by Christ on Earth in the breaking of the bread before the disciples after the long walk to Emmaus). Christ has already become the norm of history with (1); (2) and (3) are just further working out of this reality. We will therefore concentrate on this exposition.

Von Balthasar deduces from the fact that Christ is clearly truly physical during this time, as evidenced by his eating, touching, and so on, that he is also truly still a part of our world history.[33] But he is also the risen Lord, and so his time is also the eternity of his divinity. Jesus therefore inserts all of history into the context of eternity; not in spite of being historically specific, but *by* being historically specific.[34] Further, this must also be the mode of time, not merely of the risen Christ, but also of the ascended Christ.[35]

This reality is the end of history, its goal and *eschaton*, but it is present in the midst of history. In that way, as the mid-point of history, he communicates to beginning and end their total validity: "By interpreting history in both senses, from fulfillment to promise and from promise to fulfillment, he performs, here within history, an act which involves both the end of history and its totality: for as the end of history, the *eschaton*, he is present at its center, revealing in this one particular *kairos*, *this* historical moment, the meaning of every *kairos* that can ever be. He does not do this from some point outside and above history, he does it in an actual historical moment, in which he is present both to prove that he himself is alive and to be the self-utterance of the Kingdom" (*TH* 88).

It is only this dynamic of the whole in the part[36] that enables the proper interpretation of every moment of his existence in this world. "Each moment of his life is more than itself; it is the presence of all things fulfilled: the 'fullness of time' in a qualitative sense, of time exalted to the plane of eternity" (*TH* 91–92). In other words, this dynamic of particular historicity with universal validity is not something newly created by the resurrection; rather: "What the Lord reveals in the forty days is what was already in full reality present, but concealed. The meaning of this revelation is not that it continues on the same time-plane what had already been done, but that it manifests the eternal significance contained in it" (*TH* 92).

At this point, von Balthasar arrives explicitly at the problem of universals, and explains his solution to it in its theological form. The passage is as follows:

> Herein lies the solution to the theological problem of universals. The life of Christ, as was said, is the "world of ideas" for the whole of history. He himself is the idea made concrete, personal, historical: *universale concretum et personale*. There is no moment at which he is a *universale ante rem*, in essence *preceding* existence, insofar as the *res* is his own historical and temporal existence. He is *universale in re*, the supra-temporal *in* time, the universally valid *in* the here-and-now, necessary being *in* concrete fact; in the thirty-three years of his life the accent is on the *res*, and during the forty days on the *universale*. And it is only as this *universale in re* that he becomes, in relation to the time of Promise, a kind of *universale post rem*, supplying the meaning after the event, and to the time of the Church in the individual

Christian a kind of *universale ante rem*; both of these being inseparable from the *universale in re* of the Incarnation in its fullness (*TH* 92–93).

Let us take the time to unpack this very rich text. The life of Christ is the world of ideas; the word *life* is very important. For in the Ideal Metaphysic, Christ, the pre-incarnate one is the world of ideas, and thus the exemplar of things in their very beings (both that they exist, and that they are of such a sort). But in the Historical Metaphysic, the *life* of Christ, that is, the historical details of his experience and actions, is the ideal world. This is no longer understood simply in relation to the form of being of the thing, with its temporal and historical realities bracketed; Christ is now also the ideal world precisely of history, that is, of the *historical form* of things as such.

It might seem that a result of this would be that the life of Christ is therefore the exemplar of all the evils done in the world, of the horrible and unspeakable acts that history presents to us with disappointing frequency. Yet this is no more required as a conclusion in the Historical Metaphysic than we are required to believe in the Ideal Metaphysic that because Christ is the exemplar of all creatures that he must represent their twisted and godless forms. The ideal world is also the source of our word *ideal*; it represents the norm against which beings are to be measured. There is not therefore necessarily an idea in the ideal world of deformed being; just of what that deformed being ought to look like.

Now, the ideal world, or, as von Balthasar shifts to calling it, the Idea, is concrete, personal, and historical in Christ. This specificity is necessary: for the Idea is the life of Christ, and an impersonal, non-concrete, a-historical life is not a life at all. This point underscores that it is only by being a part of history that Christ can be the norm of history.

But the real work this claim does is to move us to the next idea, that it is impossible that this life of Christ be a universal that pre-exists that of which it is the universal (the thing, the *res*), as a Platonic form does. This is because what we mean by the life of Christ is Christ's historical and temporal existence. It is precisely this that will be the universal for everything else. But for Christ, this life is the *res* itself, the very thing. Christ's life cannot exist before Christ's life, therefore the universal can't exist before the thing.

There is a logical problem here. Briefly, the word *universal* is being used equivocally. For Christ's life is the universal of the whole of history. And it is as the universal of other things that it is called universal. In this sense, the phrase *universale in re* means "the Life of Christ as the universal for everything else." In this way, there is no problem.

However, normally when we speak of the *universale in re*, we mean that the humanity is real only in particulars, for example, Socrates. But Socrates is not identical with this universal, for then the universal would *be* a particular. Therefore Socrates is not humanity. In this example, *humanity* is the universal and *Socrates* is the thing.

But Christ's life is also said to be the thing. What then, is the universal of which the life of Christ is an example? If Christ is the thing, what corresponds to *humanity* in the Socrates example? This would, by analogy to the Socrates example, need to be something other than the life of Christ, and therefore it is a numerically distinct universal from the universal of all other historical things. This would mean that *universal* when applied to Christ and Peter would be applied equivocally.

This is not what von Balthasar means. For he stresses that the life of Christ is *historical*; it is therefore a particular in the category for which it is also the universal. This is the Balthasarian paradox: that one of the class is the exemplar for the class. When we approach this from the direction of the problem of universals, we end up with what seems to be a contradictory claim: a particular is universal. When we approach it from the logic of the Ideal Metaphysic, the picture is quite different: it is exactly analogous to the situation with the category *Being*. If we follow that analogy, von Balthasar's claim would be that the life of Christ is in some way History-itself, and everything else participates in its history. This does indeed seem to be very close to the claim in *A Theology of History*.

Very close, but perhaps not exactly right. Von Balthasar goes on to gloss *universale in re* with "the supra-temporal *in* time, the universally valid *in* the here-and-now, necessary being *in* concrete fact." In other words, there does seem to be something else in view here as the universal. It is not simply that the life of Christ is the universal of all historical things, of which the life of Christ is one, and so it is History-itself, or better, the Historical-itself. Rather, that which is the universal, of which the life of Christ is an example, is the supra-temporal, the universally valid, necessary being: in short, divinity. The life of Christ is part of the person of the Son.

But if this is the relation, are the conceptuality of universal and particular quite right? To say that the life of Christ is a specific instance of which the divine Son is the genus would mean that this historical existence is *a form of* necessary being. And so it is, von Balthasar would argue: the historical life of Jesus of Nazareth does in fact happen to be a form or instance of the divine second person. This is what it means for necessary being to come and dwell within history as one of us. And it is only the fact that it is necessary being within the confines of history (the universal in the thing) that enables it to become the universal for all other things.

The upshot, then, is that the universal does not exist until it is instantiated in an individual, which is consistent with the claims in the Ideal Metaphysic. This does not mean that Christ didn't exist before the Incarnation, but that the life of Christ, the historical career, didn't exist before it happened, which seems true.

Thus, the following claim is that during the thirty-three years of Jesus' life we saw the thing, the life of Christ, in the forefront; during the forty days after the resurrection, we saw the universal in the foreground. But which universal is this? Is it the divinity, or the life of Christ as universal for everything else? It can only in fact be the latter, because of what has already been said about the nature of the appearances of these forty days. He stays to show us the new universal that he has become (the accomplished fact of the transition from the Ideal to the Historical Metaphysic).

This new universal *does* become a *universale ante rem*, a universal that exists prior to being instantiated in a concrete particular. In that way, it attains the status of the Platonic forms, or better, of the exemplary ideas that were so important in the Ideal Metaphysic; but it does so only secondarily. He must fight to get to the more Platonic notion of form, and even then only through a prior affirmation of an Aristotelian picture of universals. Still, we do arrive at the Platonic (Bonaventurean) picture: the life of Christ is now the exemplary cause of the life of every Christian, and of the life of the Church, and it is the norm against which all other forms of life will be judged as deficient or disobedient.

All of this could be summed up in von Balthasar's words in *Theologic I*, speaking about the preconditions that objects place on potential knowers: "This kind of extension can be termed, in contrast to the abstract universality of laws and structures, concrete universality, for the unique as such has universal validity" (*TL* I.182).

Thus the outlines of the Historical Metaphysic begin to take shape. These outlines will be filled in more specifically in the next chapter; it is most important to note here the way in which it is structurally similar to what was said in the Ideal Metaphysic. We are seeing the type of analogical correspondence one would expect in two systems that are complimentary rather than antithetical.

This focus on concretivity has many ramifications. One is a certain nuanced understanding of the notion of the interiority of the subject: "If each and everything were nothing more than an 'instance of. . .' or a kind of algebraic 'x' that could be exchanged for other entities without loss, then things would possess absolutely no intrinsic value of their own as individuals. [. . .] In a world such as this, existence would no longer have any meaning, for being would have lost the property that alone gives the possession of being its desirability: unrepeatability and, therefore, interiority" (*TL* I.81). Interiority is therefore the result of this unrepeatability. This seems to be because of the negative description of what would be the case if beings were entirely substitutable (in algebraic fashion). "To know one cat is to know every cat" would mean that every cat as such is laid open by the violence of generality, "prostituted" such that it had no space of its own to withhold and offer only by degrees, only to the intellectual gaze that could be bothered to slow down and notice it in its particularity.

Interiority is not, then, as we might perhaps naively have thought, the space of inner reflection, the content of self-consciousness which is first for itself and only then for others (as, for instance, I have my thoughts, and you cannot know them unless I signal them to you, because they are internal to my intellectual space); rather, interiority is the ontological (rather than intellectual) being-for-itself of each thing, its *haecceity* (thisness) or closely deduced therefrom. You cannot know my thoughts because you are not *me*. It is defined not as that which does not lie open to other subjects, but as that into which other subjects must be invited if they are to have any experience of it at all. Thus, it is defined more radically in terms of its *relationality* to other subjects than in the common understanding.[37]

It should be clear how much such an account of subjective interiority owes to the commitment to concretivity and an Aristotelian take on the problem of universals. Even if it should be true that this commitment to subjective interiority was a prior intuition or even commitment for von Balthasar, the necessary ground for it, which he would have had to fight his way back to, was to be found in his reflections on the problem of universals.

III. The Relation between the Ideal and Historical Metaphysics

We cannot leave the moment of the revelation of these two metaphysical systems without comparing them to one another. I have already hinted that this cannot be an instance of one coming to supplant the other; this would run contrary to von Balthasar's deep commitments about the way grace works. But surely more can be said about the two? We therefore ask the question: "What is the relationship between these two metaphysics? Will it be possible to reduce one to the other, or to subsume both to a higher system?" Three possible strategies emerge: (1) to identify a higher system to which both the Historical and the Ideal belong; (2) to subsume the Historical to the Ideal; (3) to subsume the Ideal to the Historical. Each of these strategies has problems and ramifications for the theological system.

(1) The attempt to subsume the Historical and Ideal under an over-arching order would require the identification of a metaphysical order with greater primacy or more encompassing reach than either the Ideal or Historical could claim. The search for such a system falters from the beginning, however, when we remember that the person of Christ is for von Balthasar an irreducible fact. Since the person cannot be reduced to anything else, the systems based on it will not be reducible to anything else. The only possibility of a more fundamental reality is the Trinity itself, and we have already seen that the Trinity as such cannot be the basis of a metaphysic.[38] As it is in every case in the encounter of that which is grounded in Christ (creation) with that which grounds Christ (the Trinity) that metaphysics crosses over into theology, the search for a higher system to unify the Ideal and the Historical is as such not a search for a more fundamental metaphysic, but an expression of the openness of metaphysics to theology.

(2) If we attempt to reduce the Historical to the Ideal, we find more promise. For this may be conceived of as subordinating the first principle of the Historical (viz. the incarnate Christ) to the first principle of the Ideal (viz., the pre-incarnate Logos). The Logos certainly has temporal as well as logical priority over the incarnate Christ, as the condition of his possibility. Can we not then say that the Historical is founded upon and presupposes the Ideal just as the incarnate Christ is founded upon and presupposes the pre-incarnate Logos? This is certainly true, but it perhaps doesn't say as much as it may at first appear to. For while it may be true that the possibility of the Logos becoming incarnate requires the prior existence of the Logos, that does not give us certain and specific knowledge about the form the incarnate Logos will take. To put the matter trivially, it doesn't determine whether Christ will be a first-century Jew or a twenty-first-century American, among other things. This specificity is not even *post facto* deducible—we cannot point to necessary and sufficient reasons within the Ideal Metaphysic for the specificities of the realm of the historical Incarnation. But if we are not able to arrive at such knowledge of the Historical Metaphysic on the basis of the principles of the Ideal, then we have not yet established anything other than a purely external connection between them. The logic of the one remains opaque to the logic of the other; we have at best developed a general dependence. Knowing this general dependence of the

Historical on the Ideal will not yet count as a reduction of the Historical to the Ideal because the robust specificity of the Historical Metaphysic remains undeducible.

This is the heart of the problem for this approach, for it is precisely the specificities of the Historical that need to be accounted for, and it is precisely this that the Ideal is incapable of accounting for. The relationship of exemplarity between Christ and the world (which is the fundamental relationship for the Ideal Metaphysic) is indeterminate but determinable with respect to many possible historical outcomes; a world history which did not include the necessity of Incarnation would never in fact realize the Historical Metaphysic (which, in von Balthasar's estimation, could only be secured in the hypostatic union of God and humanity); yet such a world is truly a possible outcome of the Ideal Metaphysic.

Other strategies that attempt to reduce the Historical to the Ideal will falter in the same way. What is ultimately required is a relativizing or bracketing of the *necessity* of historicity; it must become merely an epiphenomenon or accidental property, ultimately fully explicable within the framework of the Ideal Metaphysic (and therefore to some extent able to be deduced from the Ideal). Something is lost here, and it is precisely all that was argued for in the development of the historical problematic in *A Theology of History*. This is to declare the triumph of the Ideal over the Historical, a triumph that von Balthasar claims the fact of the Incarnation ultimately blocks.

(3) This brings us to the strategies that will attempt to reduce the Ideal to the Historical. All such strategies require that in some way we understand the Historical Metaphysical order to be ascendant over the Ideal order. This is in fact the most promising of the three approaches, because von Balthasar's own reflection privileges reflection on the incarnate Christ over reflection on the pre-incarnate Christ. Thus we may also attempt the strategy here of subordinating the first principle of the Ideal to the first principle of the Historical. This would mean that Christ as exemplar of all things is understood only in the light of the incarnate Christ. This statement is not only *not* strange within a Balthasarian milieu, it actually sounds familiar.

In spite of this, there is reason to hesitate before affirming this approach. For this strategy, in making the incarnate Christ the inner meaning of Christ the exemplar, quickly raises the supralapsarian question.[39] For as the Historical order is founded on the Incarnation, any such strategy will make any explication of the original intention of creation (in the Ideal Metaphysical world) impossible without reference to an Incarnation which must have been willed from the beginning.

To make this more pointed: If one wishes to claim that there is only one metaphysic on the basis of the fact that God's eternal will eternally decreed the Incarnation, and therefore it is the Historical that is to be privileged, one has to ask on the basis of what the Incarnation was willed. If it was willed as a remedy for human sin, there remains the logical possibility of creation in which this sin was not intended, and therefore one can speak of two metaphysics, at least in the order of intention or logic. If the Incarnation was willed apart from human sin, then it was always God's plan for creation: one has succeeded in uniting the two metaphysics, but in a supralapsarian affirmation.

As with the reduction of the Historical to the Ideal, the reduction of the Ideal to the Historical loses something, though here what is lost is more subtle. What we lose is a certain *autonomy* of the Ideal order as willed in its own goodness rather than as on the way to another, greater good. It must now be seen as at best preliminary, a temporary situation that from its very first moment (and before any complication of sin enters the story) is awaiting a greater fulfillment in the eventual coming of the Historical dimension in the Incarnation. This type of understanding of the world of nature before grace is in fact already ruled out.[40]

Still, it seems that the price to be paid here is not nearly so steep as in the previous reduction. For there is something that rings true to many previous theological systems about the idea that even in the first moment of creation there is already a mysterious something more, a higher fulfillment of nature that is not only possible, but even willed by divine power. Any theology that claims that had humanity not sinned we would have received a confirming grace that would have made us unable to sin in the future is ultimately of this sort.[41] The question then arises, is there any price to be paid here higher than what is already routinely paid in theology?

Further, the supralapsarian question seems to be motivated from within the logic of the Historical Metaphysic itself. For metaphysics defines a series of relations among various realities and ultimately defines not only specific causal relations but also the general rules and models of causality. As such, one is able to make deductions on the basis of metaphysical systems, and the nature and strength of the deductions will be relative to the metaphysic that controls them. It would seem to follow that if one desires to reach necessary conclusions, the system must be rooted on something necessary. This is ultimately why metaphysical first principles are held to be irreducible—they need to be necessary, and any reducibility on their part can only be seen to endanger their necessary nature.

So, the question arises: Given creation, is Christ as incarnate necessary? If not, it would seem that the entire Historical Metaphysic will be paralyzed. It will not be able to generate statements about meaning, only facts. All its explanatory power will be deferred, and we will be left with an insufficiently differentiated field of facticity that can be interpreted only locally if at all.[42]

Yet, if we conclude that the incarnate Christ is necessary, and if this necessity proceeds from systemic rather than world-historical considerations (that is, the Fall), then we have in fact concluded a supralapsarian necessity. For example, suppose we say the following: If God relates to another in such a way as to create it, then God will ultimately relate to it via assumption.[43] In order for this to ground necessary deductions in a metaphysic based on the form of that eventual assumption, the claim will have to be strengthened to: If God relates to another in such a way as to create it, then God will ultimately *necessarily* relate to it via assumption. Before one even begins to ask on what basis the will to assumption follows necessarily upon the will to create, it is already clear that such a position has, in *necessarily* linking assumption to creation, made assumption necessary in the supralapsarian sense.

One possible way to ground necessity in the Historical Metaphysic without a supralapsarian affirmation is to claim that Christ is necessary, but he is only necessary as divine, not as incarnate. Such a position will be tasked with explaining how this allows the Historical Metaphysic at all—for the problematic that developed that metaphysic *required* a union of divinity and humanity for its solution.[44] In the realm of the Historical Metaphysic, it is *precisely* as incarnate that Christ is necessary. Thus, this position is really just another attempt to reduce the Historical to the Ideal, and it will suffer the same problems.

Whatever we may think the costs of a supralapsarian affirmation are, it is clear that von Balthasar wants no part of such an affirmation. The entire supralapsarian question is one that he wishes to disallow *a priori*. He reads Bonaventure as having transcended the question that was to become such a hot topic of discussion between Thomists and Scotists.[45] He invokes the "free and magnanimous love of God" as that which grounds the necessity of the Incarnation.[46] Here is where an answer to the question of the relations of the two metaphysics is ultimately to be found.

The truth is that the Ideal and Historical Metaphysics must resist any attempt to reduce them one to the other. The question of their relationship is ultimately one that cannot be answered, because the necessity of both first principles (the Logos as well as the incarnate Logos) is conditioned by the freedom of the divine will. What God freely wills is necessary, and no account can be given which fully explains why God chose this way rather than another;

such an account would endanger the absolute freedom of the divine will.[47] This is what grounds the necessity of the trinitarian life, and therefore of the second person who is the first image of the the Father; likewise, it is this will which grounds the necessity of the Incarnation of the Logos. Therefore the created order, in both its Ideal and Historical Metaphysical relations, is seen to be truly contingent, dependent upon the good will of the Creator—in this way, the traditional relationships theology has striven to assert between Creator and creation are re-affirmed.

It also follows, however, that discrete choices of the absolute divine freedom are not commensurable—they simply cannot be measured against one another. It is their very inscrutability that ensures this. For example, we may know that the God who had mercy on Peter when Peter placed himself properly at God's mercy will also have mercy on Paul when he does the same; but we know this because we know it is God's character to be merciful. But just because we know that it is God who creates in the image of the exemplar, we do not know that God will later choose to become incarnate in hypostatic union, because we don't know on what basis God chose to create in the first place, nor do we know the real basis for the choice to incarnate. Both choices remain inscrutable; and while love is certainly a large part of the motivation behind both, it is not a complete answer, for we could not predict on the basis of the logic of love alone the choices God would make.

The conclusion is therefore that while God may know what relationship holds between the Ideal and Historical Metaphysics, the Balthasarian system must rest content with only the fact of each. Further, if von Balthasar can shed no light on the relation between the two systems, then neither can he comment on the supralapsarian question. The question remains shrouded in the mystery of the divine freedom, which is by nature and necessarily impenetrable to us. To be fair, this is not so much transcending the supralapsarian question as expressing agnosticism about it, but it is an agnosticism that is firmly grounded systematically.

The change from the Ideal to the Historical Metaphysical realm, while of enormous importance (and the occasion of rhapsodic passages throughout von Balthasar's works), is therefore ultimately taken for granted. But since the system is to be characterized by a fascination with beauty, by a reverence before the glory of God as it appears in the world, the Historical Metaphysic, in which the glory took on decisive form in the person and (derivatively) the life of Christ, is to be privileged. Therefore, for the purposes of our remaining exposition, and for the purposes of properly interpreting the Balthasarian corpus, the pivotal point will be the Christ who is divine and human, and as such is the concrete analogy of being. From this viewpoint it is possible to analyze the nature of the analogy and its effects upon the system.

It is important to reiterate, however, that on the one hand the Logos, in assuming a human nature, does not cease to be divine, and on the other hand that grace does not destroy nature, but perfects it.[48] Therefore, the realm of the Ideal Metaphysics is not replaced or superseded with the Incarnation: rather, it finds its fulfillment in the Historical Metaphysic. Because of this, a smooth transition from the types of topics that belong properly to the one to the types of topics that belong properly to the other is not really possible. Instead, von Balthasar will speak seamlessly of a reality grounded in the divine self-expression in the Son and of a reality whose being is constituted by the loving obedience proper to the Son as the one who became incarnate. The fact that both of these realities meet in the person of Christ focuses the system on precisely that point where analogy is offered as the abiding rule of interpretation.

EXCURSUS: VON BALTHASAR AND SUPRALAPSARIANISM

Before moving to the analysis of analogy in its specificity (an analysis which brings us to the furthest reach of metaphysics, to its border with theology), there is much more to be said about von Balthasar and the dynamics of supralapsarianism. This topic is worth pausing over not just because of its relevance to the question of the relation of the Ideal and the Historical Metaphysics, but also because the logic of von Balthasar's thinking so often prompts one to wonder why a supralapsarian affirmation was so repugnant to him. It seems so isomorphic to his system that its absence is strange. We have already indicated that the reason lies in a need to protect divine freedom; the following are some considerations that question whether that answer can really stand as von Balthasar's most consistent answer at the end of the day.

In *Cosmic Liturgy*, von Balthasar says the following about Maximus: "Maximus expressly says that the incarnation—more precisely, the drama of Cross, grave, and resurrection—is not only the midpoint of world history but the foundational idea of the world itself" (*CL* 134). Now, this might seem not only to be a supralapsarian affirmation in Maximus, but, more interestingly, it could be taken as a map to relating the Ideal and Historical Metaphysics in von Balthasar. It would be a strategy of our third type, subordinating the Ideal to the Historical, and would ring true to certain other passages in the Balthasarian corpus.

It is therefore interesting that von Balthasar does not consider this to require Maximus to hold to a supralapsarian account. He says: "And because Maximus does not intend to demonstrate a necessity [for the incarnation] in the metaphysical sense, but rather [to point to] the meaning of history itself—*all* history!—he also includes the historical process of sin in the supreme synthesis" (ibid.). In other words, the Incarnation comes in to Maximus's synthesis precisely because this synthesis is carried out in Maximus's version of a Historical Metaphysic, not in the Ideal Metaphysic. One cannot give an account of the meaning of history, even from a hypothetical *a priori* divine point of view, without reference to the Incarnation (including the cross) as its goal, precisely because it is *this* history, which includes the realities of human sin, for which one wishes to give an account.

Von Balthasar attributes Maximus's ability to win his way to this viewpoint to the rejection of a Platonic idea of motion as an original fall and an acceptance of an Aristotelian account of the positive goodness of nature. As a result of this, Maximus is able to convert the first principle from world-conquering knowledge to a principle of love; finitude is no longer evil, union with God is no longer the dissolution of identity, but requires abiding distinction; rather, union becomes rooted in concrete particularity.[49] In short, the correct choice of Plato over Aristotle turns Maximus into von Balthasar, allows all of the distinctive and important features of the Balthasarian metaphysics to shine forth. "Synthesis, in reference to both God and man, can now be reinterpreted primarily in terms of a love rooted in freedom: both the Incarnation of the Son and his commandment of love, which brings to full realization the idea of humanity, presuppose and generate freedom" (*CL* 135).

This answer may be applied with great propriety to von Balthasar himself. Notable about it is the emphasis on freedom, which, as we have seen, does so much work in securing the rejection of a supralapsarianism affirmation. No matter how supralapsarian such passages may sound, this is ultimately due to a failure to attend to the nature of the necessity von Balthasar is asserting. He clarifies this with relation to Maximus: "the 'necessity' he speaks of is nothing but the inner cohesion of the divine plan of salvation, read phenomenologically from the facts of sacred history" (*CL* 202). Von Balthasar is not claiming that the Incarnation is necessary in a metaphysical sense; at most, he is saying that, given the phenomenological facts of sacred history, Incarnation is necessary, and must be thought to belong to the original unity (cohesion) of the divine plan. What this type of answer rejects is that the divine plan could be considered solely in light of the Ideal Metaphysic, which is ultimately what supralapsarianism would like to do. It asks the question about the Incarnation while suspending any possible answer about which of several possible Historical Metaphysics might follow. But if we speak of necessity at this level (that is, of necessity properly speaking) we are now talking about a kind of necessity that constrains even God. Metaphysics has transgressed on theology.

Let us consider another example, this time from von Balthasar's constructive theology: "The result is a failure to interpret and assess positively the phenomenon of *appearance*, which in reality gives the thing in itself its integrity and plenitude, its completed, meaningful essence, its radiant glory. Once we realize that the appearance, the object's emergence in the space made ready by the subject, is something original, primary, and indispensable for the object itself, the appearance takes on its for ontological weight. For it now comes to light that this appearance within the subject is the expressive field of the object's essence as intrinsically as the body is the expressive field of the soul" (*TL* I.65). Especially in light of the mention of "appearance" and "radiant glory," this could be interpreted in the light of *The Glory of the Lord* to mean that creation as the space for Incarnation was necessary for God's full essence. This conclusion is blocked by the fact that the entire subject-object reciprocity described in *Theologic* I is limited to created subjects and objects. However, *Theologic*I has also established that while God is free of this dynamic, there is something analogous to this dynamic in God. This has been shown to be enough to establish a necessary logic to the appearing of God's glory in creation (any world God creates must be capable of being the space for his appearing and will have such an appearing); yet it also turns out to be enough to block the claim that Incarnation must be the ultimate form this would take. How?

The supralapsarian claim is blocked by the analogies given in the preceding pages:, especially this one: "Just as a man who sets off on a long journey does not know what will happen to him or how he will be changed when he returns after years of absence, so, too, the subject does not know what the adventure of knowledge will bring it" (*TL* I.62). What this means in the current case is that no one can foresee how all these considerations (subject and object, the analogous reality in God, and so on) will come together. However, and this is unlike the case of created subjects and objects, God has lordly freedom to determine the form of this union. The form of the union is therefore governed by spontaneity, and its logic is the logic of freedom, that is to say, love.

The recurrence of spontaneity throughout *Theologic*I, and especially its use as the correlative of receptivity (where one would have expected *action*),[50] shows its importance. It begins to seem as if all activity is spontaneity, that what it means to be active is to be free. I think von Balthasar would sustain this assertion. But if love requires freedom, can we then say that all action is love?

No; for freedom is the necessary condition of love, but also of hate. One cannot predict ahead of time whether freedom will lead to love or hate. It does however mean that love only unfolds in the sphere of spontaneity and activity.

This returns us to the notion of *unvordenklichkeit*, the inability to anticipate what freedom will do. The importance of *unvordenklichkeit* for the discussion of nature and grace can be summed up in Barth's words, cited by von Balthasar: "Grace is a *special* work that does not simply coincide with the work of creation. Nor can it be regarded as the continuation and crowning achievement of creation (although it is that! For how otherwise is God the Creator in fact to carry on and conclude his work, making it living and effective?). Grace is in fact that moment when God outdoes even himself" (*Barth* 122). Thus, revelation "does not just draw out prior potential but exceeds all expectation" (*Barth* 122). "According to the biblical view, the covenant and its history are in no way the purpose of creation as such. Rather, the covenant is the content of the divine work of reconciliation, which is something distinct from creation. . . . [But we can also say that] creation *points toward* this other work. This other work *begins* in and with the work of creation. . . . But this does not permit us to conclude that the work of creation is the cause of this other work, or that the other work is the purpose of creation" (*Barth* 123, qting. Barth).

Von Balthasar explains this in the following way: "In other words, both works reflect each other and their respective orders and act as 'countertypes' (6, 77) to each other. But, despite this relationship whereby grace supports and perfects nature, we would do well to maintain the distinction between them, even where we make the second order the prototype of the first (5, 82)" (*Barth* 123). Von Balthasar thus consistently uses the divine freedom and sovereignty to block any supralapsarian conclusions. In spite of this, there are still many passages which get von Balthasar into supralapsarian trouble, such as the following: "But there can be no question—since the world was created with a view to the Son, who was to be born as a man and to die as the Lamb of God; and that this incarnate Son was shown to be a product of ('conceived by') the Holy Spirit—that the Spirit must have been active in the creation, explicitly or implicitly, as a Person" (*TL* III.415). He here deduces the Spirit's involvement in creation from the Incarnation of the Son, and even states the latter as that for which creation occurred. This seems not only to imply but to *require* that the Incarnation have always been the goal of the creative act.

Another objection could be motivated on the basis of von Balthasar's solution to the problem of interpreting history theologically as presented in chapter 5, I.A. There, the Incarnation was required to solve the problem. The entire theological solution to the problem of universals and the Historical

Metaphysic as such all seem to fall apart without the Incarnation. But even the Ideal Metaphysic does not seem to be immune: for the problem that *A Theology of History* attempts to solve is not a problem created by human sin, but by the dynamics of universality and particularity. Thus it seems that even in the Ideal Metaphysic, Incarnation is required. And this is could be taken as one definition of supralapsarianism: the necessity, not within the Historical, but with the Ideal Metaphysic, of Incarnation.

These seeming counterexamples do not change von Balthasar's final position about supralapsarianism, but it is illustrative of why this is such a persistent problem in the corpus. Von Balthasar believes that he has transcended the supralapsarian question: that is, he believes not that he has answered it in the affirmative, but that he has built a system such that the question is, as it were, a non-starter. Therefore, freed from the need to hold this (in his view) undesirable position at bay, he feels himself entitled to all the advantages of a supralapsarian view without having to actually claim one. Thus he will unabashedly say things that are typically said only by theologians who are comfortable with the supralapsarian affirmation.

Whether he has transcended the question or, as I have suggested, merely expressed a methodological agnosticism about it is of course relevant here. For if I am right, he is *not* in fact entitled to use its fruits, and in doing so either commits himself implicitly to a supralapsarian view or causes his system to become inconsistent. But even if I am wrong, is it still true that to have transcended the view entitles one to enjoy its spoils? Is it possible that if the argument needed to be transcended in the first place, one has also called into question whether the conclusions drawn by one side of the other in the argument should be considered riches to be captured.

Notes

1. Chapter 1, III, 36ff.

2. "Menschliches Denken hat, seitdem es zu philosophieren gelernt hat, die Dinge zu erfassen gesucht durch eine grundsätzliche Zerlegung in zwei Elemente: das Faktische, das als solches das Einzelne, Sinnliche, Konkrete und Zufällige ist, und das Allgemein-Notwendige, dessen Universalität damit zusammenhängt, daß es das Abstrakte ist, das Gesetz und die Geltung, die vom Einzelfall absieht, um ihn übersteigend zu regeln" (*TG* 9). [Human thought has, since it learned to philosophize, sought to grasp things through a fundamental breakdown into two elements: the factual, which as such is the unique, sensible, concrete and accidental, and the universal-necessary, whose universality entails that it is the abstract, the law and the validity which is abstracted from the particular instance in order, transcending it, to rule it.]

3. He cites ancient astrological systems as signs of the rationalist tendency to look beyond the concrete to a deeper explanation in the realm of the universal (*TG* 10).

4. "Doch ist es ohne Zweifel so, daß die 'rationalen' Systeme, sowohl im griechischen wie im christlichen Raum und bis zu Kant und Hegel, als die tragenden Pfeiler der hohen Philosophie galten, als die tiefere, gleichsam vornehmere Weise zu philosophieren, während der Empirismus, der die Kraft der eindringenden Abstraktion unterschätzt und bei den 'sinnlichen Fakten' stehenbleibt, die oberflächliche Antithese dazu bildet, praktisch jedoch den immer erneuten Anlaß für wahre Philosophie, ihn zu überwinden" (Ibid.). [But there is no doubt that the "rational" systems, as much in Greek as in Christian context, and all the way to Kant and Hegel were considered as the supporting pillars of high philosophy, as the more profound, and at the same time nobler ways to philosophize, while empiricism, which underestimated the power of penetrating abstraction and remained with the "sensible facts," constituted a superficial Antithesis, but in fact an ever rehashed occasion for true philosophy to overcome.]

5. "Dieser beruhigenden Reduktion auf die Wesensgesetze gegenüber scheint das Faktisch-Historische, sofern es sich dieser Auflösung widersetzt, kaum etwas Positives, eher nur ein Denkhindernis zu bedeuten" (ibid.). [Against this soothing reduction to the laws concerning essence, the factual-historical seems, inasmuch as it resists this resolution, hardly something positive, rather to indicate only a hindrance to thought.]

6. "Wer das Geschichtliche in seiner Gesamtheit zu deuten unternimmt, muß, wenn er nicht in einen gnostischen Mythos fallen will, ein in ihr wirkendes und sich offenbarendes Gesamtsubjekt ansetzen, das zugleich eine allgemein normgebende Wesenheit ist" (*TG* 11).

7. Ibid. Von Balthasar does not consider the possibility of the other class of beings which, as personal, could also be the locus of subjectivity, namely angels (and demons). On the one hand, his system evidences such a strong focus on the divine-human drama that angels are scarcely considered; in fact, *Herrlichkeit* I.649 ff. advances an argument that the angels have become nearly obsolete with the coming of the Christ-form, that they have been pushed to the side to make room for the glory appearing in Christ. (By contrast, see the extended discussion of angels in *TD* III.465 ff., which presents well the challenge of integrating angels into a story so focused on the divine-human encounter.) On the other hand, in this particular instance, to invoke angels would be to make them the subjectivity that underlies all history, which would begin to look a lot like Gnostic emanations.

8. Ibid.

9. "Aber der bedarf keiner Geschichte, um sich zu sich zu vermitteln" (ibid.).

10. This may seem like an overly simplistic reduction; however, as will become clear later (chapter 6) von Balthasar holds to a very particular view of the relations between the Trinitarian processions and the creation of the world, and thus specific conditions have to hold. Even later (chapter 7) it will be shown that the principle of eternal immutability, though not thematized as such, exerts a powerful influence on von Balthasar's doctrine of God, such that characteristic modes of divine action are discernible at the varying levels on which God acts. Although the full explication of these points would certainly serve to elucidate what is driving the rejection of God as the subjectivity of history, such an explication may not be undertaken in a short space or without some of the concepts to be developed in this chapter. Therefore they must only be mentioned now as elements of the system whose eventual appearance will lend greater plausibility to the reading offered here.

11. "Oder der Mensch, aber dieser ist, als freies, handelndes Subjekt je dieser Einzelne, der offenkundig die Geschichte im ganzen nicht überherrschen kann" (*TG* 11). [Or man, but he is, as free, acting subject, always this unique one, who clearly cannot rule over history in its entirety.]

12. Ibid.

13. "Jedenfalls führt sie, auf die Geschichte hin betrachtet, zum höchst geheimnisvollen Begriff einer Kommunikation und Kommunion aller freien Personen von identischer metaphysischer Wesenheit innerhalb der Wesenheit, so, daß diese, wenn sie als geschichtlich verwirklicht vorgestellt wird, sich in einer Schicksalsgemeinschaft der sie bildenden Personen ausfalten muß" (*TG* 12). [In any event it [the dialectic in human nature] leads, when applied to history, to a most mysterious idea of a communication and communion of all free persons from an

identical metaphysical essence within the essence in such a way that it must unfold in a common destiny of the constitutive persons, if it is conceived of as realized historically.]

14. "Philosophisch läßt sich allenfalls feststellen, daß der Einzelne in seiner persönlichen Vernunft und Freiheit in einer Solidarität mit allen Menschen stehen muß, daß seine Entscheidungen somit für die Gesamtheit nicht ohne Widerhall sind, daß aber kein Einzelner sich über die andern beherrschend erheben könnte, ohne deren Menschsein metaphysisch zu gefährden und seiner Würde zu entthronen" (ibid.). [Philosophically, at best it allows the assertion that the individual in its personal reason and freedom must stand in solidarity with all humans, that its decisions are therefore not without repercussions for the whole, but that no individual could raise himself up, ruling over the others, without endangering metaphysically its humanity and dethroning it of its dignity.]

15. "So kann . . . der positive Aspekt der Erlösung des Gesamtgeschlechtes aber nur so einer Einzelperson (als Religionsstifter und 'Erlöser') zugetraut werden, daß diese die religiöse Genialität besitzt, erstmals einen grundsätzlich *allgemeinen* und für alle beschreibaren 'Pfad der Erlösung' erspürt und aufgewiesen zu haben. Ein solcher Weg darf nur in einem äußerlichen Sinn geschichtlich sein, er muß, wenn er wirklich für alle Geltung besitzen soll, als allgemeiner und gültiger Weg in der Wesenheit wurzeln: des Menschen, des Schicksals, des Kosmos im ganzen" (*TG* 13). [But the positive aspect of the salvation of the whole race can fall on one person (as a religious founder and "Savior") only in such a way that this one exhibits the religious genius to have discovered and pointed out for the first time a fundamental, universal "path of salvation" walkable by all. Such a path is only permitted to be historical in an external sense; it must, if it is supposed to really offer worth to all, take root in the essence as the universal and available path: of humanity, of fate, of the whole cosmos.]

16. "Diese Schranke zu sprengen vermöchte nur ein dem philosophischen Denken un-erfindliches und unvermutbares Wunder: die seinshafte Verbindung Gottes und des Menschen in einem Subjekt, das als solches nur ein absolut einmaliges sein könnte, weil seine menschliche Personalität, ohne gebrochen oder überspannt zu werden, emporgenommen wäre in die sich in ihr inkarnierende und offenbarende göttliche Person" (*TG* 13–14). [Only a miracle, undiscoverable for philosophical thought and unsuspected by it, could explode this barrier: the real union of God and man in one subject, which as such alone could be an absolutely unique thing because its human personality, without being broken or strained, gets taken up into the divine person incarnating and revealing itself in it.]

17. "Die Formel, die sich ergab, ist ebenso hart wie geheimnisvoll. Hart ist sie, weil sie alle innerweltliche Norm, ihre Geltung, ihre Anwendung, und Erforschung dem 'individuellen Gesetz' der Einmaligkeit Jesu Christi als der Offenbarung des freien, konkreten Willens Gottes über der Welt unterstellt. Geheimnisvoll ist sie, weil sie diesen Anspruch auf Herrschaft (kyriotês) erhebt aus dem von keiner wissenschaftlichen Warte aus zu überblickenden und zu beurteilenden Mysterium der seinshaften (hypostatischen) Einigung der göttlichen und der menschlichen Natur in Christus, welches Mysterium nunmehr sein Licht und seinen Schatten steiler oder flacher über alle innerweltlichen Geltungen ausbreitet" (*TG* 17). [The formula which ensues is as hard as it is mysterious. It is hard because it subordinates all inner-worldly norms, their validity, their implementation, and their investigation to the "individual law" of the uniqueness of Jesus Christ as the revelation of the free, concrete will of God for the world. It is mysterious because it raises this claim to lordship (*kyriotes*) on the basis of the mystery, overseen and judged by no scientific viewpoint, of the real (hypostatic) union of the divine and human nature in Christ, which mystery shines its light and shadow, sharply or flatly, over every inner-worldly valuation.]

18. "In Jesus Christus ist der Logos nicht mehr das die Geschichte regierende und ihren Sinn stiftende Reich der Ideen, Geltungen und Gesetze, er ist selber Geschichte. Im Leben Christi fällt das Faktische mit dem Normativen nicht nur 'faktisch', sondern 'notwendig' zusammen, weil das Faktum zugleich Auslegung Gottes und gottmenschliches Urbild alles echten Menschentums für Gott ist" (*TG* 20). [In Jesus Christ the Logos is no longer the realm of ideas, values and ordinances ruling history and endowing it with meaning, it is itself history. In the life of Christ the factual and

the normative coincide not merely "factually" but "necessarily," because the fact is at the same time the interpretation of God and the human-divine image of all true humanity for God.]

19. "Das geschichtliche Leben des Logos—zu dem sein Tod und seine Auferstehung und Himmelfahrt gehören—ist als solches die eigentliche Ideenwelt, die alle Geschichte normiert, unmittelbar oder reduktiv, aber nicht aus einer ungeschichtlichen Höhe, sondern aus der lebendigen Mitte der Geschichte selbst" (*TG* 21). [The historical life of the Logos—to which belong his death and resurrection and ascension—is as such the true realm of ideas which norms, immediately or reductively, all of history; but not from an unhistorical height, rather from the living center of history itself.]

20. "Von der höchsten und abschließenden Perspektive aus betrachtet ist es der Quellpunkt des Geschichtlichen überhaupt, von wo alle Geschichte vor und nach Christus ausgeht und worin sie ihre Mitte behält" (Ibid.). [Considered from the highest and decisive perspective, [the Logos] is indeed the source of the historical from which all history, before and after Christ, emanates and in which in it maintains its center.]

21. "Alle diese Teilstrecken und Abwandlungen des einen Maßes (den Abstand Gott-Mensch, den Abstand Gott-erbsündig Gerechter und den Abstand Gott-Sünder überhaupt) kann er freilich nur messen, weil er mehr als Mensch, weil er Gottmensch ist" (*TG* 52). [He can freely measure all of these lengths and modifications of the one measure (the distance between God and humanity, the distance between God and the justified human subject to original sin and the distance between God and the sinner generally) only because he is more than human, because he is God-man.]

22. "Doch er mißt sie nicht einfach von oben her, mit dem Maß des himmelischen Blicks, er mißt sie von unten und innen, indem er sein Menschsein, Leib und Seele, als Maßeinheit gebraucht, die er solange im Willen des Vaters verwendet, ausweitet, geschmeidig macht, bis jedes Maß dieser Welt damit gemessen ist" (*TG* 52–53). [But he does not simply measure it from above, with the measure of the heavenly gaze; he measures it from below and within, by his humanity, life and soul, as the needed unit of measurement, which he applies, expands, and makes flexible in the will of the Father until every measure of this world is measured by it.]

23. *The Eschatology of Hans Urs von Balthasar* (Oxford: Oxford University Press, 2005), 21. Healy calls this "the 'concretization' of the analogy of being within the person of Jesus Christ."

24. "Das Maß der höchstmöglichen Nähe wie der tiefstmöglichen Entfernung zwischen Gott und Mensch ist fundiert, untergriffen und überholt durch das Maß der wirklichen Nähe und der wirklichen Distanz zwischen Vater und Sohn im Geiste am Kreuz und in der Auferstehung. Keiner weiß so wie der Sohn, was es heißt, im Vater leben, in seinem Schoß ruhen, ihn lieben, ihm dienen. Keiner weiß darum auch wie er, was es bedeutet, von ihm verlassen sein" (*TG* 53). [The measure of the highest possible nearness and of the deepest possible separation between God and humanity is founded, undergirded and overcome through the measure of the real nearness and the real distance between Father and Son in the Spirit on the cross and in the resurrection. No one knows like the Son what it means to live in the Father, to rest in his lap, to love him, to serve him. Likewise, no one knows like him what it means to be abandoned by him.]

25. "In diesem Sinne kann Christus die *konkrete Analogia entis* genannt werden da er in sich selbst, in der Einheit seiner göttlichen und menschlichen Natur das Maßverhältnis für jeden Abstand zwischen Gott und Mensch bildet. Und diese Einheit ist seine Person in beiden Naturen" (*TG* 53–54, note 1). [In this sense, Christ can be called the concrete analogy of being, because in himself, in the unity of his divine and human nature, he constitutes the proportion for every distance between God and humanity. And this unity is his person in both natures.]

26. "Er ist so sehr das Konkreteste und Zentralste, daß im allerletzten nur von ihm her gedacht werden kann, und daß an diesem Punkt jede Frage, was wäre, wenn er nicht wäre, oder wenn er nicht Mensch geworden wäre, oder wenn die Welt ohne ihn gedacht werden müßte, sich als vollkommen überflüssig erübrigt" (ibid.). [He is so much the most concrete and most central that in the end thinking can only start from him, and that at this point every question of

what would be if he were not, or if he had not become human, or if the world had to be thought without him, is entirely, redundantly superfluous.]

27. Ibid., 146.

28. Cf. ch. 3, I.B, von Balthasar's reading of Fichte.

29. Regarding my naming of these systems as "ideal" and "historical," it is worth noting that von Balthasar introduces a distinction between a "real" and an "ideal" realm (metaphysic) in Gregory of Nyssa (*Presence and Thought* 57ff). My distinction is not intended to apply von Balthasar's analysis of Gregory in that early work to von Balthasar himself; it is, however, an interesting parallel.

30. *GL* II.187

31. *GL* II.283 ff., Bonaventure, I *Sent.* d. 35, a. un., q. 1.

32. This content consists in the analysis of the relationship between Creator and creatures opened up in the union of both in a person. This relationship, which is the unfolding of the concrete content of the analogy of being, will be examined in the next chapter.

33. "If Jesus is not a spirit but tangible flesh and blood, if he eats the same fish and honey and bread as the disciples, then his time too is not ghost-time, not some fictitious appearance of duration, but time in the most genuine and real sense possible" (*TH* 84).

34. "The fact that it is simultaneously his eternal time makes no difference. That would only be a contradiction if one postulated that time and eternity could not be united, and consequently that time could not be redeemed and preserved within eternity; in the most positive sense, taken up into it" (ibid.).

35. "And since it is not possible that the mode of time belonging to the risen Christ should have altered with his Ascension (this being rather in the nature of a signing-off gesture, purely for our benefit), it is necessary to grasp that the mode of time revealed during the forty days remains the foundation for every other mode of his presence in time, in the Church, and in the world. His manner of being, revealed during those days, is the ultimate form of his reality. His Ascension did not make him a stranger to our world. He inserted those forty days between his Resurrection and Ascension in order to show his disciples in a direct and tangible way to reality with which he is to remain with them 'all the days even unto the consummation of the world' (Mt 28:20)" (*TH* 87).

36. *Das Ganze im Fragment*, the German title of von Balthasar's *Theological Anthropology*, which makes many of these same points. It also calls to mind the mode of Eucharistic presence, in which, according to Scholastic theology, the body of Christ is whole in the whole and whole in the parts.

37. The common understanding also includes the idea of its hiddenness, but bases this on the primacy of subjectivity at the end of the day, or on a physicalist model of subject-object encounter (which again respects the inviolability of each before setting them in motion to collide with each other). Von Balthasar is against this picture of subject-object relations.

38. Chapter 1, III, 35. The Trinity is not the ground of creation, but that reality which creation must confront as it seeks its affirmation. Creation under the Ideal Metaphysic received this affirmation at the beginning, when the Lord surveyed all things and declared them good; creation under the Historical Metaphysic awaits its final affirmation in judgment, when the blood of Christ will be the sharp dividing line between the divine "yes" and "no" to each creature.

39. The theological question which asks whether the Incarnation was part of God's original intention for creation, apart from sin. For a philosophically driven historical introduction to this question, see Edwin Christian van Driel, *Incarnation Anyway* (Oxford: Oxford University Press, 2008).

40. See chapter 3, II.A.

41. Augustine's *non posse peccare* is of this sort (*De Civitate Dei* XXII.30), and Anselm is certainly of this opinion (cf. *Cur Deus Homo* Bk. 1, ch. 18). The major Medieval theologians, including Bonaventure, will follow to a large extent this.

42. Such may be seen to be the result of the great twentieth-century systems that have excised anything like a necessary center from metaphysics. Derrida and Foucault come to mind.

43. I have used *assumption* and not *incarnation* here to preserve the generality of the claim—in this form, the claim does not require that the created reality be fleshly.

44. For a more complete presentation of this problem, see the Excursus.

45. "Damit holt Bonaventura weitgehend die Christologie der vornicänischen Väter ein, für die der Logos (endiathetos und dann prophorikos) die Vermittlung vom höchsten Gott zur Schöpfung war, vermeidet aber vollkommen deren Subordinatianismus. Mehr noch: er übersteigt, im Fall, daß Gott wirklick eine Welt zu erschaffen beschließt, durch seinen Liberalitas-Gedanken von vornherein die thomistisch-skotistische Kontroverse über das Motiv der Menschwerdung. Der Logos mag noch sosehr als der 'Erlöser' von der Sünde in der Welt erscheinen, sein Menschwerden wird letzlich nicht von diesem Motiv bedingt, sondern durch die alles Weltliche übersteigended freie und großherzige Liebe Gottes" (*TLg* II.154). [Bonaventure thereby wins back the expansive Christology of the pre-Nicene Fathers, for whom the Word (*endiathetos* and then *prophorikos*) was the mediator of the highest God to creation; but he avoids completely their Subordinationism. Even more: in the event that God really decided to create a world, he overcomes from the beginning, through his idea of *liberalitas*, the Thomist-Scotist controversy over the motive of the Incarnation. However much the Logos may appear as the 'savior' from sin in the world, his incarnation is not conditioned by this cause, but rather by the free and magnanimous love of God transcending all worldly things.]That von Balthasar is right in his reading of Bonaventure here is certainly not a given. At the very least, Bonaventure, whose system perhaps more than any other Medieval system would be so welcoming to the supralapsarian claim, joins his friend Aquinas in being unwilling to attribute any motivation to the Incarnation other than redemption of human sin, though he admits that in doing so he is taking a position that is less subtle (III *Sent.* d. 1, a. 2, q. 2).

46. "Sein Menschwerden wird letzlich nicht von diesem Motiv bedingt, sondern durch die alles Weltliche übersteigended freie und großherzige Liebe Gottes" (*TLg* II.154). See Angelo Scola, "Nature and Grace in Hans Urs von Balthasar," *Communio* 18, no. 2 (1991): 207–26: "Beyond the quarrel between Thomists and Scotists over the end of the Incarnation, a question that finally cancels itself out because it excessively pretends to penetrate the *futurabilia Dei*, Balthasar joins his friend Przywara in affirming that man, the image of God, is a simple *silhouette* which finds its luminous figure [*Gestalt*] only in Christ" (211–12).

47. See *TL* I.240: "Because this sovereign majesty is immediately one with infinite being and infinite knowledge, it coincides with infinite and unconditional necessity, and even in God it is impossible to distinguish necessity from his self-determination and to make the latter in any way dependent on the former. God's truth is an identity of necessity and freedom: God is freely what he necessarily is and necessarily what he freely is. God grounds himself, and this self-grounding is an expression of his essence and of the fact that he is absolute person."

48. *H* I.26

49. "It is here, for the first time, that Maximus' work of correction can be seen in its full breadth of its implications. As soon as motion (*kinesis*) is no longer seen simply (in Platonic fashion) as a sinful falling away but is seen (in Aristotelian fashion) as the good ontological activity of a developing nature, the highest ideal [for existence] can also be transformed from a Gnosis that conquers the world by seeing through its reality into a loving, inclusive affirmation even of finite things. Now finitude is no longer evil; now union with God, from which we come and which, in the end, we hope to regain, no longer includes the destruction of all the boundaries between beings. This union, in fact, may not be imagined here as a concept that excludes differences but as a concrete idea that includes particularity" (*CL* 135).

50. Cf. *TL* I.75

6

Analogy of Being in Trinitarian and Christological Keys

Participation turned out to play an important role in the analysis of the Ideal Metaphysic. Participation was found to require primary reference to the analogy of being; in fact, our analysis of the Ideal Metaphysic supports the conclusion that the analogy of being *is* the content of participation. Moving forward, the question now becomes how to understand the participation of creatures in the Creator within the realm of the Historical Metaphysic. To do this, we must ask about the relationship of the human to the *trinitarian*divine, to examine the way in which the image of God that creation is has been grounded in the image of the Father that Christ is. In this investigation, the nature of analogy at last comes into full expression as the non-identity of identity, or as the differentiation within unity that is characteristic of uncreated being, and that analogously marks the nature of created being.

If therefore the divine love seeks to communicate the incommunicable (whether ontologically or epistemologically) in a non-trivial way to those beings outside the divine nature who are first and foremost called into existence to be objects and willing participants in this cosmic love, unmeasured love must find a measure according to which it will communicate.[1] Much as Plutarch's divinity sought the measure by which to relate ideas and matter,[2] God will have to find (or be found to have) a medium of commensurability that can render the communication understandable. Unlike Plutarch, however, there is nothing outside the divinity not created by and in reference to the divinity. And since the *maior dissimilitudo* rules out that any creature could be a standard of commensurability with reference to God, we find that love has eternally had its own measure in itself. For the infinite, being unable to be compared to anything else, can only be measured and contextualized in terms of itself.

This is the furthest moment of the *maior dissimilitudo*, the *maxima dissimilitudo*, if you will. And this furthest distance from the creature is the realm of *aseity*, which is denied to creatures by their very name. Here indeed the doctrine of divine aseity finds its ultimate realization in two fundamental truths: (1) God is from Godself in such a way as to not need another, and (2) God is defined by Godself in such a way as to be incomparable. It is this latter sense which is the insuperable distance between God and creatures, and which prevents any effort at collapsing the one into the other.[3] However, the fact of God's incommensurability means that if God is to be "measured" at all (*mensurabilis*) it cannot be on the basis of a being like unto God (something *co-mensurabilis*), and therefore it can only be on the basis of God's self that such a measuring be possible. It will be claimed that such measuring is not only possible, but has actually happened in the Son, who as intra-trinitarian measure is also the only conceivable measure for the self-communication of God to creatures. It is for this reason that the divine love, consubstantial and identical with the eternally self-subsisting divine being, infinite in quality and quantity, wellspring of God's creative act and the first thought of God, beyond all comprehension or limit, the primal infinity, the original unmeasured and unfathomable quantity, took on flesh: to become the common ground for the communication of divinity to creation.

Indeed, we must allow our understanding of the relationship between the human and the divine to be guided by the fact, developed in Anselm and Bonaventure, that the discussion is grounded in the divine desire for self-expression outside of itself and for communication to the creature that stands outside of the divine. Put more simply, we must allow the analogy of being to be ruled by a fundamental top-down orientation in all its aspects. For if the analogy is read in the other direction, starting with the human suitability for relationship with the divine, we will in fact be re-interpreting von Balthasar in the sense of Schleiermacher rather than letting him speak for himself.[4]

I. FROM THE ONE TO THE MANY: MULTIPLICATION IN THE IDEAL METAPHYSIC

In spite of the promises made in the last chapter, we begin this portion of our journey with a return to the Ideal Metaphysic. This is necessary, because we have not quite followed it to its absolute end, to the heart of the nature of the multiplication made possible by analogy. We cannot leave this unsaid.

Here at the fruition of the Balthasarian conception of the analogy of being, we now understand that it the fundamental metaphysical relation between the first principle and every created reality. Our analysis to this point has secured the first unity that underlies the system; now it remains to turn to the moment of multiplication. In this moment in the development of a metaphysical system we see simultaneously emerging the rules and patterns of causality and the scope of possibilities for each creature.

Yet even before turning to the analogy of being as the explication of multiplication, we have already learned that the measure that this analogy represents is a concrete measure, found in the first principle itself (the incarnate Christ). In order to explicate the dynamics of this analogy, both as the measure of immeasurable love (Christ's position within the Trinity and the grounding conditions of creation in the Trinity) and as the expression of that love toward creatures (both in creation through Christ and assumption/redemption in Christ), it is important not to get stuck at the *Theodrama* and not press on to the *Theologic*. Focused as it is on Incarnation and the God-human drama, the dramatics allows us to bracket and ultimately neglect the metaphysical questions of being which are its ground. The danger of this is that in the dramatics, von Balthasar's voice sounds most like what we long to hear, are used to hearing and are comfortable hearing: Through the dramatics we can domesticate the transcendence of the aesthetics. We would accept that Being and love are co-extensive, and then we would reduce Being to our modern conception of love and end up with a fairly anthropocentric communalism.

The Logic, were we to read further, complicates the picture. It forces us to realize that it is not just our concept of Being, but also our concept of love that must be revised. It forces us beyond the most recent kenosis (assumptive-kenosis in the Incarnation) to the first temporal ground of our being (creative-kenosis in creation), and then on to that first kenosis, the ultimate ground of our being (processive-kenosis in the Trinity). If, as von Balthasar has it in the *Epilogue*, the True is self-expression,[5] then it becomes clear how important Bonaventure, with his emphasis on the centrality of expression for analogy of being, is for this final challenge.[6]

All that has come before has prepared us for understanding the meaning and import of analogy of being as it functions within the Balthasarian system. Now at last we are prepared to turn to analogy of being proper. Here, we will discuss two aspects: the trinitarian dimensions of the analogy, and the Christological dimensions.

A. TRINITARIAN DIMENSIONS OF THE ANALOGY OF BEING

It may seem strange, in light of the argument so far, to suppose that there is anything like a trinitarian dimension to the analogy of being. For the analogy of being terminates in Christ, not in the Trinity as such. But Christ is himself a trinitarian reality: as the expressive midpoint of the Trinity, he offers that which is imitable about the Trinity for imitation. Even if that should turn out to be very little, it is significant to von Balthasar's metaphysics that the first principle is itself defined by its participation in an eternal trinitarian life.

1. GROUNDING THE POSITIVITY OF DIFFERENCE IN GOD

The classic formula for the analogy of being, developed at Lateran IV and often quoted by von Balthasar,[7] is as follows: "inter creatorem et creaturam non potest similitudo notari, quin inter eos maior sit dissimilitudo notanda" (DS 806).[8] This formula is often abbreviated by von Balthasar to "similitudo, sed semper maior dissimilitudo."[9] It is thus a principle of both nearness and distance, which allows it to fulfill its role as standing between identity and pure difference without collapsing into either.

Von Balthasar is always clear, however, that any conception of the analogy of being that will be theologically acceptable must begin with the difference.[10] For this reason, even the Biblical revelation cannot begin with *Imago Dei* theology, but after an initial indication must work its way back toward it only once the radical transcendence of God has been firmly asserted.[11] Unlike the negative theological traditions, however, von Balthasar doesn't find it necessary to attempt to protect the divine being from too close a *rapprochement* with created being—divine *aseity* sees to it that the creature can never, through grace or any other means, ascend to the level of the divine. For, however lofty it may become, the creature is always metaphysically marked as having its being from another, while God alone has being from Godself and not another.[12]

Once that has been established, however, it is possible to note that the otherness within the divine persons in some way founds the otherness of the creature; and this precisely because there is something in God, namely this otherness, which allows the positing of a creature that is an image in just this sort of way (that is, marked in a fundamental ontological way by an irreducible difference from the divine).[13] Put very simply, there is otherness in creation because there is otherness in the Creator, though the strength of the separation is magnified in the case of creation.[14]

This is a difficult concept in the Triptych. The first hint comes in *The Glory of the Lord* with an oblique reference to the Anselmian analogy of being: "The formula, so typical of Anselm, of the God-creature analogy: *one sees that one is not able to see more on account of one's own darkness*" (H II.224);[15] here, the analogy is the measure of the difference and is grounded inescapably in the *maior dissimilitudo*: One is aware that one is not able to see more of God because of one's own darkness, that is, the weakness of one's own nature in comparison to the greatness of that nature to be measured by the intellective faculty.[16] It is precisely this inability, which stems from the metaphysical distance between knower and object, that is, according to von Balthasar, Anselm's "formula for the analogy."

The point comes to the fore in a passage from the *Theologic* that is at once the most difficult and most important statement about the nature of the analogy in the whole of the Triptych: "This likeness in 'greater unlikeness' already begins in the non-identity of being and essence (real distinction) within the identical existing creature, wherein 'the structural image of trinitarian being' shows itself. For, according to Thomas, the difference itself is '*quoddam ens*' (*De. Pot.* 3 a 16 ad 3), and the being of the (differing) essence is not derivable from the '*esse*' (De Ver. 21 q 5 ad 8); in this respect, the specific creaturely non-identity refers in its original constitution back to that in God which (with Hegel) can be called the identity of the identity (of the essence) and the non-identity (of the hypostases)" (*TLg* II.77).[17] The claim here is on the one hand that the fact that the creature's being and essence are not identical (as they are in God) is itself a mirror of the triune being.[18] This might seem counter-intuitive from a Thomistic perspective, where one tends to focus on the divine being considered in abstraction from the persons—in that case, it does not seem possible that a non-identity of being and essence could in any way reflect the divine being, which is characterized by an identity of these two elements; *maior dissimilitudo* is the required theological conclusion of this comparison. However, when one considers the divine being as triune, there is what may be called an identity of identity and non-identity, that is, an identity of the essence (which is simple and one) and the hypostases (which are differentiations, but which are not really distinct from the essence and thus, in a real sense, identical with it). In this way, there is a reflection, there is *similitudo*.[19]

A second claim is implicit in this analysis, and one that is far more important for the understanding of von Balthasar's construal of the analogy of being, namely that that which grounds the *dissimilitudo* is identical to that which grounds the *similitudo*.[20] And that thing is the most fundamental ontological characteristic of creaturely make-up, the very sign of creatureliness, namely the fact that one's being and one's essence are not the same. Because of this, creatures differ maximally from a Creator whose essence is to be, is his very act of being; but also because of this, creatures greatly resemble a God who is three persons in one essence.

This turns a corner in the history of the analogy of being, for it places the Trinity centrally in view as that to which man's being is analogous in a way that is philosophically specific and robust. Further, the Trinity has been brought into the story of analogy by a greater emphasis on the person and centrality of Christ, for not only is it only in Christ that the analogy of being appears, but Christ himself is concretely this measure of the likeness and ever greater unlikeness, and becomes in himself the living analogy. As such, he is the measure of Trinitarian being itself, which both expresses and grounds likeness and unlikeness.

This knot of concepts is expressed more clearly in the second section of the *Cosmic Liturgy*, which is von Balthasar's consideration of Maximus's doctrine of God. The starting point there is the idea we are considering in this section, namely that the positivity of otherness is grounded in God's very being. This is established in a very general way through Denys.[21] But in Denys there remained a hidden contradiction between Being and Nothingness, light and darkness: it is the achievement of Maximus, von Balthasar says, to overcome these tensions with the doctrine of analogy.[22]

The features of this analogy are strikingly similar to the account we have just been following in *Theologic*: God's identity with Godself in transcendence and immanence makes it possible for God to ground not only unity but also *difference* among creatures;[23] passivity in creatures takes on a positive, affirmed role, *because* it is different from God, because even being different from God is a way of imitating God.[24] This leads to the consideration of the dialectic of God's immanent name (Being) and his transcendent name (Not-Being); here von Balthasar is defeated in his ability to use Maximus as the conveyer of Balthasarian content. For Maximus turns here to the ascendency of negative theology, where von Balthasar does not wish to go. Even the attempt to recast the Maximian picture in terms of the real distinction between existence and essence doesn't get von Balthasar any further than an epistemological reduction of Maximus's apophaticism. Von Balthasar accepts that the dialectic of being and non-being must "limit itself to the statement of opposites" (*CL* 90).

Here there is a clever move. Von Balthasar attempts a different dialectic, that of motion and rest. This too, fails;[25] but in doing so, it causes the real distinction between being and essence in creatures to appear, and thus arrives at the same conclusion reached above: "It simply brings us, once again, back to the focal point of this polarity within creaturely existence, where the creature's precise difference from God and his precise similarity with God stand inseparably linked" (*CL* 90). There are steps missing to get us from the dialectic of motion and rest to this statement about the polarity (real distinction) in creaturely being as simultaneously the likeness and greater unlikeness to God. Those steps are the very ones filled in above in the argument from *Theologic*.

The conclusion is also stated in *Theodrama*: "Every limited being (*essentia*) participates in real being (in the *actus essendi*), but none of them is identical with it, nor can the totality of limited beings exhaust it. From Thomas onward this mystery is called the 'real distinction.' Evidently, this specifically creaturely constitution of being has something to do with the distinction in God between that being which is common to the Persons and the qualities that distinguish them, although the 'real distinction' is a characteristic of the creature in its irreducible otherness vis-à-vis God" (*TD* V.68).

It is this unity of the referent of both likeness and unlikeness that makes possible the "basic relationship, on the level of ideas, of God and the world. Distance grows with increasing nearness" (*CL* 92). The converse of this is also true: "The highest union with God is not realized 'in spite of' our lasting difference from him, but rather 'in' and 'through' it. Unity is not the abolition of God's distance from us, and so of his incomprehensibility; it is its highest revelation" (*CL* 96). This grounding of creaturely difference in God may be taken as a particular instance of what is a more general axiom for von Balthasar: "the Trinity contains the purely positive archetypes of what, within creation, is reflected in potentialities and in the negatives that result from sin" (*TD*V.173).[26] This surprising doctrine, which would have to be given a full explication in any thorough treatment of von Balthasar's theology, is pursued with a seriousness and rigor that underscores how fundamental it is for von Balthasar. Not content to merely assert this but remain skeptical about our ability to determine what the positive form of these potentialities would be in God, von Balthasar will seize the cataphatic reins and describe several such equivalences and their divine counterparts in specific detail.[27]

A defense of this claim is difficult, because it is in fact axiomatic, and so more in the nature of an assumption than a deduction. For just this reason it is problematic at this stage: for one wonders what the grounds are that would motivate the acceptance of this claim. The answer ought already to be clear to us, however: analogy is the ground. Analogy is the measure of *every*relation between God and the creature, and that means that nothing creaturely comes *from nothing* in the sense of not being the image of anything. And if any creaturely x is in the image of some y, that y can only be God. Thus, for every x, there is some aspect of y that it images. The qualification need only be added that the image may have been significantly altered by a) finitude or b) sin to arrive at von Balthasar's claim. It is a necessary corollary of his version of the Analogy Thesis, and underscores the nature of the analogy he has in mind.

2. GREATER UNLIKENESS

We come now to the clear and definitive statement of the greater unlikeness of analogy. This is ultimately that on which the entire doctrine of analogy must hang, because analogy asserts that whatever likeness one can reasonably predicate must be matched by a greater unlikeness. The securing of that greater unlikeness will therefore ground the possibility of asserting a sufficiently non-trivial likeness as well as set the definite limits to how far that likeness may go. As we have seen that von Balthasar would like to push the likeness quite far (to the archetypality of *everything* in the creaturely realm in God), he will need a very strong unlikeness.

This unlikeness appears at the end of *Theologic* I as the "mysteriousness of truth" (*TL* I.230). It is the nature of worldly truth that it cannot appear without at the same time expressing an abiding mystery, what von Balthasar calls a "comparative."[28] What this amounts to is appearing and greater non-appearing, where the "greater" is obliquely referenced by "comparative." The reason for this is because of the analogy that holds between divine truth and worldly truth: "*Because* divine truth, being the truth of an *absolute* interiority, necessarily remains a mystery in all its manifestations, all worldly truth has some share in this mysteriousness" (*TL* I.231).

The "share" that it has is a participation that it receives as a gift (because it is not Truth-itself, it can only be truth if Truth makes room in itself, if divine Truth graciously allots to worldly truth a share in its being). This means that the mystery of truth as such is beyond the power of the creature: "However hard it may try, in fact, the creature can never betray and profane its mystery as completely as it might intend by its sin. The mystery, in other words, is never given into the creatures possession in such a way that it ceases to remain, at the same time, in God's safekeeping. This is the seal that the Creator has imprinted upon his creature, thereby branding it as his property" (ibid.). This is then used to explain a concept invoked earlier in the book, that worldly truth is groundless.[29] What this now means is not that worldly truth has no ground, but that its ground is not in itself, but rather in another: the transcendent truth of God.[30] God's truth also turns out to be groundless, but this not because it is grounded in another, but because it is grounded only in Godself.[31]

How can the same thing (whether one rest on oneself) be both the condition for grounding and a sufficient condition for groundlessness? This seems to be what von Balthasar is claiming: on the one hand, the creature's truth is groundless because its ground is not in itself; on the other hand, God's truth is groundless because it is grounded only in Godself. How can these both be true?

Von Balthasar is speaking in a compressed fashion, and probably moving a bit too quickly here. The creature's truth is groundless because it is open to and dependent upon a higher truth that controls and contextualizes it. This is not groundlessness simply speaking (probably not even properly speaking); what it really means is that the creature's truth has no *immanent* ground. It is in fact grounded in God's truth, and therefore not groundless. God's truth, by contrast, is not founded upon anything transcendent to God. It is self-grounded, and therefore self-determined. But if it therefore needs nothing other than itself in order to be, it is sufficient to be the cause of itself, and therefore stands upon nothing else as a necessary condition. What it means for God's truth to be groundless is that it has no *external* ground. This sense of "groundless" as "having no external ground" is something that may be affirmed of the creature immanently, and of God simply, and thus it is applied analogously between the two.

Yet God's groundlessness also rests on infinity, and that means that it is also groundless in the sense that one never reaches the end of that on which it is founded. There is always more, a dynamic of ever-greater. Thus a transcendent dimension is not missing even in divine truth, although it is not transcendent in the direction of another, but in the direction of its own infinite depths.

Von Balthasar confirms this interpretation of an analogical predication of *groundlessness* in this passage: "in other words, the groundlessness of all worldly grounds is itself analogous to the groundlessness of the divine ground" (ibid.). This leads to the conclusion: "Of course, the structure of this analogy entails that the unequivocal creatureliness of the world's groundlessness—the fact that the world does not stand in itself and the distance from God that this implies—is the locus where we glimpse the unequivocal godliness of God's groundlessness—the fact that, unlike the world, he stands wholly in himself" (ibid.). The talk about groundlessness is here converted from the realm of truth to the realm of *standing*, that is, existence. We are therefore speaking of the relation of the fact that the creature is from another to the fact that God is from Godself, *a se*. The world's lack of aseity demarcates a distance from God, and there is no more unequivocal divine attribute than aseity. Aseity *is* the expression of the greater unlikeness.

This was, in fact, the conclusion in *Theologic* II, reached in the same passage we were analyzing in the previous section. For the identity of essence and existence in God is the Thomistic expression of the divine aseity, and the decisive point of distinction between Creator and creature. If, as we found in the last section, the real distinction is the ground of both the likeness and the greater unlikeness, and if it is a statement about aseity, then we have found that in God which surpasses creatures in such a way that it surpasses any possible likeness between God and creatures. This is expressed very well in *Theologic* II: "There can, of course, be no question of violating the creature's *maior dissimilitudo* [greater dissimilitude] with respect to God (DS 806), for the creature, no matter how high grace may lift it, can never overtake the divine aseity" (*TL* II.82).

The space this opens for the positive affirmation of likeness is huge. Now, no matter what may be said about the creature, it is still decisively distanced from God by its very creatureliness. Even if, *per impossibile*, every divine predicate (omnipotence, omniscience, etc.) were conferred upon the creature, there would remain something divine that is *incommunicable*, namely aseity. For no one can give to another that the other not be from another: aseity must be possessed properly or not at all.[32] Thus, even in that extreme case, a greater unlikeness would remain.

Further, likeness and unlikeness are not just true of the creature taken as a whole: every aspect of creatureliness ought to fall under this, to the extent that the creature is free only analogously to God, a being only analogously to God, and so forth. And the greater unlikeness is secured for every possible predicate precisely in aseity: for God is free in Godself; the creature only has freedom through another. To be sure, this is not, to von Balthasar's mind, something for the creature to lament;[33] nevertheless, it means that the creature possesses whatever predicates it possesses as gifts, as from another, and so the very nature of our freedom, goodness, etc. are both like and unlike that which is possessed properly (through oneself).

All predicates are therefore analogical. We might have wondered how to interpret this analogy: whether it is likeness or unlikeness that is more decisive in understanding the *quality* of our predicates compared to God; von Balthasar has clarified that it is the unlikeness which is decisive. Even given this, we could still end up in an apophatic agnosticism about the nature of our predicates in the following way: predicates applied analogously between God and creatures are applied primarily to God, and secondarily to creatures. But we do not know them in their primary significance, because we are unable to inspect them except as they are applied here in a secondary sense. There is therefore some act of faith by which we assert that "God is good" is true, because we don't know what *good* really means. Nevertheless, we are not wrong in supposing this, as we will understand when we see (in the beatific vision) what it really means that God is good.[34]

This last claim is one that von Balthasar can deny. Since we know not just *that* there is a greater difference, but that this greater difference is in fact aseity, we can begin to describe just how our freedom differs from God's freedom.

Even if such a description may not be exhaustive, it can still go a long way in reflecting on the differences between what freedom which is possessed properly is like compared to freedom possessed from another (the overall project of *Theodrama*).

As an interesting side note, this forms a response to one of Barth's concerns about analogy of being, expressed this way by von Balthasar: "The concept of being does not suffice for expressing the decisive element in the relation between God and creature. [. . .] This basis is supposed to be what both subjects have in common; but the real basis is what is most unique about both subjects, where there is no similarity. The one subject is self-positing, that is, exists *a se*. The second is other-posited and exists *ab alio*. This is the indissoluble contrariety" (*Barth* 162). Von Balthasar's view has converted this from being a disproof of the analogy of being into an aspect of it. It is in this sense that the following passage is to be interpreted: "Though we must not fall into direct contradiction and say that the creature is dissimilar to God where it is similar, yet we must assert something only slightly different: that, in everything where it is similar to God, the creature is in fact also dissimilar. Analogy is an ultimate relational term: it cannot be explained by any more fundamental identity or non-identity" (*Barth* 109). That is, the claim that it is direct contradiction to say that the creature is unlike God precisely where it is like God is denied, but what is substituted is only slightly different. The difference will simply avoid the contradiction of any statement that entails that the unlikeness and the likeness are the same; it will not rule out the claim that unlikeness and likeness are *grounded*in the same thing.

Ultimately, von Balthasar has found his solution to the argument over an analogy of faith versus an analogy of being in precisely the place where Barth anchors the analogy of faith: Jesus Christ. His entire exposition of Barth's conversion to analogy (to which the passage just cited belongs) is his argument that the logic of Barth's position had already answered Barth's own objections.[35]

B. CHRISTOLOGICAL DIMENSIONS OF THE ANALOGY OF BEING

Pedro Escobar dubs von Balthasar a "Christologian,"[36] where *Christologian* is defined as one for whom knowledge of God is mediated only through Christ and nothing else, for whom theology *is* Christology. We have now arrived at the point where, for von Balthasar, Christology and analogy meet; a point which will show the fittingness of Escobar's claim.

In the second volume of the *Theologic*, von Balthasar reminds us that analogy is originally a Pythagorean term meant to describe two quantities that were in proportion (*ana logon*) to each other.[37] He goes on to say that Plato released the term from the type of mathematical exactitude it has in Pythagoras, using it to compare the place the idea of the Good holds in the realm of ideas to the place the sun holds in the sensible realm, and even introducing a causal relationship (and thus, in a way, prefiguring the exemplary cause). From here, von Balthasar notes, it is not far to the Christian idea that all created things are termed *beings* only by analogy, because of their causal and formal (*sic*) dependence on God.[38]

However, he concludes that this "general relationship between God and the creature distinguished by their immeasurable distance from each other" is not the focus of Christology.[39] Rather, Christology is concerned with "the relationship of the Logos, who is himself essentially God and identical with God, to his human nature, assumed in highest freedom, with which he has also made himself identical."[40] In effect, though he doesn't say so explicitly, von Balthasar is retrieving the etymological sense of the Pythagorean *ana logon* (as the measure of a proportion) by placing the proportion which is the analogy of being into the Logos. In that case, the central fact of Christology becomes the relation of the natures internal to the hypostasis of the Logos; or simply put, the central fact of Christology becomes the mystery of the Incarnation.[41]

The analogy of being, however, is a doctrine which is tied to the theological locus of creation, for it deals with the eternal being of the Creator and the contingent created being that is modeled on it, irrespective of any questions about sin or a fall.[42] Subtly, then, the Christological shift von Balthasar executes here also shifts the doctrine of creation from a primary concern with the multitude of created beings in their relation to their infinite ground to the Incarnation as the place where alone the relationship between Creator and creature may appear in its truest light.[43]

This proportion between the Creator and the creature that is realized in the hypostatic union is also exemplified prototypically in the Logos who is the beginning and end of all creation.[44] Further, because this proportion, which is a measure of difference, is beyond all human ability to conceive, it remains what Bonaventure calls *proportionalitas*, a "proportional relation between proportional relations." Von Balthasar unpacks this rather dense definition by clarifying exactly what is being compared to what here: The difference between God and creature on the one hand is being compared to the difference between the intra-Trinitarian persons on the other.[45]

What is asserted, then, is that Christ contains the measure of the Trinity (as perfect expression, and therefore as medium of communicability) *and* the relation between divine and human being, and that these two "measures" are placed in relation to one another in Christ—first prototypically in Christ as exemplar of all things that are to be made in the Ideal Metaphysic, and then in a realized form in the Incarnation, when Christ causes the two proportions to coexist within a single hypostasis in the most robust metaphysical way in the Historical Metaphysic.[46]

Christ not only contains this proportion or measure, but is in fact identical to it, is himself the measure within the Trinity[47] and the measure of the distance between Creator and creation.[48] This returns us to the notion of Christ as the concrete analogy of being. von Balthasar grounded this claim, it will be remembered, in the fact that the unity of divine and human nature in the person of Christ encompasses every possible interval between God and humans.[49] Every similarity and dissimilarity between Creator and creature is concretely exemplified in the one who in his person *is* both Creator and creature.[50] The true fittingness of this only emerges when one remembers that Christ does not for the first time come to express this measure in the Incarnation, but was always eternally the measure by being the perfect expression of the Father and of all created things.[51]

With this concretization of the analogy of being in the person of Christ in the Incarnation, we have effected the final move from the Ideal to the Historical Metaphysic. The understanding of analogy operative in the Historical Metaphysic is therefore controlled from the midpoint of its concrete instantiation in the person of Christ as the proportion that holds between the trinitarian and divine–creature relations. Let us now examine this proportionality.

II. *PROPORTIONALITAS*: MULTIPLICATION IN THE HISTORICAL METAPHYSIC

If it is true that "the trinitarian relation is the primal measure in God" (*H*II.71),[52] then it is with this relation that we must begin. "For it is rightly said that the immeasurable Father himself is measured by the Son, the measure of the Father is in fact the Son, because he gauges him. . . . And for that reason God created all things according to measure and rhythm (*metro kai taxei),*and nothing is without measure with him, because nothing is without number (*anarithmêton)*" (*H* II.71).[53]

What is this measure? In the first place, it is a right proportion from which alone fullness may be said to spring. The nature of this concept of fullness is established by a clarification of what is in von Balthasar's view the correct term to oppose to *lack*: He takes issue with the opposition *lack-excess* because excess also is a kind of lacking, namely a lack of proportion. A better opposition is *lack-fullness*. From this it becomes clear that proportion is the harmonious regulation of inflow and overflow, as it were a wise administration; and therefore wisdom is the measure governing the soul, and for the same reason the Trinity is governed by wisdom in the person of the Son.[54]

Thus the "relationship of the primal numbers" in which created relationships participate finds its fulfillment, and indeed, its archetype, in the relations among the persons in the Godhead.[55] One can therefore say that even God, though infinite, is not without measure, for a complete and perfect likeness such as the Son *does* in fact measure the Godhead.[56] This is possible because in the Son there is the possibility (and ultimately, the reality) of an infinite measure, such that the dignity of the divine essence is not imperiled.

In the last section, *proportionalitas* was called a "proportional relation between proportions." The first of these two proportions that are to be co-related appears now as a relation of equality, of full measure. It is not, however, a relation of identity, for in spite of the looseness of the language here,[57] it is still a relation between the persons that prevails and not a relation of one person to the essence.[58] The first proportion, therefore, is one of perfect expression or likeness.

Now, it is this from which springs the possibility and reality of a measured world.[59] It is that measure which secures the existence of truth;[60] it is the fixed point to which everything else is referred and in which everything else participates, even while at the same time grounding the possibility of any participation, or as Bonaventure would have it, expression.[61]

The first volume of the *Theologic* expands on this idea: "The artwork that a sculptor or composer brings forth has a truth whose measure lies in the conception of its creator" (*TLg* I.41).[62] This is true because the human artist is sharing in the divine power, which contains the measure of the truth of things within the divine archetypes.[63] But this measure cannot be external to being because everything that exists participates in being. Being, therefore, must in some way be able to measure itself, be able to use itself as measure.[64] This is really just underlining again the point that the exemplar in God is not other than the divine essence: In God, the measure of the truth of created beings must be the divine being itself.

The conclusion, "insofar as this measure is a measure that is itself measured by infinite truth, it partakes in divine truth; but insofar as it is not itself the infinite measure, the sphere of divine truth remains transcendent to it" (*TLg* I.45–46), is therefore justified.[65] Human reason's ability to measure (which amounts to its ability to know) stands necessarily upon a transcendent measure that has first measured all things.[66] The underlying motivation for this claim remains the desire to secure God's exemplarity: God alone primarily possesses knowledge that is not an image but the archetype of reality, whose truth is not measured by things but measures them.[67] God's knowledge is generative of truth; it is pure spontaneity without any admixture of receptivity in relation to the things he knows. The truth that his knowledge posits in being is the measure of the truth of things. Human knowledge can never be archetypal knowledge in the absolute sense. Yet the law of the analogy of being and of secondary causality implies that God allots to the creature something of God's creative power even in the domain of truth.[68]

The foregoing provides firm grounding for the created intellect's activity within the prior working of the divine intellect; but the measure that is in the divine is not merely an epistemological measure, but also an ontological one. The discussion in the first volume of the *Theologic* limits itself to the examination of inner-worldly truth, casting only a preliminary eye at the divine ground that is the condition of the possibility of anything like worldly truth at all; for that reason it is primarily the epistemological relation between the Creator and creature that comes into view, the being of worldly things already being taken for granted (as phenomenologically appearing and mutually conditioning). In the second volume, however, when the view is broadened to include the "truth of God", the same truth is applied to the very being of created things: "in the face of the worldly realm created by him, in whose essential ground the word is hidden, through which it has its truth of being in the first place" (*TLg* II.32).[69]

"For the true idea of these things, through which all existing things are measured, lies only in God, and this relationship between things and their true idea is accessible to no finite intellect" (*TLg* II.94–95);[70] this relationship is the other proportion in the Bonaventurean *proportionalitas*, namely the relation of Creator and creature, that which commonly is thought to be signified by analogy of being.[71] It is no more accessible to the human mind than the relations between the persons in the Trinity is, because one of the terms is the incomprehensible Trinity; and yet it is not totally inaccessible. It also depends, as has been discussed, on the other proportion, the intra-Trinitarian relations, for it has already been stated that it is only on the basis of the complete expression of the Father in the Son that an expression in creation can be allowed.[72] This relation reveals itself as love, both in the Trinity and in its subsequent outward expression in creation.[73]

The result is that two proportions are set in relation to each other, and one is the image of the other. Yet neither is accessible to the human mind. And it is *this*relation, the *proportionalitas*relation of the proportions between the persons in the Godhead on the one hand and the proportion between God and creatures on the other hand that is the analogy of being properly speaking. This point must be emphasized, for it underscores that creaturely being is not related merely to a generic category of being, or to the divine nature considered in abstraction to the persons, but rather to the Godhead in its trinitarian fullness.

The question of the possibility of a relation of these two proportions is one which von Balthasar admits could at first seem to be solvable only in the negative: one would be forced to say that there can be no relation.[74] This admission would be forced by the *maior dissimilitudo*, the great distance that holds between them.[75] But as the problematic of the theology of history was solvable only by the unpredictable fact of the Incarnation, so this fundamental metaphysical problem is solvable only by the undeducible revelation that God is Trinity. Here, in the revelation that there is an Other in God who is the image of the Father and the archetype of all that can be created as well as in the revelation of a Spirit who is the free love of the "One" and "Other," then the otherness of creaturely being as well as the existence of creaturely being are positively grounded in the being of God.[76] This is the insight that no other religion can match; for lacking the Trinity, a ground in the original unity of divinity for the goodness of creaturely difference cannot be found; it can only be thought to be a fall.[77]

Therefore, there is some relation of comparability that holds between divine and creaturely being. The creature comes from God, not just in the bare metaphysical relations of origin, conservation, and goal but in the specificity of personal difference.[78] Creaturely difference is only intelligible in a positive sense on the basis of difference in the primal, divine unity.[79] Von Balthasar says that to explain this properly, he would have to insert a full treatise on metaphysics at this point. All that we have developed to this point may be taken as an outline of such a treatise.[80]

Thus the answer to the problem of the possibility of *proportionalitas* is ultimately grounded in the prior of the two relations within *proportionalitas*, the intra-trinitarian relations. This must be so: *proportionalitas* is not a neutral ground in which the divine and the divine-human proportions will meet, for nothing that stands outside of God can be properly understood without primary and fundamental reference back to God.[81] Rather, *proportionalitas* is the point of contact between the derived proportional relation of creatures to their archetype with the grounding proportion which constitutes that archetype.[82]

Creation is the outward self-expression of God (compared to the inward self-expression in the Son); therefore each outward self-expression must be referred back to the first expression in the Son if it is to be properly interpreted in the light of its true being and if its highest created possibilities are to be understood.[83] "It never has its norm in itself in such a way that it no longer needs to receive [the norm] from God."[84] This is to finally and completely enshrine the proportion between the internal divine expression and the external divine expression (that is to say, the analogy of being) in the central place cosmologically speaking.[85]

The discussion of the assumption of a human nature by Christ could not do other than bring the relation of the cosmos to the Logos into view, for man is the midpoint of creation,[86] and it is precisely as *incarnate* that Christ is the midpoint of all things.[87] This leads us into the heart of the fundamentally cataphatic character of von Balthasar's Christology: It hinges on the image, but an image that is archetypal precisely on account of its image character. Jesus is a metaphysical Janus, facing God with one face and humanity with the other—and it is the divine face that is toward the human and the human face that is toward the divine—therein lies the mediation. In this archetypal imaging, Christ is the image that the prohibition against idolatry forbade humanity to set up.[88] It is not that we were to have no images, only that it was not in our power to construct an image of appropriate dignity, and so we were commanded to abstain from images until such time as the divinely appointed image could appear. This image is the truth, and "this truth beheld is nothing other than what the first part of this trilogy termed 'glory': the exhibition without worldly analogy of God in the world" (*TLg* II.16).[89]

There is no worldly analogy because Christ is himself the analogy, and worldly being is always already transcending itself in the direction of the divine being which, far from being antithetical to it (as the Greeks tended to think), has always had the intention of making room within itself to receive and beatify finitude.[90] The first thought of creation for God was one of union or, put another way, one of love.[91]

This theme of love resumes and completes the theme of participation that it has been so important for von Balthasar to highlight in all of his theological sources. The payoff of exemplarity is that it provides a basis for participation;[92] in participation, the trinitarian life of God is extending itself toward us.[93] It is in this that we learn that a self-giving rooted in love, which is perhaps the very definition of love, is the fundamental character of God.[94]

Notes

1. That is to say, it must find that on the basis of which communication is possible at all. *Communicatio* is etymologically based on *communis*, something that is common. The concept is therefore that there must be something in which the uncreated and the created meet if there is to be true influence—but for there to be something of this sort, the communicating love cannot remain unmeasured. For that which is without measure cannot have anything in common with another. The dependence on number evident in this logic is analogical, and is rooted in Augustine's *De Musica* (and thus in the Pythagorean roots of Platonism). See chapter 2, II.C.

2. See Dörrie, H. "*Formula Analogiae:* An Exploration of a Theme in Hellenistic and Imperial Platonism" in *Neoplatonism and Early Christian Thought*, (London: Variorum, 1981), 38.

3. D. C. Schindler underlines this point for quite different reasons as he seeks to ally von Balthasar's project with the continental philosophical project, claiming that they both share "the desire to overcome what is often called today a 'metaphysics of presence,' that is, a reduction of the object of knowledge to its immediacy to the knower, or, in other contexts, 'identitarianism,' that is, the privileging of identity over difference in relation" (*Hans Urs von Balthasar and the Dramatic Structure of Truth: A Philosophical Inverstigation* (New York: Fordham University Press, 2004), 1. As Kevin Mongrain rightly says, "if God is the world and the world is God, either tragedy is not real or God is tragic. Neither option is Christian, von Balthasar thinks," *The Systematic Thought of Hans Urs von Balthasar: An Irenaean Retrieval* (New York: Crossroad, 2002), 58.

4. This type of anthropological turn, which begins from the structures of dependence in creatures, is essentially the misstep Larry Chapp makes: "If such a strongly universalistic concept of Christ's role in human history is to be taken seriously, then a study of the general human 'thirst' for God is necessary" (*God*, 43). Again, "Balthasar turns to the history of the dialectical interplay between mythological and metaphysical thought for clues concerning the real outlines of the human longing for the divine" (ibid., 43–44). The text given in support of this last claim is from *GL* IV.24: "Metaphysics, in the breadth of myth, philosophy and religion already offers an interpretation of man that radically directs him to the divine." Chapp is redirecting von Balthasar's statement, which is one about man's fundamental analogous relation to the divine, into a fundamentally anthropological statement about man's longing for the divine. This is precisely the kind of anthropological turn von Balthasar wishes to avoid. Such analyses can only arrive at a general notion of God, and will therefore not from the beginning think through the whole God-creation story in a trinitarian light.

5. *Epilogue*, 77 ff.

6. The discourse of the divine love in its dispensational configuration of grace will accordingly depend not merely on the understanding of analogy to be developed here, but also on the dynamics of kenosis to be developed in the next chapter. As such, it can only be appended as a theological epilogue to the properly metaphysical concerns of this project.

7. *TL* II.76 *et plures*.

8. "A likeness is not able to be noted between Creator and creature unless a greater unlikeness is to be noted between them."

9. "Likeness, but always greater unlikeness"

10. As Gerard O'Hanlon reminds us: "there *is* an enduring and incommensurable difference between God and the world, between the divine and the human 'unmixed' natures of Christ. Any facile attribution of change and suffering to God, based on the fact that the person of Christ is affected by his human nature, represents a failure to maintain the distinction between the natures; it is a relapse into monophysitism and results in a mythical notion of God," *The Immutability of God in the Theology of Hans Urs von Balthasar* (Cambridge: Cambridge University Press, 1990), 43.

11. "Der Alte Bund hat über die analogia entis nie anders nachgedacht als die Tatsache bedenkend, daß der hinfällige Mensch dem freien Gott alles verdankt: das lebendige Sein (aber Gott ist auch noch Herr über die Sheol der Toten) und alles ihm im Bund darüber hinaus Geschenkte" (*TLg* II.62). [The Old Testament reflected on the *analogia entis* in no other way than

as the considered fact that frail humanity owes everything to the free God: living being (although God is also still the Lord over the Sheol of the dead) and all other things given to him in the covenant.]

12. Cyril O'Regan makes this point in "Von Balthasar and Thick Retrieval: Post-Chalcedonian Symphonic Theology:" "Chalcedonian christological discourse, specifically discourse about the unconfused (*asynchutos*) natures in the hypostatic union, actually proves regulative. This discourse sets limits to what can be said about human beings even and especially when the possibility of *theosis* is granted. And it sets limits by specifying the gulf between the human and the divine that is mysteriously and uniquely surpassed and retained in the hypostatic union" (240). Cf. Rowan Williams, whose statement seems to attempt to ally von Balthasar's analogy with the Pure Difference Thesis: "The *maior dissimilitudo* not only insists upon the folly of treating God and world as two 'cases' of existence; it also, certainly in Balthasar's hands, evokes the dynamic of dissimilarity. Difference is always an *excess*; as, in Balthasar's trinitarian theology, the divine Persons transcend each other in freedom, so in the relation of creature to Creator difference unceasingly opens out—as space for movement, not as alienation," "Balthasar and Trinity" in *The Cambridge Companion to Hans Urs von Balthasar*, Edward T. Oakes and David Moss, eds. (Cambridge: Cambridge University Press, 2004), 43.

13. "Wenn es aber absolut gut ist, daß es den Andern gibt, dann ist diese Andersheit innerhalb der vollkommenen Wesenseinheit das Fundament für die mögliche Andersheit auch des mit Gott nicht wesenseinen Geschöpfs und für die diesem eigentümlichen unaufhebbaren Differenzen. Ohne daß die dem Geschöpf eignende ,maior dissimilitudo' von Gott (DS 806) angetastet würde, da Gottes Aseität in keinem noch so gnadenhaften Zustand des Geschöpfs eingeholt werden kann, muß in Gott trotzdem eine Voraussetzung liegen, die es ermöglicht, ein Geschöpf zu planen und ins Dasein zu setzen, das in seinem Sein und Wesen eine abbildhafte Ähnlichkeit mit Gott, dem Dreieinigen, hat" (*TLg* II.76). [But if it is absolutely good that the other exists, then this otherness within perfect Being is the foundation also for the possible otherness of the creature not identical in essence with God and for the particular, ineliminable differences. Without the creature possessing the "*maior dissimilitudo*" being impinged on by God (for the condition of the creature, however graced, can in no way catch up to God's aseity), there must nevertheless lie in God a presupposition that makes it possible to plan and to bring into existence a creature that in its own being and essence has an imitative similarity with the triune God.] Cf. Bonaventure, *Hex* 11.9: "ante dissimile necesse est esse consimile, ante inaequale est aequale, ante essentialiter differens est essentialiter idem." [Before the dissimilar it is necessary that there be the consimilar; before the unequal is the equal, before the essentially different is that which is essentially the same.]

14. Johann Roten connects this idea with the divine love, which for von Balthasar as for Bonaventure is a central theme of the trinitarian processions: "The reading of finite reality leads to the discovery of receptiveness and openness to infinity. The meditation of being opens the understanding for the ontological difference and its ultimate rootedness in love (*ens et amor convertuntur*)," "Hans Urs von Balthasar's Anthropology in Light of His Marian Thinking," *Communio* 20, no. 2 (1993): 319.

15. "Die für Anselm so kennzeichnende Formel der Gott-Geschöpf-Analogie: *videt se non plus posse videre propter tenebras suas.*"

16. Werner Löser quotes the following passage from "Warum ich noch ein Christ bin": "Faith must recognize the validity of the claim sufficiently in the claim itself to allow of assent. But it would not be faith if it were able to work out this validity in a rational system and expound it exhaustively. There must always be something which eludes or obstructs faith when it thinks that it is able to see through the conditions for the possibility of the reality that stands before it. When Jesus says, 'I am the Truth,' 'I am the Resurrection,' he is saying that God is present in him. But: *Si comprehendis, non est Deus.* If God interprets himself in Jesus Christ then Anselm's formula for God applies to this manifestation too: '*id quo majus cogitari non potest.*' The context makes it clear that this means neither exhaustive knowledge—as though the objective, utter 'greatness' of God

corresponded to a subjective, ever-expanding thought in man. It is rather that the *majus* of the one who manifests himself takes possession of the *cogitatio* in such a way that the latter, by acknowledging its being over-mastered, praises the perfect victory of the inscrutable truth of God. Other formulas of Anselm confirm this interpretation: *videt se non plus posse videre*: the little eye can encompass only so much, although the object seen extends farther than its power of vision: and the eye (in being over-mastered) terms this farther field of vision *quiddam majus quam cogitari potest*. And so we come to the ultimate formulations which open up vision into a higher sphere, without allowing what is seen there to be dragged down into the realm of sight: *evidentissime comprehendi potest, ab humana scientia comprehendi non posse*. Or yet again, in other words: *rationabilitier comprehendit incomrehensibile esse*" (Löser, "Being," 488–99).He goes on to comment on the above passage: "In the background of this assertion stands the conviction that the formula of the *analogia fidei* of the Fourth Lateran Council—according to which God, no matter how much he might approach the world, still remains all the much more inconceivable (DS 806)—not only holds true philosophically but also, and even more so, in a christocentric theology" (Ibid., 489). Although Löser falls prey here to a common tendency among contemporary thinkers to reduce the ontological to the epistemolgical, (for it is *not* an analogy of faith but of being, and it was not stated in an epistemological but rather an ontological form by Lateran IV) he is nevertheless right to see the Lateran IV formula underlying the Anselmian reflections given here.

17. "Diese Ähnlichkeit in der ‚größeren Unähnlichkeit' beginnt schon bei der Nichtidentität von Sein und Wesen (Realdistinktion) innerhalb des identisch daseienden Geschöpfs, worin sich ‚das strukturelle Abbild des dreieinigen Seins' anzeigt. Denn nach Thomas ist die Differenz selbst ‚quoddam ens' (De Pot. 3 a 16 ad 3), und das Sein des (differenten) Wesens nicht aus dem ‚esse' ableitbar (De Ver. 21 q 5 ad 8); insofern verweist die spezifisch geschöpfliche Nichtidentität in seiner ersten Konstitution zurück auf das in Gott, was man (mit Hegel) die Identität der Identität (des Wesens) und der Nichtidentität (der Hypostasen) nennen kann."

18. Angelo Scola underscores that triune being entails difference: "Already on the ontological level, but even more so in the context of a christocentric interpretation of the relation between nature and grace, one can see the emergence of Balthasar's Trinitarian doctrine in the thesis of Triune Love which admits difference in God himself, quite different from the difference which appears in the sphere of created being" ("Nature," 212–13).

19. See von Balthasar's statements in *Heart of the World* p. 35: "This is a new mystery, inconceivable to mere creatures: that even distance from God and the coolness of reverence are an image and a likeness of God and of divine life. What is most incomprehensible is, in fact, the truest reality: precisely by not being God do you resemble God. And precisely by being outside of God are you in God. For to be over against God is itself a divine thing. As a person who is incomparable you reflect the uniqueness of your God. For in God's unity, too, there are found distance and reflection and eternal mission: Father and Son over against one another and yet one in the Spirit and in the nature that seals the Three of them together. Not only the Primal Image is God, but also the Likeness and the Reflected Image. Not only the unity is unconditional; it is also divine to be Two when there is a Third that binds them together. For this reason was the world created in the Second One, and in this Third One does it abide in God." See also *TL* II.315–316. Cf. John O'Donnell ("Truth as Love"): "The act of existence which is common to all created being never exists except in the diversity of distinct essences. The identity of *esse* exists concretely in the non-identity of essence and existence in any given creature. Therefore any given being reflects both the unity of being and the real distinction between existence and essence. Hence any finite being mirrors in a faint way the unity-in-diversity of the divine life" (207).

20. This has been commented on by several writers: Fergus Kerr points out that "the more we recognize that all our being is in God's image and likeness, then the more is God known as 'the One ever beyond all similarity, the ever more improbable, the ever ungraspable One'" ("Balthasar and Metaphysics," 227); Rowan Williams adds: "arising from all of this, the third fresh contribution, though the least easy to pin down in any one explicit text or group of texts, is the way in which Balthasar effectively makes trinitarian difference the basis of all analogy, all identity

in difference, so that there is truly a metaphysic, an account of reality as such, that emerges from doctrine" ("Balthasar and Trinity," 49–50).Nicholas Healy says: "My aim is to establish an account of the *analogia entis* as a structure of unity-in-difference such that the affirmation of the transcendent perfection of God always includes the affirmation of the goodness of its finite participant and image precisely in its otherness from him" (*Eschatology*, 39). (He goes on to discuss *similitudo* in Aquinas, when he ought to have gone to Bonaventure.) Later, he adds: "Rather, in crossing the trinitarian threshold, we enter into what is at once the ultimate justification and the ultimate form of analogy itself" (ibid., 83).D. C. Schindler says it best, however: "Balthasar's 'analogia entis,' by contrast, begins with God, not as a simple positivity but as an absolute poor-wealth, in relation to the relative rich-poverty of the creature. In this case, the difference between God and creature is not compromised by similarity, but rather it paradoxically increases directly with similarity. More concretely, it means that what is negative or imperfect in the creature on account of its finitude is not to be merely 'opposed' to God's (positive) perfection (for what can be opposed to the absolute?) but becomes rather, in and because of its very finitude, an image of the divine" (*Dramatic*, 49).

21. "Even greater than a God who defines himself only by his absolute otherness from the world, this God proves his very otherness in the fact that he can give positive Being to what is not himself, that he can assure its own autonomy, and for that very reason—beyond the gaping chasm that remains between them—assure it a genuine likeness to himself" (*CL* 83).

22. "But it is Maximus who banishes even the hidden contradictory influences of these things and who finally reconciles the idea of a hierarchy of being with the assumption of a structural analogy between God and the world" (*CL* 84).

23. "The theme, then, that will be with us throughout this study is the reciprocal relationship of God's transcendence and God's immanence; from this relationship it follows that God is so completely identical with himself that he is able to form all the things that participate in him both into integral units marked off from each other by mutual dissimilarity and into a whole built out of the mutual similarity of the parts" (*CL* 85–86).

24. "Rather, the very passivity of creatures comes from God, is inseparably tied to their createdness, and is not pure imperfection because even being different from God is a way of imitating him" (*CL* 87).

25. "The dialectic of motion and rest teaches us no more than the dialectic of being and not-being" (*CL* 90).

26. This is stated again later in the volume: "Everything that, in the created world, appears shot through with *potentiality* is found *positively* in God" (*TD* V. 389).

27. *TD* V.146 describes hope as based in the trinitarian life; more importantly (and controversially), *TD* V.243 describes the eternal self-surrender of the divine persons to one another as the ground of suffering in the world.

28. "We saw above that the infinite ground appears in the background of every finite truth. Indeed, we saw that by the very nature of all worldly truth, of all that is expressed in any way, there can be no expression without the concomitant appearance of a permanent mystery, without the comparative that intrinsically characterizes truth" (*TL* I.230–31).

29. *TL* I.131ff, esp. 206.

30. "All created truth is groundless to the extent that it does not have its ground in itself, to the extent, in other words, that it breaks through its own ultimate ground into the depth of God's ultimately inexhaustible mystery" (*TL* I.231).

31. "God's truth, too, is groundless, in the sense that it rests upon nothing other than itself, nothing other than its own infinity" (ibid.).

32. Even in the Trinity, where the Father may be said to give aseity to the Son, the Son, is thereby from the Father in an enduring way, reflected in their names. For von Balthasar, this marks the Son enduringly as the one who is sent.

33. "The fact that finite freedom is always embedded in and surpassed by infinite freedom, unequivocally expressed here, does not put the former at a disadvantage: on the contrary, it speaks

of God's prevenient care in preparing the necessary breadth and scope for the creature's freedom (cf. Eph 2:10)" (*TD* V.403).

34. Cf. Aquinas, *ST* Ia, q. 13, a. 6. It is not clear to me that Aquinas should be read according to the opinion I have described in the text: I think much would depend on how one were to interpret Aquinas' claim that goodness and wisdom exist "more eminently" (*eminentius*) in God. George Lindbeck (and others following him) interpret this to mean that Aquinas thinks that we are unable to specify in what way goodness is more eminent in God, *The Nature of Doctrine* (Philadelphia: Westminster, 1984), 66.

35. This is the purpose of *Barth* 163ff.

36. In his article "Hans Urs von Balthasar: Christo-logian," *Communio* 2, no. 3 (1975): 300–16.

37. The Pythagorean formula is ὁ κατ᾽ ἀνάλογον λόγος, λόγος τῆς ἀναλογίας, cited Liddell and Scott, *Greek-English Lexicon* (Oxford: Oxford University Press, 1940), 1057, literally: "The measure according to proportion, the measure of the proportion."

38. "Analogie was ursprünglich ein von den Pythagoreern verwendeter mathematischer Begriff, der zueinander auf verschiedene Art 'im Verhältnis' (ana logon) stehende Größen zu bestimmten geeinigt war (je nachdem war das Verhältnis arithmetisch oder geometrisch oder—beides verbindend—'harmonisch'), aber von Exaktheit solcher Art kann in der Christologie keinesfalls mehr die Rede sein. Gelockert war diese mathematische Strenge schon bei Platon, wenn er die Bedeutung der Idee des Guten für das Ideenreich mit der Sonne für die sinnliche Welt vergleicht und dabei noch von einer kausalen Abhängigkeit des zweiten vom ersten ausgeht (da 'das Gute [die Sonne] als sich selbst analog gezeugt hat'). Von hier zur christlichen Idee, daß alles geschaffene Seiende aufgrund kausaler und formaler Abhängigkeit vom göttlichen Sein schlechthin als nur 'analog seiend' zu bezeichnen ist, ist nur ein Schritt" (*TLg* II.284–85). [Analogy was originally a mathematical concept used by the Pythagoreans, which was applied to specify measurements standing "in relations" (ana logon) in different ways (whether this was an arithmetic, geometric, or (joining the two) "harmonic" relation), but one can in no way speak any longer of exactitude of such a sort in Christology. This mathematical severity was loosened already in Plato, when he likened the meaning of the idea of the Good in the realm of ideas to the sun in the sensible realm, and thereby even posits a causal dependence of the second on the first (because "the Good has begotten the sun as analogous to itself"). From here there is only a step to the Christian idea that all created being is to be referred to the divine being *par excellence* because of a causal and formal dependence as only "analogous being."]

39. "Aber in der Christologie wird nicht das allgemeine Verhältnis zwischen den beiden in unmeßbarer Distanz voneinander unterschiedenen Größen Gott und Geschöpf bedacht" (ibid.).

40. "Das Verhältnis des Logos, der wesenhaft Gott selber ist und mit ihm identisch ist, zu seiner in höchster Freiheit angenommenen Menschennatur, mit der er sich ebenfalls identisch gesetzt hat" (ibid.).

41. "It is not simply that he Son is a sort of container for the structures of created things: his active relation to the Father, as seen in the incarnate life which represents the eternal life, is a prototype for the relation of all things to the Father—the foundation of analogy, to touch on a pervasive theological interest in Balthasar's work" ("Balthasar and Trinity," 40).

42. Louis Dupré quotes von Balthasar's definition of glory as "the divinity of the Invisible radiating in the visibleness of Being in the world" (*GL* I.431); he goes on to say: "As it functions in the revelation, aesthetic form does not arbitrarily restrict what in itself is formless. Rather than pointing to an Absolute beyond itself, it *manifests* the 'divine super-form' (I, 432). In Christ, God himself appears as expressive in his very nature," ("The Glory of the Lord: Hans Urs von Balthasar's Theological Aesthetic," *Communio* 16, no. 3 [1989], 386). Thus it becomes clear that aesthetics is concerned first with the recognition of the originary exemplarity, that is, with the representation of the *analogia entis*, then with the Incarnational exemplarity, and lastly, with the eschatological exemplarity. As Nicholas Healy has it: "According to Balthasar, analogy, in its first and deepest meaning, is neither a logical principle nor a linguistic tool governing speech about

God, but is the ontological relationship that obtains between God and creation" (*Eschatology*, 21). This serves as a corrective to John Saward's understanding of analogy: "With the divine will that he has received from the Father, the Son from eternity is willing to assume human nature and to suffer for sinful mankind on the Cross. This is analogical obedience. Obedience in the full sense as implying service and submission, duty and command, comes into operation with the Incarnation," John Saward, *The Mysteries of March: Hans Urs von Balthasar on the Incarnation and Easter* (Washington, DC: Catholic University of America Press, 1990), 23. The contrast of the "analogical obedience" of Christ to "obedience in the full sense" makes clear that Saward's use of the word "analogy" is to weaken the meaning of that to which it is adjectivally applied. This use of analogy seems to be about *predication*, and privileges the human semantic realm as the proper one. Ultimately, therefore, we have to do with an analogy that is *merely* epistemological, and not also an analogy *of being*.

43. "According to Balthasar, the central difficulty for christology concerns the preservation and fulfillment of the analogy of being within the hypostatic union" (Healy, *Eschatology*, 93).

44. "Will man auf die scholastisch überkommenen Analogiebegriffe zurückgreifen und sie dem Gesagten einpassen, so ist von einer primären ‚attributio' aller Dinge an den Logos auszugehen, der selber als Grund und Ziel der Schöpfung dieser die rechte ‚proportio' zwischen Gott und Geschöpf vorlebt und durch seinen Geist mitteilt" (*TLg* II.288) [If one wants to fall back on the traditional Scholastic concept of analogy and insert it into what was said, then the starting point is a primary "*attributio*" of all things to the Logos who himself, as ground and goal of creation, demonstrates and communicates the right "*proportio*" between God and creation through his spirit.]

45. "Wobei die letztere, als jeden menschlichen Begriff übersteigend, bei aller Zueignung (attributio) an Christus und gnadenvollen 'Teilnahme an der göttlichen Natur' eine 'proportionalitas' bleibt, ein 'Verhältnis von Verhältnissen', nämlich des Differenz-Verhältnisses zwischen Gott und Geschöpf und desjenigen von Vater, Sohn und Geist" (*TLg* II.288). [Whereby the latter, as exceeding every human concept, in every dedication (*attributio*) to Christ and graceful 'participation in the divine nature' remains "*proportionalitas*," a relationship between relations, namely the relation of difference between God and creation and the one between Father, Son and Spirit.] For more on this, see also *H* II.297–98: "Eine similitudo participationis zwischen Gott und Kreatur ‚ist überhaupt nicht vorhanden.'" [A *similitudo participationis* between God and creature "is certainly not extant."]

46. "Wohl aber bleibt innerhalb der christologischen Analogie die ursprüngliche und immer unendliche Distanz zwischen Gott und Geschöpf, eine für das Geschöpf nie meßbare und deshalb auch nie als Analogie überblickbare Distanz, die jedoch—und das ist die andere Seite—nur innerhalb der Rekapitulation der Schöpfung in Christus bestehen bleibt und deshalb, ohne aufgehoben zu werden, in die unendliche Distanz zwischen den göttlichen Personen innerhalb der identischen göttlichen Natur hinein *verklärt* wird." (*TLg* II.288). [But certainly the original and always infinite distance between God and creation remains within the Christological analogy, a distance never measurable by the creature and for that reason also never surveyable as analogy, which however—and this is the other side—only remains extant within the recapitulation of creation in Christ, and for that reason, without being transcended, gets transfigured into the infinite distance between the divine persons within the identical divine nature.] Cf. Dupré: "By assuming human nature God transformed the very meaning of culture. Henceforth all forms have to be measured by the supreme form of the Incarnation" ("Glory," 385).

47. This claim could be said to be analytic in the title *Logos*, if this is understood in a Pythagorean sense.

48. Kevin Mongrain notes: "Von Balthasar thinks that the first corollary of the Irenaean version of *corpus triforme* Christology is that creation and redemption are united" (*Systematic Thought*, 53). Peter Casarella adds: "The analogy of the gift has its measure in the giving person of Christ (Eph. 4:7). Von Balthasar never allows the analogy of the gift to dissipate into a formless mystery. Positive and negative theology are kept in balance by the christological measure,"

"*Analogia Donationis:* Hans Urs von Balthasar on the Eucharist," *Philosophy and Theology* 11, no. 1 (1998), 148.

49. Chapter 5, I.A. What von Balthasar means by "interval" is difficult to describe. It is a metaphor which describes the relationships that could or do hold between God and creatures. A theology of Pure Difference would in essence deny that there are any intervals between God and creatures, and a theology based in the Identity Thesis would, by asserting the relationship to ultimately be one of sameness, reduce the interval to zero. Only in analogy is there an abiding interval, and therefore an abiding relationship, between God and creatures.

50. Cf. Healy: "The relation which is established in the act of creation is ordered to a gratuitous fulfillment within the person and mission of Christ, who is the pattern, the primary instance, and the accomplisher of the unification of God and creation. In his movement from birth to death and resurrection, Christ provides the final measure for both the similarity and the distance between created and uncreated being. In this sense, Christ can be called the 'concrete analogy of being', or 'the analogy of being in person'" (*Eschatology*, 21–22). Contrast this with Larry Chapp's take on this notion: "However, if Christ is the concrete analogy of being, then two mutually conditioning principles can be held: (1) that creation does participate in some sense in the act of Being and is, therefore, analogous to God's act of existence; and (2) that this analogy is based on a divine initiative where God himself 'bridges' the gap between creation and himself through the Son's free obedience in the Incarnation. This latter point is central to Balthasar's entire approach. The initiative in bridging the gap is God's, and therefore any 'analogy of being' which does not take into account the world's existence within the 'kenoses' of the trinitarian God is doomed to fall back into one of the false polarities" (*God Who Speaks*, 90). To speak of the *analogia entis* in a way which involves the positing of a gap to be overcome *in the order of creation* is wrong. Christ doesn't *overcome* the gap between the divine and human in the *analogia entis*, he *measures* it.

51. Healy again makes the point nicely: "Thus, to speak of Christ as the analogy of being is to do more than to say that he reproduces in himself the analogically structured relation between God and the creature. It is also to say that he enacts that relation in himself. His doing so obviously presupposes the reality of God and the reality of the creature. On the other hand, he is the primary measure that regulates the relation between them. As such, Christ is the concrete *locus* in which the experience of the reality of God and of the reality of the creature presupposed to Christology takes its truest shape" (*Eschatology*, 96). Only the reference to "experience" makes one hesitate—the question in von Balthasar is not about experience, but about metaphysics.

52. "Das dreieinige Verhältnis aber ist das Urmaß in Gott"

53. "Denn mit Recht wurde gesagt, der unermeßliche Vater selbst werde vom Sohne gemessen, des Vaters Maß ist nämlich der Sohn, weil er ihn ermißt. . . . Und deshalb erschafft Gott alles nach Maß und Rhythmus (metro kai taxei), und nichts ist maßlos bei ihm, weil nichts ohne Zahl (anarithmêton) ist."

54. "Die ästhetische Seinsschau der Jugendschriften drückt sich in einer höchsten Wertschätzung des Maßes und der Mäßigung aus, die den Begriff modus nicht nur auf das christliche Leben im ganzen anwendet, sondern auf Gott selber. ‚Modestia kommt von modus, und temperantia von temperies (das heißt harmonische Mischung). Wo aber Mäßigkeit und Wohlgemessenheit herrscht, da ist kein Zuviel und Zuwenig. Das ist die Fülle, die wir dem Mangel entgegensetzten, was viel wichtiger ist, als wenn wir Überfluß gesagt hätten. Im Überfluß nämlich liegt ein Zuströmen und ein allzu heftiger Erguß. Wenn das in größerem Maß geschieht, als was genügt, dann mangelt auch darin das Maß, und das Übermäßige zeigt eine Mangelerscheinung. . . Das Maß der Seele ist also die Weisheit. . . Es ist das, wodurch sich die Seele ein Schwergewicht gibt, um nicht ins Übermäßige auszulaufen noch durch mangelnde Fülle beengt zu werden. . . Was aber ist die Weisheit, wenn nicht die Weisheit Gottes, Gottes Sohn?'" (*H* II.120). [The aesthetic intuition of the young writer expresses itself by a very high regard for measure and restraint, which applies the concept *modus* not only to the Christian life, but also to God himself. "*Modestia* comes from *modus*, and *temperantia* from *temperies* (that is, harmonious mixture). But where moderation and due solmenity rule, one finds neither too much nor too little.

This is the abundance that we oppose to lack, which is much more important than if we had said 'excess.' For in excess lies an influx and an all too violent eruption. If this were to happen in greater measure than is needed, then too measure is lacking, and the excessiveness is a sympton of deficiency…The measure of the soul is therefore wisdom…This is that wherewith the soul lays heavy importance in order that nothing runs out into excess nor becomes restricted through lack…But what is wisdom, if not the Wisdom of God, God's Son?"] The "wo aber Mäßigkeit und Wohlgemessenheit herrscht" calls to mind Mozart's *Die Zauberflöte*, at a moment in the opera when Tamino is engaged in an aesthetic judgment about the beauty of Sarastro's temple.

55. John Saward will use this correspondence of creaturely and trinitarian realities as the basis for his approach in *The Mysteries of March*: "Moreover, precisely because they are united in the Trinitarian hypostasis of the Son, we can conclude that all he does or suffers in his human nature has its analogue in the divine nature of the Blessed Trinity" (18). As such, he is most immediately interested in how the "christological analogy of being" can lead to an understanding of the "Trinitarian dimension of the Incarnation and Easter" (ibid.).

56. "Es gibt den Einklang von Gott und Welt auf Grund dieses Verhältnisses der Urzahlen, die sich im Sein und Wesen alles Weltlichen darstellen, obwohl immer nur annäherungsweise und partizipativ; es gibt ihn noch höher deshalb, weil auch das Unendliche Gottes nicht ohne Maß ist, sondern vom Sohn als dem Gleichbild des Vaters durchmessen wird" (*H* II.141). [There is harmony between God and the world on the basis of this relationship of the original numbers, which show themselves in the being and essence of all worldly things, although always only approximately and in a participatory way; therefore there is something still higher than them, because even the infinite God is not without measure, but gets thoroughly measured by the Son as the express image of the Father.]

57. The suggestion that the Son measures God is loose—more strictly speaking, it ought to be that the Son measures the Father. For the Son is not the image of the divinity, he *is* the divinity; he is the image of the Father.

58. Such a relation could not in any sense be said to express the whole triune Godhead.

59. "Weil an dieser Stelle in Gott die Möglichkeit und Wirklichkeit einer gemessenen Welt entspringt" (*H* II.141). [because the possibility and reality of a measured world has its source in this locus in God.]

60. "'Damit aber Wahrheit sei, braucht es ein höchstes Maß, aus welchem sie hervorgeht und zu dem sie sich, vollendet, zurückwendet. Diesem höchsten Maß selbst ist kein anderes Maß mehr auferlegt, denn ist das höchste Maß durch das höchste Maß Maß, dann ist es durch sich selber Maß. . .So ist Wahrheit nie ohne Maß und Maß nie ohne Wahrheit'" (*H* II.120) ["In order that there be truth, a highest measure is required, from which it springs and to which it, completed, returns. No other measure is subjected to the highest measure itself, for if the highest measure is measure through the highest measure, then it is measure through itself…So truth is never without measure and measure is never without truth."].

61. "Daß der Sohn, indem er Ausdruck des Vaters ist, zugleich Ausdruck überhaupt, nämlich von allem ist [. . .] Der Sohn ist also nicht etwa nur das Urbild, nach welchem weltliche Abbilder geschaffen werden, er ist Gott als Ausdruck, somit als Wahrheit, und deshalb Prinzip sowohl des Ausgedrücktwerdens der Dinge in der Schöpfung wie ihres Sich-Selbst-Ausdrückens als geschaffene Wesen: ,ratio exprimendi est ipsius exemplaris: das Ausdrucksein (des Geschöpfs) stammt vom Urbild her. . . . Alle Dinge sind wahr und fähig, sich selbst auszudrücken kraft der Ausdrucksmacht jenes höchsten Lichtes', nämlich des Wortes" (*H* II.294–95). [That the Son, because he is the expression of the Father, is at the same time the expression *par excellence*, namely of all things. […] The Son is therefore not only the archetype after which worldly images were created, he is God as expression, therefore as truth, and therefore the principle both of the expression of things in creation as well as their self-expression as created beings: "*ratio exprimendi est ipsius exemplaris*: the expressivity (of creation) comes from the archetype. . . . All things are true and capable of expressing themselves thanks to the expressive power of that highest Light," namely the Word.]

62. "Das Kunstwerk, das ein Bildhauer oder Komponist hervorbringt, hat einen Wahrheitsgehalt, dessen Maß in der Konzeption seines Schöpfers liegt."

63. "Hier nimmt das menschliche Subjekt in besonderer Weise teil an der wahrheitsetzenden Macht des göttlichen Verstandes, dessen Urbilder das Maß der ins Dasein gesetzten Dinge und ihrer Wahrheit enthalten" (*TLg* I.33). [Here the human subject participates in a special way in the truth-making power of the divine reason, whose prototypes contain the measure and truth of things brought into existence.] This participation of the subject in the higher divine intellect is a fundamental part of von Balthasar's theory of knowledge, and the primary result of a phenomenological reflection on epistemology: "Denn die Lichtung seiner selbst, in der es sich selbst ergreift und darin erfährt, was Sein ist, lichtet ihm nicht das Sein im ganzen, sondern lichtet das Sein nur soweit, daß es begreift, daß alles Sein *an sich selbst* gelichtet sein muß. In der punkthaften Identität von Sein und Bewußtsein, in dessen Licht das Subjekt das Maß sowohl seiner selbst wie des zu messenden Objekts gewinnt, wird ihm klar, daß das absolute Sein ein von sich selbst gemessenes, sich selbst gegenwärtiges und darum ein Selbstbewußtsein sein muß. Denn es erfährt, daß die Wahrheit, in deren Licht es das Objekt mißt, und die nichts anderes ist als die Lichtung des Seins, nicht auf die Punkthaftigkeit seines Selbstbewußtseins eingeschränkt ist. Es weiß, daß es, indem es den eigenen Maßstab zur Erkenntnis des Objekts anlegt, keinen subjektiven Maßstab teilnehmen darf. Es weiß also, daß es in seiner messenden Funktion zugleich von einer es selbst umgreifenden Wahrheit des Seins schlechthin gemessen wird. Sein Licht ist begrenzte Teilnahme an einem unendlichen Licht." (*TLg* I.44–45). [For the clearing of itself, in which the subject seizes itself and therein experiences what being is, does not illuminate being as a whole to it, but illuminates being only as far as it understands that all being must be illuminated in itself. In the pointlike identity of being and awareness, in whose light the subject gains the measure as much of itself as of the measured object, it becomes clear to it that absolute being must be measured by itself, present to itself and therefore self-aware. For it experiences that the truth in whose light it measures the object and which is nothing else than the clearing of being is not limited to the punctiliarity of its self-awareness. It knows that it, by employing its own standard for the knowledge of the object, is permitted to participate in no subjective standard. It knows therefore that it is measured in its own measuring function at the same time by a self-possessing truth of being itself. Its light is limited participation in an infinite light.]

64. "Dieses Maß kann nichts dem Sein Fremdes, von außen daran Angelegtes sein, denn außerhalb des Seins ist nur das Nichts. Das Sein muß vielmehr sein Maß in sich selber tragen, es an sich selber nehmen, und diese Maßnahme ist eben nichts anderes als die Enthüllung seiner selbst" (*TLg* I.35). [This measure cannot be foreign to being, applied to it from the outside, for outside of being there is only nothing. Being must rather carry its measure in itself, it applies it to itself, and this measure-taking is really nothing other than the unveiling of itself.]

65. "Sofern dieses Maß ein von der unendlichen Wahrheit selbst gemessenes Maß ist, hat es teil an der göttlichen Wahrheit, sofern es aber nicht selbst das unendlich messende Maß ist, bleibt ihm die Sphäre der göttlichen Wahrheit transzendent."

66. "Maß und Licht aber sind die beiden untrennbaren Eigenschaften der Wahrheit. Es kann daher nicht angenommen werden, daß ein Seiendes Maß und damit Erkennbarkeit besitze, wenn es nicht zugleich im Licht des wirklichen Gemessenwerdens steht." (*TLg* I.50). [But measure and light are the two inseparable characteristics of truth. It can therefore not be assumed that a being possesses measure and thereby recognizability if it does not at the same time stand in the light of the true measuring.] A few paragraphs later: "Ein Seiendes, das von Gott nicht erkannt wäre, könnte auch von keinem endlichen Subjekt erkannt werden, letzlich darum, weil es als Seiendes gar nicht existieren würde. Es würde aber darum nicht existieren, weil es von Gott nicht erkannt wäre, also kein Maß seines Seins und darum keine Wahrheit besäße. Vor dem göttlichen Erkennen sind daher alle Dinge restlos enthüllt und von ihm gemessen. Bei Gott liegt ihre Wahrheit, und wer sie erkennen will, der muß sie in der Angleichung an den göttlichen Geist erkennen" (*TLg* I.51). [A being that were not known by God could also not be known by any finite subject, in the end because it would in no way exist as a being. It wouldn't exist because it would not be known by God, therefore it would possess no measure of its being and thus no truth.

All things are therefore completely unveiled before the divine perceiving, and measured by him. Their truth lies with God, and whoever wishes to know them must know them in adequation to the divine mind.]

67. "Denn Gottes Erkenntnis ist keine nachbildende, sondern eine urbildliche, die das Seiende selbst grundlegt und in allen seinen Beziehungen feststellt. Gott nimmt nicht das Maß des Objekts an seinem bereits vorhandenen Sein, sondern dieses hat sein Maß an der Idee, die Gott von ihm hat" (*TLg* I.51). [For God's knowledge is not imitative, but rather archetypal, which grounds the existent itself and establishes it in all of its relations. God does not take the measure of the object from its existing being, rather this has its measure in the idea that God has of it.]

68. Cf. *TL* I.127.

69. "Angesichts der von ihm geschaffenen Weltdinge, auf deren Wesensgrund das Wort verborgen ist, wodurch sie allererst ihre Seinswarheit haben."

70. "Denn dessen wahre Idee, durch die alles Existierende gemessen wird, liegt einzig in Gott, und diese Beziehung zwischen der Sache und ihrer wahren Idee ist keinem endlichen Verstand zugänglich."

71. See Ellero Babini, "Jesus Christ, Form and Norm of Man According to Hans Urs von Balthasar," *Communio* 16, no. 3 (1989): 450–51: "At this Christological level, the original axis, the *analogia entis* into which the Son, becoming incarnate, had entered, is surpassed and inserted within another relation, which is revealed as more original, indeed as grounding the creaturely relation of the *analogia entis*; the Trinitarian relation of the Son with the Father in the Holy Spirit. The distance between man and God, between the world and God, is contained within the intratrinitarian distance between the Son and the Father, which is a communion in the Holy Spirit who proceeds from both and who maintains union even in remoteness."

72. "Vielmehr kann es die vielen Schöpfungsgedanken Gottes nur deshalb geben, weil der Sohn der Einzige, Eingeborene des Vaters ist, auf dessen Einheit hin und von dessen Einheit her alle äußern Ausdrucksformen und nachahmenden Bilder entwerfbar sind. Das Weltbild Bonaventuras wird somit zwar im Höchstmaß christozentrisch sein—weil alle unvollkommen ausdrückenden Nachbilder auf das eine vollkommene Bild des Vaters, das ihn mit höchster Präzision ausdrückt, bezogen und durchsichtig gemacht werden müssen, um verständlich zu sein—, es wird aber gerade deswegen nicht platonisch sein" (*H* II.288–89). [Much more can God's many ideas of creation only exist because the Son is the unique, only-begotten of the Father, from whose unity and toward whose unity all external expressive forms and imitative images are designable. Bonaventure's worldview thus will be christocentric to the highest degree—because all incomplete, expressive imitations must be in relation to and become transparent to the one complete image of the Father that expresses him with the highest precision—but precisely for that reason it will not be Platonic.]

73. "Das Sein selbst enthüllt sein letztes Antlitz, das für uns den Namen trinitarische Liebe bekommt und erst mit diesem letzten Mysterium das andere Mysterium erhellt, warum überhaupt Sein ist und warum es uns als Licht und Warheit und Güte und Schönheit aufgeht" (*H* I.151) [Being itself here unveils its final countenance, which for us receives the name trinitarian love and for the first time, with this last mystery, sheds its light at last on that other mystery, why there is Being at all and why it appears as light and truth and goodness and beauty.]

74. "Zunächst scheinen die beiden Differenzen in keinem Verhältnis zueinander zu stehen" (*TLg* II.165). [Initially, these two difference seem to stand in no relation to each other.]

75. "Zwar unterstreicht die Offenbarung vom ersten Vers der Genesis an die absolute Freiheit und Souveränität Gottes der geschaffenen Welt gegenüber, und die ganze Schrift läßt keinen Zweifel darüber, daß die Welt für Gott nicht notwendig ist, sondern sich seiner liebenden Freigebigkeit verdankt. Damit wird die Kluft zwischen Schöpfer und Geschöpf auch bei aller Begnadung und 'Teilnahme an der göttlichen Natur' des letztern, in 'noch so großer Ähnlichkeit' unüberschreitbar und allen Versuchen natürlicher Religion und Mystik der Weg zur Identifikation abgeschnitten" (ibid.). [Indeed, from the first verse of Genesis revelation underlines the absolute freedom and sovereignty of God over and against the created world, and the whole Bible leaves no

doubt that the world is not necessary for God, rather it owes itself to his loving magnanimity. Thereby the chasm between Creator and creation, even amidst every grace and "participation" of the latter "in the divine nature," even in the midst of "still so greater a likeness," becomes untraversable, and the path to identification is cut off from every searching of natural religion and mysticism.]

76. "Anderseits aber wird über diesen (bleibenden) Abgrund durch die Offenbarung der Trinität eine unvermutete Brücke geschlagen: wenn es in Gottes Identität den Andern gibt, der zugleich noch Bild des Vaters und damit Urbild alles Erschaffenbaren ist, wenn es in dieser Identität den Geist gibt, der freie, überschwengliche Liebe des 'Einen' und 'Andern' ist, dann wird das Anders der Schöpfung, das sich am Urbild des göttlichen Anders ausrichtet, und ihr Überhaupt-Sein, das sich der innergöttlichen Liberalität verdankt, in ein positives Verhältnis zu Gott gerückt" (*TLg* II.165–66). [But on the other hand, an unsuspected bridge over this (abiding) abyss is hewn through the revelation of the Trinity: if there is another in God's identity, which at the same time is also the image of the Father and thereby the archetype of all created things, if there is the Spirit in this identity, who is the free, effusive love of the "One" and the "Other," then the otherness of creation, which orients itself to the archetype of the divine Other, and its actuality, which owes itself to the inner-divine liberality, is moved into a positive relation to God.]

77. *TL* II.166

78. "Damit rücken göttliche und geschöpfliche Differenz immerhin schon in eine gewisse Vergleichbarkeit. Die Kreatur ist nicht bloß 'aus Gott' und damit ihrem ganzen Sein (und dessen Differenzen) auf ihn als Ursprung, Bewahrung und Endziel verwiesen, sondern ebenso ausdrücklich auf die Hypostasen" (ibid.). [Thereby the divine and creaturely differences always finally move into a certain comparability. The creature is not simply "toward God" and thereby referred in its entire being (and its difference) to him as origin, continuance, and goal, but equally expressly to the hypostases.]

79. "Dieses Verwiesensein erfolgt ebenso aufgrund des primären Unterschieds gerade auch der geschöpflichen Differenz wie kraft deren Unverstehbarkeit in sich selbst ohne den (in ihrer Unterschiedenheit von Gott liegenden) Verweis auf die innergöttliche Differenz. Das Nichtzustandekommen-Können der Identität innerhalb der weltlichen Differenz im konkreten endlichen Wesen setzt innerlich eine Form von Differenz innerhalb der göttlichen Identität voraus" (ibid.). [This reference results as much because of the primary differences inherent in the creaturely difference as because of the inexplicability [of the creature] in itself without reference (lying in its difference from God) to the inner-divine difference.]

80. Specifically with respect to this point about creaturely difference, section I.A.1 of this chapter.

81. It is for this reason that the relations are intra-divine:divine-human, not intra-divine:intra-human. Created being lacks *aseity*, and so it does not contain its measure within itself, but only has measure outside of itself, in the archetype.

82. "Denn wie könnte die weltliche Differenz in ihrer 'major dissimilitudo' der göttlichen Identität gegenüber nicht doch als ein Abfall, und nicht als ein 'sehr Gutes' gewertet werden, falls diese Differenz nicht in Gott selbst eine mit seiner Identität nicht konkurrierende Wurzel besäße, zumal die weltliche Differenz (in allen Seienden!) ja wesentlich dem von Gott in seiner 'liberalitas' dahingegebenen vollkommenen, aber nichtsubsistenten und somit nicht faßbaren Sein mit Gottes Willen und Urbildlichkeit entspringen muß?" (*TLg* II.169). [For how could the worldly difference, in its *maior dissimilitudo* to the divine identity, not indeed be assessed as a decline, and not as a "very good thing," if this difference did not possesses a ground in Godself not incompatible with God's identity, especially since worldly difference (in all beings!) must spring essentially from the perfect but nonsubsistent and thereby incomprehensible self-giving being of God in his liberality and from the will and archetypality of God?]

83. "Sofern deshalb auch jeder nach außen erfolgte Selbstausdruck Gottes umschlossen und getragen bleibt von seinem göttlichen Selbstausdruck und zu diesem hin gelesen, gedeutet, zurückgeführt, aufgelöst werden muß, um aus den ihn ermöglichenden Bedingungen verstanden und in sie hinein vollendet zu werden" (*H* II.289). [Insofar as for that reason also every self

expression of God occurring outside remains enclosed and supported by his divine self-expression, and must be read, interpreted, returned, resolved toward it in order to understand it from the conditions making it possible and to become complete in them.] Cf. Angelo Scola: "Leaving behind the narrow confines (rooted in Molinism) of a christocentrism of the Risen Christ who fails to grasp the whole of being and of history, Balthasar affirms with great conviction the centrality of the theme of creation in Christ" ("Nature and Grace," 211).

84. "Es hat die Norm seiner selbst nie so sehr in sich, daß es sie nicht jeweils mehr von Gott her sich geben lassen müßte" (*TLg* I.55).

85. "Aber da dieser Mensch Jesus darin zugleich der Ausdruck des ganzen Gottes ist (der Vater und der Geist sind in ihm), kann die menschliche Logik, in der er Gott ausdrückt, selber nichts anderes sein als ein ‚Bild und Gleichnis' des dreieinigen Gottes. Der Mensch könnte dieses ‚Bild und Gleichnis' Gottes unmöglich sein, wenn Gott in ihm nur sein einiges ‚Wesen' unter Ausschluß der dreieinigen Lebendigkeit dieses Wesens hätte abbilden wollen. Die Identität der göttlichen Hypostasen mit dem Wesen Gottes verunmöglicht eine solche Annahme. Es muß deshalb im weltlichen Bereich eine Abbildlichkeit des Trinitarischen geben, an die der sich auslegende Logos zu seinem Selbstausdruck wird anknüpfen können und müssen" (*TLg* II.33). [But because the man Jesus is thereby at the same time the expression of the whole God (the Father and the Spirit are in him), human logic can, inasmuch as it expresses God, itself not be other than an "image and likeness" of the trinitarian God. Humanity would be unable to be this "image and likeness" of God if God had wanted to reproduce in it only his unified essence with the trinitarian liveliness of this essence excluded. The identity of the divine hypostases with the essence of God makes such an assumption impossible. Therefore, there must exist in the worldly realm an imaging of the Trinity, to which the self-displaying Logos can and must refer in its self-expression.] To this must be added Gerard O'Hanlon's comments. He says: "In other words the kind of emptying and self-giving we see in the incarnation is both the image and the effect of the eternal 'externalisation' of God that is involved in the intra-trinitarian life" (*Immutability*, 14). He continues: "In other words, unlike the Kenoticists, he is saying not that kenosis is the central concept in God which subsumes all others in such a way that incarnation and cross are seen as natural and necessary to God, but rather that God's sovereign power is revealed as love and self-giving in such a way that divine kenosis is real, is an expression of this divine power and love, and can and does freely reveal itself in human form in such forms as the incarnation and the cross" (ibid.).

86. "*Der Mensch* ist für Bonaventura wesentlich Weltmitte und darin Weltinbegriff; das muß denen entgegengehalten werden, die seine Lehre als eine einseitig spiritualistisch-weltflüchtige, ekstatische auslegen möchten. Die Impressio der Stigmen ist Eindruck Gottes in die sinnliche Welt. Und der Excessus erfolgt, wie schon gezeigt, als Akt der Bewunderung vor Gottes Nähe und Weltimmanenz" (*H* II.317–18). [Man is for Bonaventure essentially the center of the world, and therefore the epitome of the world; this must be objected to those who would prefer to expound his doctrine as a one-sided, spiritual, ecstatic flight from the world. The impression of the stigmata is the expression of God in the sinful world. And the excess takes place as has already been indicated, as the act of admiration before the proximity and world-immanence of God.]

87. "*Christus* ist als Verbum incarnatum Mitte von allem; nichts hat Bonaventura lieber und ausführlicher gesagt. Aber ebenso stark betont er, daß Christus Mitte als Mittler ist, also vermittelnde Mitte" (*H* II.328). [Christ as Word incarnate is the middle of all things; Bonaventure said nothing more fondly and concisely. But he stresses just as strongly that Christ is the middle as mediator, therefore a mediating middle.]

88. "Vom Menschen her betrachtet, erhält die Eikon-Bezeichnung Jesu den Sinn von ‚Ur-bild', ‚Bild schlechthin', was sich aber sogleich mit dem zweiten Gesichtspunkt koppelt: er ist das endlich von Gott selber hingestellte Bild, das dem Menschen aufzurichten verboten war" (*TLg* II.68). [Seen from the human side, the icon-character of Jesus obtains the sense of "arche-type," "quintessential image," which couples itself immediately with the second point of view: he is the image finally set up by Godself, that humans were forbidden to set up.] See Angelo Scola: "In what

does the absolute singularity of Jesus Christ consist? In the fact that his humanity is the place in which the archetype itself, the Son (the perfect Icon of the Father) transfers himself into the image without ceasing to be the archetype" ("Nature," 213).

89. "Diese geschaute Wahrheit ist nichts anderes, als was wir im 1. Teil dieser Trilogie als ‚Herrlichkeit' bezeichnet haben: die weltlich analogielose Darstellung Gottes in der Welt."

90. "Es wurde hinzugefügt, daß sich Gott und Welt aber nicht starr wie Urbild und Abbild gegenüberstehen, vielmehr Gott das weltliche Abbild von vornherein über sich auf das Urbild hin geschaffen hat, so daß alle Immanenz sich stets auf Gott hin transzendiert. Weltliches Sein ist bestimmt, in göttliches Sein eingeborgen zu werden, weltliche Zeit in göttlich ewig bewegte Ewigkeit, weltlicher Raum in Gottes unendliche Räume, weltliches Werden nicht in ein regloses göttliches Sein, sondern in das ewig Ereignishafte göttlichen Lebens" (*TLg* II.78). [It is added that God and the world do not stand rigidly against one another as archetype and image, rather God created the worldly image from the outset on the basis of the archetype, so that all immanence transcends itself immediately toward God. Worldly being is destined to be nestled in divine being, worldly time in divine eternally moved eternity, worldly space in God's infinite space, worldly becoming not in a motionless divine being, but in the eternal eventfulness of divine life.] Note the appropriateness of the Janus metaphor to this passage also. See von Balthasar, *Epilog* 59: "Man erkennt hier endgültig, daß die ganze unverkürzte Metaphysik der Transzendentalien des Seins nur entfaltbar ist unter dem theologischen Licht der Weltschöpfung im Wort Gottes, der sich zuletzt in göttlicher Freiheit als sinnlich-geistiger Mensch ausspricht, ohne daß die Metaphysik selber zu Theologie zu werden bräuchte." [One learns definitively here that the entire, unabridged metaphysics of the transcendentals of being is only explicable in the theological light of the creation of the world in the Word of God who expresses himself definitively in divine freedom as sensory-spiritual humanity, without requiring that metaphysics itself be turned into theology.]

91. Johann Roten, "Hans Urs von Balthasar's Anthropology": "The eccentricity of the theological understanding of the human person is our acceptance and admission into the trinitarian love-cycle" (322). What von Balthasar has been pushing at all this time is that to be properly constituted, one's center must be in God. For the persons of the Trinity, this center therefore remains intrinsic to them, because it is who they are, and so the result is *perichoresis*. For human persons, since we are not God, it is extrinsic, which means *ekstasis*.

92. Peter Casarella: "By viewing the world symbolically, the subject sees itself participating through its own likeness in the divine archetype (*Urbild*). As in Gregory of Nyssa's theory of participation, the image is dynamically drawn from within the spatio-temporal confines of history to an always greater union with its eternally begotten archetype. The expression of the divine archetype in finite images points to a unique exemplary form which measures all forms. Against all subordinationist schemes, the expression of the singular divine form in an image is not a diminution of its power. Bonaventure, in a passage cited by Balthasar, states succinctly the core of this theory of the expressing image: 'The likeness which is the truth itself in its expressive power…better expresses a thing than the thing expresses itself, for the thing itself receives the power of expression from it" ("Experience as a Theological Category: Hans Urs von Balthasar on the Christian Encounter with God's Image" *Communio* 20:1 [1993], 121–22).

93. See Kevin Mongrain: "God reveals the meaning of history as the opening of this trinitarian life for participation by humanity. This participation involves incarnating the trinitarian unity-in-difference in creation" (*Systematic Thought*, 57). See Larry Chapp: "For Balthasar the 'what' of revelation is more appropriately referred to as the Who: revelation is given once and for all in a definitive manner in Jesus, but *what* is given is nothing less that the offer for historical humanity to participate in trinitarian eternity" ("Revelation" in *The Cambridge Companion to Hans Urs von Balthasar*, edited by Edward T. Oakes and David Moss [Cambridge: Cambridge University Press, 2004], 22).

94. Gerard O'Hanlon: "This is a decisive turn-about in our way of seeing God (32). It means that God is not first and foremost 'absolute power' but 'absolute love', and that God's sovereignty is shown primarily not in holding on to what is proper to him but rather in

abandoning it in such a way that all inner-worldly opposition between power and weakness is overcome" (*Immutability*, 14).

7

Participation, Love, and Kenosis

We saw in the previous chapter that the highest moment in the explication of the metaphysics was at the same time the beginning of the ability to speak in a properly theological mode. The point where the highest principle of created reality, as both its source and goal, comes into view is simultaneously the point at which a doorway is opened into the eternal life of the uncreated, and to as much as can be known about the grounding of creation in the uncreated being of God. The seamless transition we find at this point in von Balthasar's thought is the desired and natural result of focusing the discourse on Christ, on the one who is himself at once the meaning of creation and the exposition of the Trinity. The ontological problem of existence (why is there anything at all, and why is it of this sort?) and the epistemological problem of the divine (how can we know that it exists, and what it is like?) are alike solved in Christ as the revelation of the divine life and the blueprint of creaturely reality.

The explanatory power of this privileged midpoint is only heightened by the divinization of creaturely reality, a divinization that, although it fails to absolutize creaturely being (which must always remain relative and subordinate to uncreated being), nevertheless valorizes it in the most lofty and final way. In Christ a common space is made in which creation and Creator can meet; but it is a commonality secured not by being a point higher than both or outside of both in which they can meet as equals, but rather it is the space of the divine interiority making room within itself for the reality of created being.

In this way the intersection and ultimately the union of theology and metaphysics may be seen to be a reflection of the encounter and union of God and creation. Metaphysics remains controlled by theology, for the true measure of Christ remains the measure of trinitarian love, and every worldly interval is to be correlated to this. Creation remains subordinate to God, for it can only come to exist, come to understand itself, and come to fruition in the person of the one who expresses fully and uniquely (as Word and therefore *expressio*) the trinitarian dynamic of love.

Love, as inner dynamic of the being of God and therefore the transcendental transcendental, is the logical point at which metaphysics expands into theology. It is with this theme that we will bring this study to a close—at precisely that point where one will be most capable of seeing the ramifications and payoff of the choices von Balthasar has been making from the beginning.

Much secondary literature has focused on the idea that Being and love are co-extensive.[1] This is a fundamental statement for von Balthasar, theologically as well as philosophically. Many of these writers correctly identify kenosis as key to von Balthasar's treatment of love; this insight must be expanded if it is to cover the entire field of metaphysics and theology treated here. The analogy of being is the kenotic love of God in creation, the "second kenosis" which is preceded by the self-giving of the Trinity and followed by the emptying unto death on a cross in the Incarnation.[2]

Therefore, before we can turn to speak of the divine love, we must examine these three important kenotic moments in the life of God and cause them to appear in their proper light. Only once that has been accomplished will it be possible and profitable to look at the movement of unifying grace; for kenosis is the divine *exitus*, a movement that finds its fulfillment in the return (*redditus*) of unifying grace. These two taken together describe the dynamics of love, which would be incomplete were either theme to be neglected. In the process, both kenosis and grace will appear as having primary reference to the donation of the being of God in such a way as to make them nearly synonymous. It will also become clear that what we see in this dynamic is no mere addition to the philosophical system examined so far, but rather the very life and energy implicit at every moment in the theoretical metaphysical deductions on the one hand and the practical encounter between persons (divine-divine as well as divine-human) on the other.

I. The Concept of Kenosis

In the Introduction to *The Glory of the Lord*, when the great Balthasarian system is still young, we find a surprising, tender ode to the "tragic" figure of Johann Georg Hamann.[3] His importance for the Balthasarian project is that he represents a theology that could have restored a sense of the place of the beautiful to Christian thought, had he not been shunted into marginality; of equal importance for von Balthasar, though it will not appear again as a major topic of discussion until the last volume of the *The Glory of the Lord*, is the fact that it is on the basis of the kenotic love of God that Hamann opens a space within theology for the beautiful. Before turning to von Balthasar's own statements about kenosis, it will be worthwhile to pause on his analysis of Hamann's use of the theological notion.

In Hamann's context, von Balthasar says, beauty is taken as coextensive with the natural world.[4] Against this, Hamann recognizes that for the Christian, the glory of God in a created realm which is subject to sin has been veiled, and the speech of God in nature has to a greater or lesser extent ceased; correspondingly, even the proper glory nature itself has is veiled.[5] In this situation, God's glory can only be unveiled in lowliness and suffering.[6]

In this way, there emerges a kenotic logic of kenosis—now the proof of majesty is the proof of self-emptying.[7] Von Balthasar's very brief analysis here notes that Hamann saw this kenotic constitution of glory not just in the Incarnation, but even in creation: "Glory as kenosis, not first of the incarnate one, but already of the Creator."[8] Beyond this, through the notion of archetype, Hamann finds access to the "innermost mystery-core of all reality," the union of the Logos with the Church.[9]

This is not ultimately the scheme that von Balthasar will follow, but it does bear strong structural similarity to the picture he will eventually draw of a kenosis in creation, and of a grounding kenosis behind even that. This deduction is carried out in the final volume of *The Glory of the Lord*, empowered by the theological reflections on the glory of God as appearing in the New Testament witness to the historical appearing of the glory in Christ.

The character of what is said in that volume can now be seen to be no mere add-on to the project, driven by a purely external need to engage the most authoritative texts of the Christian tradition, or by an equally external compulsion to bring theology and biblical studies together. Rather, given the metaphysical centrality of the historically incarnate Christ, the witness to that event, which participates in the person to such an extent as to merit sharing in his title as "Word of God" must be considered to be of fundamental importance for understanding the metaphysics that person grounds. It is to this account of the conditions of the incarnating movement of the Logos that we now turn.

Von Balthasar begins by equating the kenotic hymn of Philippians 2:6-11 with a claim that there is a free choice of a divine being at the heart of the Incarnation. Such a free choice is indeed the presupposition for an individual who was to be God and human in such a way as to have always been God.[10] This is, ultimately, the only way of being God—any being that became God would lack perfections that God *must* possess in order for the *maior dissimilitudo* to hold. Such a being would, for example, depend on another for its deity (for no being can raise itself to a level higher than its original powers through its own efforts), and therefore would lack aseity. But we have seen that aseity is precisely that which protects the space of discontinuity between creatures and Creator, and in doing so, provides for a more radical similarity than one might otherwise have expected.[11]

This reaffirmation of the necessity of the full divinity of the Son is soteriologically driven, and aims to establish that the obedience of the Son is not understandable by analogy to human terms, and is not explicable in terms of the human situation into which he comes; rather, only his unique relationship to the Father, in which he totally and freely receives all that he is from the Father and totally and freely surrenders all that he is back to the Father, can make clear the character of this obedience.[12] Such an obedience unto total emptying is not after the manner of creaturely obedience—von Balthasar clearly asserts this, but does not make clear in what sense this is true.[13] Certain clues are present in the context, however.

What is expressly *not* attributable to God is the creature's way of changing, suffering (being affected from the outside) and obeying. The first two are just statements of the divine immutability and impassability—but what is it about creaturely obedience that makes it unfitting to attribute it to God? Von Balthasar immediately turns to Hilary's argument that the Son had the power to make himself powerless without losing his power.[14] Von Balthasar rejects this approach on the basis that it focuses too much on the inherent power of the divine nature,[15] and even goes on to say that the logical result would be an "almost Docetic formulation" that would see the divine power and glory in the powerlessness of the cross.[16]

The true starting point, he claims, is the personal relationships in God. Therefore the true starting point is, along with Bulgakov, "to take the 'selflessness' of the divine persons as pure relations in the inner-divine life of love as the ground of everything."[17] This trinitarian giving will therefore ground a kenosis earlier than that of the Incarnation, namely the restricting of the divine freedom in order to make space for a creature that is itself free.[18]

Therefore, if it is necessary to look to the relationships between the trinitarian persons to understand the obedience of Christ, and if these relationships are to be parsed with a selflessness that is the complete pouring out of the self into the other, then it is precisely in this that the decisive difference between divine and created obedience lies. In creaturely obedience there is the submission of one's self to another, but there is always something held back, something which allows the one obeying to remain particular and unique. But in the Trinity, the individuals are constituted as who they are precisely in not holding anything back: the uniqueness of the Son is secured rather than threatened in the complete donation of self to the Father in loving response to the Father's initial and total self-donation.

In this way, kenosis may be seen to be the "decisive act of the love of the Son":

"In this, kenosis as the abandonment of 'Godform' becomes in fact the decisive act of the love of the Son who lets his procreation (and therefore his derivedness) from the Father migrate into the expressive form of creaturely obedience" (H III.2.2.198).[19] The Son is able to become the "expressive form of creaturely obedience" in a way that the Father is not, for the Son is derived, and therefore is able to image the type of obedience proper to beings which are ontologically marked in every moment of their existence as being from another.[20]

Thus, in the course of underscoring the type of obedience proper to the Son, and in setting up what may be called an analogical relationship between his obedience and ours, von Balthasar has, through Bulgakov and in agreement with Hamann, introduced a kenosis beyond that of the Incarnation—the kenosis of creation, where God limits his all-sufficiency in order to make room for creatures with a will so free that it creates at least the possibility of the necessity of a second kenosis. The two moments of kenosis are connected in the concept of freedom—for it is the absolute character of the divine freedom which must be restricted to make room for human freedom, and it is the (inappropriate) exercise of human freedom that creates the necessity for the second kenosis. Even more, the kenosis of Incarnation does not merely repair the damage wrought by the exercise of human will—it is the ultimate affirmation on the part of God of the human will, the full divine acceptance of the consequences of the human will. The fact of the God-man on the cross offers the most persuasive evidence of the reality of freedom of the will in humans, according to this view.[21]

In this way is Christ the lamb "slain before the foundation of the world" (Rev. 13:8): both because the necessity of kenotic death upon the cross was foreseen *and* because the clearing away within the divine freedom of a space destined to be the proper realm of action of human freedom required the acceptance of the consequences of the misuse of the human will, even though that misuse was neither necessary nor intended.[22]

Thus von Balthasar distinguishes a "first" and "second" kenosis, of which the second (that which is traditionally meant by the term *kenosis*) is the "proper" one, for in it alone may one speak of emptying and not merely limiting. But behind both of these moments the text allows the discerning of a third moment, an original moment which grounds the "first" and therefore also the "second" kenosis, namely the processions of the persons within the Trinity. To these processions one would rightly give the name of kenosis (more so than in the creation of human freedom), because here there is absolute self-emptying, complete pouring out with nothing held back, even though one does not thereby become empty.[23] But emptiness is avoided because of the free and spontaneous response of love that gives everything it has and is back to the one who first gave—the trinitarian persons are who they are because of *both* the complete self-abandonment and the complete openness to receive the return gift.

One might therefore speak of three kenoses in the Balthasarian scheme. To do so arouses the suspicion that one is dealing not merely with three strikingly similar moments, but with a law of the divine being which is imaged in the world here below. The extent to which von Balthasar would allow this extension will be discussed; first, it is necessary to look more closely at each of these moments of kenosis.

II. The Last Kenosis—Incarnation

If we are to speak of the Incarnation of the Logos, we are to speak of a kenosis that takes the form of obedience—that much is clear from the starting point of the reflections on kenosis in *The Glory of the Lord* VII. In order to explain this, von Balthasar offers a series of quotations from Karl Barth's *Church Dogmatics* IV.1, in which Barth is describing the Incarnation as being a divine self-confirmation: "God confirms himself as God in the fact that 'he betook himself to the bond and adversity of the human creature; that he, the Lord, becomes a servant and in this, differing from the false gods in precisely this, humiliates himself" (*H* III.2.2.199).[24] Yet such an action on God's part, Barth continues, does not decrease the unfittingness of attributing any antinomy to God. The necessary conclusion is that if God does this thing, then it must be within the possibilities of the divine nature to do such a thing. It must not be foreign to the divine nature to abase itself in obedience, and thereby we learn that the divine is indeed richer and more expansive than we had previously guessed. "Everything depends on the trinitarian love of God."[25]

From these statements of Barth, von Balthasar believes that one can formulate an idea capable of accounting for the possibility of the type of divine affirmation of creaturely freedom that it is theologically necessary to claim. The affirmation is the absolute obedience of love, which is an emptiness that makes itself available for every possibility, which means to be both used and abused. Such a radical self-surrender, shadowed in every act of human love, is the final "emptiness" which nevertheless is precisely that kind of thing that can be affirmed of God without paradox or contradiction. And if we feel the sting of this emptiness in our own human experiences of love (negatively in betrayal and loss, positively in the unself-conscious reciprocity of mutual love), how much deeper are the possibilities for divine love, of which our love is but a shadow?[26]

This concept of obedience also explains von Balthasar's earlier statement that the Hilarian theology, taken to its extreme, would produce a Docetic formulation that equated the cross of Christ with the glory of God.[27] The Docetism lies in equating the humanity of Christ with pure suffering, for such is not a true human life, which is always a mixture of joy and suffering.[28] In order to fulfill the kenotic demands of Philippians 2:7[29] and the kenotic implications of Romans 8:3,[30]

Even this move to allow that it wasn't necessary for every moment of Christ's life to be only suffering all the time doesn't go far enough in the desired direction. For the Son will not know the depths of absolute abandonment if he doesn't have the experience of being united to the Father. His sense of abandonment can, von Balthasar says, only be as deep as his experience of union. Further, he must know this experience not only in his awareness as the Logos, but even as the man Jesus.[31] This is to be a feature of his human life, which far from removing him from the common space of a true human existence by exalting him with divine attributes and prerogatives challenges our very notions of what true humanity ought to consist in. the thing undoable for the law, in the one weakend by the flesh, God did, sending his own son in the likeness of sinful flesh, and on account of sin condemned sin in the flesh.][/footnote] it is not necessary to see the emptying in the cross, and therefore the humanity of Christ as being consummated on the cross. The sufferings of the cross are not something Christ does to himself, but something that he, in absolute obedience, allows to be done to him. The emptying is fully and most fittingly explained in a type of obedient submission which is truly ready for anything, which has set no previous conditions, and thus which does not balk even in the face of death on a cross and absolute separation from God.[32]

All of the foregoing logic serves to underscore that kenosis does not consist in suffering *per se*, but in the act of emptying oneself of one's rights in loving obedience. In the first place, for the divine Logos which as such cannot be touched by any suffering or pain, which cannot be separated from the Father, which bears no consequence of sinful separation, kenosis will necessarily entail the giving up of invulnerability, the opening of oneself to the possibility of suffering. This first step is itself a much bigger deal than the actual suffering which follows upon the availability for suffering. Metaphysically speaking, this is the shock that we would not have expected. We are surprised and astounded that God could become a human; having once become human, it comes as no great shock that this human can suffer.

The extent to which it is a surprise that God can become human, which is the extent of the scandal of the Incarnation, is measured differently in von Balthasar than in Barth. "[T]hat the incarnating Word 'came into his own' (John 1:11), thus he does not simply (as Karl Barth says) go somewhere foreign, rather into a land whose language he knows: not only the Galilean Aramaic that the child learned in Nazareth, but more deeply the speech of creaturely being as such. The logic of the creature is not foreign to the logic of God; one could liken it to a dialect, whose pure form is spoken by God" (*TLg* II.78).[33] This simile, perhaps the most poetic statement of the analogy of being in the entire Triptych, underscores that it is a consequence of the Balthasarian logic that the surprise of the Incarnation is to some extent attenuated by the likeness between God and creatures. The Incarnation must come as a great shock because of the *maior dissimilitudo*; yet because of the *similitudo*, we may look back on the accomplished fact and marvel at the fittingness of the path chosen.

This principle also comes into play in comparing the divine obedience of Christ to creaturely obedience. Although we have already seen that they cannot be the same, even here there must be *similitudo*, and therefore it is true that "to obey God and to anticipate his will lies in the fundamental constitution of the creature" (*H* III.2.2.201).[34] The *maior dissimilitudo* is invoked here again, lest we think that the readiness for obedience of the Son is qualitatively identical with the readiness for obedience of creatures.[35] If this were so, then the work of Christ would be nothing more than the realization of a potential that already lay in creatures—he would light the way down the path that all humans were always meant to follow and were to some extent capable of following.[36] The result of this would be perhaps a new way of being in the world in which humanity is at last freed to stride down a path long closed to it—here von Balthasar names Rahner, and we could with perhaps even greater propriety name Tillich.[37] What such a theology would lack, however, is any sense of Christ carrying the burden of sin for the world.[38]

Such a viewpoint was already ruled out by the *Theology of History*.[39] There must be a qualitative difference between what Jesus is able to do and what other humans are able to do. In the *Theology of History* the consideration of this problem led to the necessity of a person who was both human and divine—this conclusion is necessary in the Balthasarian logic, and so there can be no other answer here or anywhere else such questions arise. It is therefore decisive that the obedience of Christ be human *and* divine if he is to be able to carry the sins of the world.

This is possible because of the kenosis—because kenosis describes an act whereby the divine Son empties himself of everything that is not obedience to the Father's will in order to become human. Thus, it is an act of his divine will to be found in the conditions of humanity; but it is the result of this act that makes it possible for him to offer an obedience to the Father that is *human* and therefore applicable to Adam's race. "Kenotic readiness" encompasses the full range of what is required for Christ to be the one savior of all.[40]

This describes the kenotic *condition*; in order to fully explicate the kenosis, however, it is necessary to look at kenosis in its directedness toward a goal. Christ is not just to be obedient, but to be obedient *unto death* (Phil. 2:8). This fact marks an endpoint to the obedience, a goal by which one can recognize when the obedience has been fulfilled. The kenosis is for the purpose of making room in Christ for the collision of the sin of world;[41] therefore "the Last Supper and the cross are together the 'hour' for which he came" (*H* I.549).[42] It follows from the supposition that the kenosis is required if Christ is to be able to carry the sins of the world that this can only be accomplished in the death that all sinners owe.[43]

At the end, when the time comes to bear all sin, in that hour, Christ must be absolutely empty, "pure space" that can be filled up with all the sin of the world, which will then be judged in him. The kenosis will not therefore be merely an emptying of the divine qualities, even if this must be viewed as the starting point, rooted in a divine decision, which controls the subsequent process of emptying. The man Jesus must "set his face to Jerusalem" (Luke 9:51), must in his human nature echo the divine emptying of the Logos in order that when the time comes, space will have been made for the burden which is to be borne. This emptying will not be set in opposition to the divine, but will rather be a continuation of it, the final working out of what was begun in the first moment of decision, when obedience was chosen, but chosen precisely with an eye to this end, the final rejection by both the ones he came to save and the One he must obey. Yet this human emptying will create the deepest paradox with the divine, for he must go absolutely as far as possible from his starting point: Life must die and the Word must dissolve into silence.

This theme of abandonment, in which the Word dissolves into silence, is the decisive center of the idea of the Word made flesh, and a topic von Balthasar treats frequently and with fondness.[44] It is here above all that we must keep in mind that kenosis has a directed character if we are to follow von Balthasar's formulations. It is precisely to this sense of forward motion that the paradoxes point: Life cannot ultimately die, and the Word cannot be overcome by silence, because it is the divine Life and Word at stake here, and therefore we are driven on in our theological reflection to the inevitable surprise of Easter morning. In this too the principle of analogy protects us, for as the self-emptying Christ comes more and more to resemble us in the form of our utter powerlessness and meaninglessness, there remains the ever-greater dissimilarity of the reality of his identity as very God, which must ultimately break through the bonds with which we are fettered. It is a descent *in order* to rise again, and this dimension is always in view, even and perhaps especially in the most tragic moments.

Therefore this purposefulness at precisely the moment when the metaphysic is being grounded anew (in the change in the hypostasis of Christ who is the center and ground of all things) will transform the descriptive measure of the distance between divine and creaturely being into a prescriptive mode of being for the creature in the encounter with the divine. Read correctly, we see in the abandoning, kenotic obedience of Christ the demand that will be placed on every creature, the demand that uncreated being places on created being as such, which is once again to decisively be what it always was: a fundamental defining of creaturely being only in terms of uncreated being.

The condition desired of creaturely being has already been hinted at, for we have been told already that radical obedience lies in the fundamental nature of the creature: this is the condition the Son enters into in the Incarnation. But in the Incarnation, God has something of supra-human weight to say. The question rightly arises whether or not the human mode of being is even capable of conveying this message.

Here we have come to the question that is the fundamental question of the Triptych, and each of the parts of the Triptych attempt to tackle it in the way proper to its own discourse. In *The Glory of the Lord*, the question takes the form of recognition: How are we to recognize the difference between the glory of God appearing in Christ from the glory of worldly being?[45] In *Theodrama*, the question is concerned with understanding how the absolute freedom of God in Christ confronts the relative freedom of humanity.[46] In *Theologic*, von Balthasar poses the problem in its most penetrating form: "How can God come to make himself understood to man, how can an infinite Word express itself in a finite word without losing its sense?"[47] In every part of the Triptych, the answer lies in the analogy of being. For the questions begin from the *dissimilitudo*; however, with the assertion of *similitudo*, and a *similitudo* of a more robust nature than orthodox theology might have dared to believe possible, we realize that in the divine and human encounter one is not faced with two utterly different realities. This becomes the basis for communication between them—not a shared, common space, but a likeness which creates precedent, provides as it were a point of grammatical contact such that address is possible.

This answer cannot be left in so simple a state, however. It is as yet unclear whether the metaphysical similarity is strong enough to allow the message to be conveyed, and how this could happen at all. This problem is only surmountable in the person of Christ, in the reality of the two natures in the person of Christ. But to make this possible, a radical obedience, a radical abandonment to the divine uses is required of the human nature: "But if the divine, eternal Word should wish to express itself adequately in mortal flesh (in however mysterious a way), this could not happen through humanity itself, unless in such a way that [humanity] makes available its entire fleshly, mortal-vain existence for such a self-exposition of the divine Word, in which it *abandons* itself as entire, with birth and death, with speech and silence, waking and sleeping, success and futility and whatever else still belongs to the essence of human being, like an alphabet or a keyboard, for the exposition" (H III.2.2.131–32).[48] Thus, in order for the divine to speak through the human nature, the human nature must be characterized by "an increasing self-abandonment to the command of the One who alone can extract from the whole lived existence that definitive word that God needs to conclude his new and eternal covenant" (H III.2.2.133).[49]

On the other side of this two-natured self-emptying there blossoms the return to the authority proper to the Son, a return which is not an undoing of the kenosis, nor a denial of it, but is rather its inner fulfillment.[50] For this reason, when Christ has passed the boundaries of death, there is no longer talk of his "entitlement and poverty" and self-abandonment—all that remains is the pure obedience. And because it is kenotic obedience defined by his free choice to be the Obedient One, he alone is free in the place of the absolute extremity of "coercion and unfreedom," Hell.[51] The descent proves and indicates [*besagt*] the return, and in the blink of an eye the outermost Hell is changed into the intimacy of Heaven.[52]

This is the last kenosis, Incarnation, and it is the one that opens up to the realms of Heaven that have been promised to the faithful. In it, the ethical archetype of the Christian way of being in the world (exemplified by the kenotic obedience of Christ and, derivatively, in the Marian *fiat*)[53] is established. It is, in the final analysis, the transformation of the old into the new, and sets the stage for an eschatological elevation. It would therefore be proper to go on to the theme of love, which we are so obliquely approaching. Such a move, natural as it may be, would still be premature, and must await the addition of the ground of this last kenosis, and ultimately the ground absolutely speaking.

II. Second Kenosis—Creation

"God is pure being-for-himself that needs no other being. His infinite light is complete on its own, it does not naturally trail away *ad extra*, but if it is to be imparted, is only revealed through a free donation" (*TLg* I.106).[54] There is, in other words, a problem (from the standpoint of creation) with the being of God, in that its very fullness and completeness would not seem to leave room for the existence of anything else. This is a problem with which Neo-Platonism is all too familiar, and is ultimately resolved in that context by pantheistic strategies: the many things we see are not really other than the One, as will become evident to the one who contemplates properly.

We have already seen that von Balthasar will endorse an Augustinian position against this, that the multitude can only exist outside the plenitude of the highest being if the being of the multitude is a participation in the highest being.[55] Even this situation is only possible, however, if the highest being makes room, by limiting itself, for the existence of those things that will participate in its being without ultimately being reducible to it. To employ a simplistic spatial analogy, if the being of God is everywhere, and all other beings, if they are to exist, must be *some*where, then other beings can only exist if the divine being withdraws from some places in such a way as to make room for them.

This analogy may be deeply repugnant to certain philosophical sensibilities as hopelessly entangled in physicality. By what logic, such would say, is being to be understood such that it must submit to laws of exclusivity analogous to the way in which two physical bodies impede one another from occupying the same space? And yet, we find the logic relentlessly maintained in von Balthasar—God is the all in all, and therefore there can be nothing else without God's prior act of limitation. Whatever one may think of the ontological version of this position, the version that bases itself on the freedom of God and the freedom of the creature, which we encountered earlier,[56] would seem to have enough evidentiary force to at least be allowed into consideration.

This is the kenosis of the act of creation, and as such it references the Ideal Metaphysical realm grounded on the pre-Incarnate Logos as archetype. This is the mythical (in a sense that need not be taken in opposition to *historical*) world of the Old Covenant, where the Creator so often is seen to come down to visit his creation. This image of the Creator stepping down to creation will become a major image through the reflections on the writings of the Hebrew scriptures (*H* III.2.1).

The image ultimately becomes one of the God who descends in order to meet with humanity, to establish a covenant. Because God comes down, relation is possible.[57] This involves a transposition into the earthly realm of heavenly realities,[58] which enables God to come and dwell with God's people.[59] Therefore it must be said both that humanity is transported to the divine realms and that God comes down to involve Godself in human affairs.[60] This means that we cannot say that at the Incarnation God no longer stands aloof, but enters into the history of the world; for God has already been deeply involved with the history of the world, had already come down long before the Logos did so metaphysically in hypostatic union. The eternal God did not merely stand aloof, guiding things from above, but came down to the level of the creature.[61]

This theological reading of the implications of the giving of the Covenant to the Israelites has far-reaching effects. At the very least, it outlines the general conditions that are extant when God enters into a covenant with human beings: there is something of a coming down in order to meet with us. God, in making promises to us, is by that very action limiting Godself, choosing to be toward us in a certain respect, and not in just any respect whatsoever, not just according to any rules whatsoever. We have no power, by our actions, to force God's blessing—it is self-abasement when God promises to bestow divine blessings on the people if they obey.[62] This is "absolute sovereignty," and is the necessary condition of the creature coming to share in intimacy with the divine.[63]

This is the logical bridge that connects the statement in *The Glory of the Lord* quoted above about God's entering into covenant history[64] with the notion in *Theodrama* that in creating the world, God binds Godself to the world.[65] *Theodrama* is concerned primarily with this freedom, with the encounter and interaction between the infinite divine freedom and the finite human freedom. Finite freedom is always understood as posited by infinite freedom, and embraced by it in its most authentic uses.[66] It is the freedom of this choice that leads back to the heart of the kenosis understood with reference to creation.

This freedom grounds itself in "absolute love," which gives itself away, and in so doing, allows others to be—in fact in its giving constitutes those others. This is the divine "making space" for the creatures to be.[67] In order to make space, God necessarily has to withdraw; but God does not will to cease to be infinite, so even in this withdrawal, there is fullness. God is now no longer expressly filling all reality, but is now latent in all reality.[68] The act of making space for creation therefore explains and establishes the radical immanence of God to all creatures; at the same time, it grounds God's ongoing journey with creation, for it can only occupy a space that is properly God's, and therefore it must always be of concern to God.[69]

IV. First Kenosis–Trinitarian Processions

If the path to understanding the kenotic character of creation lies through freedom, then it must have its roots in love, for freedom is that which above all characterizes love.[70] This realization is expansive—once love is touched upon, it will bring all the ways of God under its banner. For von Balthasar especially this is true, and love conquers all precisely as a kenotic love that is best characterized as the giving away of oneself for the good of the other: "reception and mission, service and creation, justice and love" all show themselves now as characteristics of that deeper and more fundamental way of being, which is kenotic.[71]

Such an expansive extrapolation, which begins to make kenosis look like the most fundamental of all realities, seems to be resisted in the last volume of *The Glory of the Lord*. The freedom of the gracious decision in which kenosis (whether it be in the Incarnation, in creation, or in the Trinity) consists must not be deducible on the basis of created structures—for such would destroy its character as *freedom*, would render it explicable within a network of causality which ultimately determines it. By the same token, this free decision cannot be extended to become a universal law of the created world.[72] But it is already clear from these statements that what von Balthasar is ruling out is not the idea of mapping kenotic love onto the Trinitarian persons, but rather of either claiming that because God is such kenotic love, it was inevitable that God create, or that because God is kenotic love, all innerworldly structures may be explained in terms of this. Once this has been excluded, it remains true that we learn something of the dynamic of the immanent Trinity through God's dealings in salvation history.[73]

We have come to the furthest point of the Balthasarian system—beyond the metaphysics, we will be speaking of the ground of the metaphysics in the very freedom (and therefore ultimately personality) of God. The Trinitarian processions ground who the Son is and are the content of his being as the first image. As such, they will also control the logic of creation—not by means of a necessary law, but as a characteristic *mode* of action within God, as characteristic of the types of things God likes to do. After this there can be only implications: the divine love in grace will appear as the logical outworking of the decisions and commitments God has made concerning and on behalf of the creature from the very beginning. All of the remaining theological topics (soteriology, ecclesiology, sacramentology, even Mariology and missiology) will find their place ordered to the fundamental markers sketched here as the ground of their logic and proper understanding.

Von Balthasar approaches the trinitarian love from multiple angles. But as our concern is with the ground for metaphysics in the life of the Trinity, it is specifically the being of God that we ought to question. For von Balthasar, this comes in the *Theologic*, when he turns to the katalogical dimension of the truth of being. This is fitting, because truth comes down from above, addressing humanity; and above all the unsearchable truth of the Trinity, which for all the resonances von Balthasar will allow must still remain for him a non-deducible fact. This is to ask the question of the "image of the Trinity in created being."[74]

At this juncture, von Balthasar turns to the Medieval metaphysical project, which started from the transcendental properties of being. As transcendental, they apply equally to divine and created being, and therefore allow us to meaningfully think about the characteristics of uncreated being.[75] At this key point, it is once again to Bonaventure that von Balthasar turns to help him develop the conceptuality.

Although von Balthasar begins by applauding Bonaventure's grasp of the necessity of applying the transcendentals to God, quoting a long passage from the *Breviloquium*,[76] it is the basis of this idea in the *Hexaemeron* that most interests him. Bonaventure starts there from the threefold relations in the divine essence: "from itself and according to itself and for the sake of itself." The meaningfulness of this is only established, however, in comparison to worldly being which is "from another and according to another and for the sake of another." Thus worldly being is correlated to the Father, Son, and Holy Spirit respectively.[77] This gives rise to a metaphysical question that is threefold in its structure: How are things to be understood insofar as they are related to their origin, archetype, and final end? The metaphysician must deal with all three aspects of the question; and while such a thinker is joined by the natural philosopher in considering the origin and by the ethicist in considering the final end, when it comes to the contemplation of creation as image of the archetype, the metaphysician has found a territory that belongs to no one else.[78]

This threefold question that confronts the metaphysician can only be answered in the knowledge that God is triune.[79] The answer thus revealed is expressed in terms of the transcendentals: because every creature comes into being through a cause, is patterned after an archetype and is directed toward a goal, they become one, true, and good.[80] Further, it is not the case that the transcendentals are merely properties of the essence the persons all share, such that they only come to express them through their share in a common nature: for the Son is properly called *imago*, the *secundum se* of the Godhead, and therefore is the very truth of being.[81]

Von Balthasar now begins to turn from Bonaventure, for he has to reach for modern writers to fill out his concerns. Now he points out that although it is where being becomes spirit that the transcendentals find their fulfillment, and if perfect love presupposes perfect knowledge, nevertheless the primal self-outpouring of God into the Son is due to a love that surpasses being and self-knowledge.[82] In other words, the transcendentals and knowledge, which would seem to offer themselves as the necessary ground of love, are outstripped by a love that trumps them all with its absolute unconditionedness: the love that governs the self-emptying of the generation of the Son. This can only mean that love transcends even being, that it comprehends being.[83]

This is, in effect, to deny that love presupposes knowledge. For von Balthasar thinks that this could be taken two ways: either that the Father begets the Son in order to come to know himself, or that the Father generates the Son *because* he knows himself perfectly. The first position would be the Hegelian dialectic of Spirit, which must suffer estrangement in order to come into true possession of knowledge of itself; the second position would lead to an Arianism that saw the Son as a creature produced after the fullness of God (now located in the Father and not in the Trinity) was already established.[84] The procession of the Son cannot be in order to bring the Father into the self-possession of Spirit, nor can it be based on the Father's thorough knowledge of himself. It can only proceed on the basis of love, which can be given no other ground without endangering its very character as free love. This unpredictable act of God is self-outpouring, or, as von Balthasar finally says explicitly, self-relinquishing (*hingabe*).[85]

All of this is only explicable if we again turn to Bulgakov and speak of an inner-trinitarian kenosis.[86] Here at last we see the union of the notion of love and self-giving; and at this point it is clear why the Christology must be kenotic (though this is still the minority opinion in the theological traditions von Balthasar draws upon): because it is the very nature of love to pour oneself out for another. This formulation makes clear also why the system cannot be content with only one kenosis, but must on to speak of kenosis in creation and in the processions of the persons. Above all, however, the equation of kenosis with love makes clear the necessity for the adjective *kenotic*, which will now need expansive use. For far from it being beneath the dignity of God to empty Godself on behalf of creatures, it is now seen that nothing is more like God. Thus, all divine actions, *ad intra* as well as *ad extra*, insofar as they demonstrate the character of love, will demonstrate the character of abandonment, of emptiness.

At the same time, the basis in the trinitarian processions challenges our conceptions of what abandonment and emptiness mean. For God is eternally and profligately pouring Godself out—and yet God is never empty, but is infinite and perfect fullness. Here the paradox of the one who loses his life in order to save it takes on its deepest meaning as a fundamental principle that undergirds all innerworldly rules.

Notes

1. For a notable example, see Werner Löser, "Being Interpreted as Love: Reflections on the Theology of Hans Urs von Balthasar."

2. In this light, we can agree that Werner Löser is on the right track when he asserts that "the formula of the analogy of Being, insofar as it is primarily a theological statement, means nothing more than the statement of the convertibility of Being and love" ("Being Interpreted as Love," 482).

3. *H* I.76. In spite of the conspicuous (some might even say jarring) position this brief glimpse at Hamann occupies in the Tryptich, von Balthasar's relationship to Hamann's theology has received very little critical attention. Martin Simon's "Identity and Analogy: Balthasar's Hölderlin and Hamann" (in *The Analogy of Beauty*, edited by John Riches [Edinburgh: T&T Clark, 1986]) is much more concerned with Hölderlin than Hamann, and is at any rate too flawed by a lack of understanding of the philosophical and theological background of von Balthasar's thought to shed much light on the relationship.

4. "Das Schöne ist die ursprüngliche Weltnatur selbst, in ihrer Sinnenhaftigkeit, ja Sinnlichkeit und Erotik" (*H* I.77). [The beautiful is the primitive worldly nature, in its sensuousness, indeed in its sensuality and eroticism.]

5. "Aber der Christ weiß und fühlt: Natur ist dem Ursprung entfremdet: nicht mehr spricht Gottes Wort durch alle Wesen, und mit der Hülle auf dem Anlitz Gottes ist auch die Herrlichkeit der Natur verhüllt" (ibid.). [But the Christian knows and feels that nature is alienated from the origin; the Word of God no longer speaks through all beings, and the glory of nature is also veiled with the veil over the face of God.]

6. "Christus allein, und das Gottes-Wort in ihm in der Gestalt des Leidens, der 'Verborgenheit sub contrario', das geschichtliche Wort in der Heiligen Schrift, enthüllt von neuem Gottes Glorie" (ibid.). [Only Christ and the word of God in him in the form of suffering, the "concealedness under a contrary," the historical Word in the holy Scriptures, unveils anew the glory of God.]

7. "*Ein* Beweis der herrlichsten Majestät und leersten Entäußerung!'" (ibid.). ["*One* proof of the most glorious majesty and the most empty outpouring!"]

8. "Herrlichkeit als Kenosis nicht erst des Menschgewordenen, sondern schon des Schöpfers" (ibid.).

9. "In der Torheit des Kreuzes, für die ihm aber auch die Torheit der Pythia, die Narrheit und das Nichtwissen des Sokrates, das 'μῶρον der Götter Homers', welches 'das wunderbare seiner Muse' ist, stellvertretend sind, findet er den Zugang zu jener ursprünglichen Schönheit unserer Existenz, zur archetypischen Kraft des echten, zeugerischen Wortes, und zuletzt zum innersten Mysterienkern aller Wirklichkeit: zur bräutlichen Einheit des Gott-Logos Christus mit seinem abgefallenen, zerspaltenen und im Tod wieder heimgeholten Leib" (*H* I.78). [In the foolishness of the cross (but for which according to him also the foolishness of Pythia, the folly and the

ignorance of Socrates, the "*moron* of the gods of Homer," which is "the wonder of his muse," are representations) he finds access to that primal beauty of our existence, to the archetypal power of the true, fruitful Word, and lastly to the innermost mystery-core of all reality: to the bridal unity of the God-Logos Christ with his fallen, broken, and in death brought home again body.]

10. "Wenn also der Aufprall des Willens Gottes in Gestalt der Weltsünde nicht ein beliebiges, sondern ein einzartiges Subjekt fordert, das nicht nachträglich bei der 'Erhöhung' zum Gott werden kann, sondern es immer schon gewesen sein muß, um es zu 'werden', dann setzt die Konstituierung dieses Subjekts den Entschluß einer präexistenten göttlichen Person voraus, wie ihn der Hymnus Phil 2,6-11 beschreibt" (*H* III.2.2.196). [If then the collision of the will of God in the form of the sin of the world requires not an arbitrary, rather a unique subject, which is not able to become God retroactively through an "exaltation," but who must have always been this in order to "become" this, then the constitution of the subject presupposes the decision of a pre-existent divine person, as the hymn in Phil. 2:6-11 describes it.]

11. Chapter 6, I.A.2.

12. "Weil sein Gehorsam nicht dem Geliefertsein des Menschen in den Tod entspringt, sondern seiner einmaligen Beziehung zum Vater" (*H* III.2.2.197). [Because his obedience springs not from the fact that man is handed over to death, but from his unique relationship to the Father.]

13. "Dafür muß wenigstens der Denkversuch gemacht werden, wie eine solche Preisgabe für den Gott möglich sei, dem wir keine kreatürliche Veränderung und kein kreatürliches Leiden und Gehorchen zuschreiben können" iIbid.). [Therefore at the very least the investigation must be made, how such a surrender is possible for God, to whom we can ascribe no creaturely change and no creaturely suffering and obedience.]

14. "Unter den Vätern hat Hilarius sich bemüht, dem göttlichen Sohn eine Macht zuzuschreiben, sich—ohne Einbuße der eigenen Macht in Freiheit—sich selbst zu verohnmächtigen (intra suam ipse vacuefactus potestatem)" (*H* III.2.2.197–88). [Among the Fathers, Hilary strove to ascribe to the divine Son a power to make himself powerless without forfeit of his proper power in freedom.]

15. "Das ist aber allzusehr von der göttlichen 'Natur' (und ihrer naturhaften Mächtigkeit) her gedacht" (*H* III.2.2.198). [But this is thought too much from the divine "nature" and its natural powerfulness.]

16. Ibid., note 7. This would not seem to be so distant from what Hamann claims (*H* I.76 ff.), and serves to underscore that von Balthasar wishes to distance himself to some extent from Hamann.

17. "Die 'Selbstlosigkeit' der göttlichen Personen als reiner Relationen im innergöttlichen Leben der Liebe zur Grundlage von allem nehmen" (*H* III.2.2.198).

18. "Diese begründet eine erste Form von Kenose, die in der Schöpung (zumal des freien Menschen) liegt, da der Schöpfer hier gleichsam einen Teil seiner Freiheit an das Geschöpf abgibt" (ibid.). [This grounds a first form of kenosis, which lies in the creation (especially of free humanity), because the creator here hands over as it were a part of his freedom to the creature.]

19. "Damit wird zwar die Kenose—als Preisgabe der 'Gottgestalt'—zum unterscheidenden Akt der Liebe des Sohnes, der sein Gezeugtsein (und damit seine Abhängigkeit) vom Vater übergehen läßt in die Ausdrucksform geschöpflichen Gehorsams."

20. Always bearing in mind that this is an image that causes the reality it images, rather than being caused by it. I have intentionaly translated *Ausdrucksform* with "expressive image" in order to call to mind an echo of Bonaventure, which I detect in von Balthasar here.

21. "Diese begründet eine erste Form von Kenose, die in der Schöpfung (zumal des freien Menschen) liegt, da der Schöpfer hier gleichsam einen Teil seiner Freiheit an das Geschöpf abgibt, dies aber letzlich nur wagen kann kraft Voraussicht und Inkaufnahme der zweiten und eigentlichen Kenose, der des Kreuzes, in der er alle äußersten Konsequenzen der geschöpflichen Freiheit ein- und überholt" (*H* III.2.2.198). [This grounds a first form of kenosis, which lies in the creation (especially of free humanity), because the creator here hands over as it were a part of his freedom to the creature. But ultimately he can only dare to do this because of the foreknowledge

and acceptance of the second and proper kenosis, that of the cross, in which he secures and surpasses all the extreme consequences of creaturely freedom.]

22. "So ist 'Christi Kreuz in die Weltschöpfung eingeschrieben seit deren Grundlegung', wie die johanneische Theologie vom 'Lamm Gottes' (1,29.36) es zeigt, das 'seit Grundlegung der Welt geschlachtet' (Apk 13,8) auf dem Thron des Vaters steht (5,6), das die in seinem Blut Gewaschenen weidet (7,17) und als Lamm-Hirt sein Leben für seine Schafe dahingibt (Jo 10,15), aber auch im 'Zorn der Lammes' (Apk 6,16) zum Richter der Seinen und der ganzen Welt wird" (Ibid.). [Thus is the "cross of Christ written into creation from its foundation," as the Johannine theology of the "Lamb of God" (1:29, 36) shows: the one "slaughtered from the foundation of the world" (Rev. 13:8) stands upon the throne of the Father (5:6), the one feeding those washed in his blood (7:17) and as Lamb-shepherd giving his life for the sheep (John 10:15), but also in the "wrath of the Lamb" (Rev. 6:16) he becomes the judge of his own and of the whole world.]

23. Von Balthasar does not see a conflict with the persons being constituted by what is a self-emptying that would seem to presuppose personal constitution. The problem is a classic trinitarian one, for in whatever the processions are said to consist, they are always reducible to personal actions, and yet the Father is not the Father except by generating the Son. The processions are therefore acts of the persons which simultaneously constitute the persons—only thus is a subordinationism that goes too far in the Arian direction avoided.

24. "Gott bestätigt sich als Gott darin, 'daß er sich in die Bindung und in das Elend des menschlichen Geschöpfs begibt, daß er, der Herr, Knecht wird und insofern, gerade darin von den falschen Göttern unterschieden, sich selbst erniedrigt."

25. "In Gott ist bei alldem 'kein Paradox, keine Antinomie, kein Zwiespalt'; indem er 'solches tut, beweist er uns, daß er es *kann*, daß solches zu tun durchaus in seiner *Natur* liegt. Er erweist sich dann eben als souveräner, größer, reicher, als wir zuvor gedacht hatten.' Alles hängt an Gottes dreieiniger Liebe, die allein es erklärt, 'daß ein Akt des Gehorsams Gott selbst nicht fremd sein' muß" (*H* III.2.2.199–200). [In God there is with all that "no paradox, no antinomy, no dichotomy"; inasmuch as he "does such a thing, he proves to us that he *can* do such a thing, that to do such a thing lies completely in his *nature*. He proves himself then as more sovereign, greater, richer than we had suspected before. Everything hangs on the trinitarian love of God, which alone explains "that an act of obedience need not be foreign to Godself."]

26. "Damit wird erahnbar, daß Gott die ins Nichts der Verlorenheit entsinkende Freiheit der Kreatur einholen und untergreifen kann durch ein noch tieferes, weil eigentlich-göttliches 'Nichten': das Leersein des absoluten Liebesgehorsams für den absoluten Befehl, für jeden Gebrauch und 'Misbrauch'" (*H* III.2.2.200). [With this it is divinable that God is able to recover and undergird the freedom of the creature, sinking into the nothingness of lostness, through an even deeper because truly divine "annihilation": the emptiness of absolute love-obedience for the absolute command, for every use and "misuse."] The German word *untergreifen*, which I have translated as God's ability to "undergird," comes from the realm of musical analysis, and refers to a method of prolongation of a musical line by supporting the movement of an upper voice with movement from an inner voice. The result is both an extension and an expansion of the upper voice as the movement of the inner inserts its own particularity into the leading of the upper line. The image here in von Balthasar is therefore that the divine music dives deeper than the human music goes in order through that very depth (by therefore becoming an inner voice to humanity's upper voice) to transform and sustain the motion of the human music. von Balthasar is far too familiar with musical anaylsis, and specifically with Mozart, who uses *untergreifen* to brilliant effect, not to be aware of the tender and powerful note the concept strikes in its usage of the divine kenosis.

27. Supra, 110, n.19.

28. "Es ist deshalb theologisch unrichtig, Jesu Leben von der Empfängnis bis zum Kreuz als ein einziges maximales Leiden zu deuten, ganz abgesehen davon, daß dies einem wahren Menschenleben nicht entspräche, das aus Freude und Leid gemischt und als christliches von Glaube, Liebe und Hoffnung getragen ist" (ibid.). [It is therefore theologically incorrect to

interpret the life of Jesus from the conception to the cross as a single maximal suffering, quite apart from the fact that this would not correspond to a true human life, which is mixed with joy and suffering and which, as Christian, is comprised of faith, love and hope.]

29. "ἀλλὰ ἑαυτόν ἐκένωσεν μορφήν δούλου λαβών, ἐν ὁμοιώματι ἀνθρώπων γενόμενος καὶ σχήματι εὑρεθεὶς ὡς ἄνθρωπος." [But he emptied himself, taking the form of a servant, having been turned into the likeness of men and found in appearance as a man.]

30. "τὸ γὰρ ἀδύνατον τοῦ νόμου, ἐν ᾧ ἠσθένει διὰ τῆς σαρκόσ, ὁ θεὸατὸν ἑαυτοῦ υἱὸν πέμψας ἐν ὁμιώματι σαρκὸς ἁμαρτίας καὶ περὶ ἁμαρτίας κατέκρινεν τὴν ἁμαρτίαν ἐν τῇ σαρκί" [For the thing undoable for the law, in the one weakend by the flesh, God did, sending his own son in the likeness of sinful flesh, and on account of sin condemned sin in the flesh.] it is not necessary to see the emptying in the cross, and therefore the humanity of Christ as being consummated on the cross. The sufferings of the cross are not something Christ does to himself, but something that he, in absolute obedience, allows to be done to him. The emptying is fully and most fittingly explained in a type of obedient submission which is truly ready for anything, which has set no previous conditions, and thus which does not balk even in the face of death on a cross and absolute separation from God.[footnote]"Es wird aber auch gleichzeitig sichtbar, weshalb das Menschsein des Menschen Jesus nicht schon identisch zu sein braucht mit dem absoluten Leiden des Kreuzes. Denn seine Existenz ist zwar als ganze durch die Kenose Gottes bestimmt (wie Phil 2,7 klar sagt, und worauf Rö 8,3 wenigstens hinweist), aber die dieser Existenz zugedachte Last bürdet er sich nicht selber auf—das widerspräche gerade dem kenotischen Zustand—,er ist nur bereit, sie sich in der 'Stunde,' die der Vater bestimmt hat, aufbürden zu lassen" (ibid.). [But it becomes at the same time visible, for what reason the humanity of the man Jesus does not need to be identical with the absolute suffering of the cross. For his existence is indeed entirely determined by the kenosis of God (as Phil. 2:7 clearly says, and to which Rom. 8:3 at least alludes), but he does not himself impose the burden intended for this existence on himself—this would certainly contradict the kenotic condition—he is only ready to let it be imposed on him in the hour which the Father determined.] See ibid., 208: "Jesus ist zuerst und vor allem der von Gott und—werkzeuglich innerhalb des Handelns Gottes—von allen Menschen Preisgegebene." [Jesus is first and above all the one abandoned by God and—instrumentally within the action of God—by all men.]

31. "Man muß noch mehr sagen: die tiefste Erfahrung der Gottverlassenheit, die stellvertretend in der Passion real werden soll, setzt eine tiefste Erfahrung der Gottverbundenheit und des Lebens aus dem Vater voraus, eine Erfahrung, die der Sohn nicht nur im Himmel gemacht, sondern auch als Mensch erlebt haben muß, selbst wenn sein Geist nicht deshalb schon in einer immerwährenden visio beatifica zu weilen braucht. Wirklich verlassen (nicht bloß einsam) kann nur sein, wer wirkliche Intimität der Liebe gekannt hat" (H III.2.2.200–1). [One must say even more: the deepest experience of God-forsakenness, which is to become substitutionally real in the Passion, presupposes a deepest experience of God-unitedness and of life from the Father, an experience which the Son had not only in heaven, but also must have lived as a man, even if his spirit does not need for that reason to already tarry in a perpetual *visio beatifica*. Only he who has known the true intimacy of love can be truly abandoned (and not merely lonely).]

32. "Es wird aber auch gleichzeitig sichtbar, weshalb das Menschsein des Menschen Jesus nicht schon identisch zu sein braucht mit dem absoluten Leiden des Kreuzes. Denn seine Existenz ist zwar als ganze durch die Kenose Gottes bestimmt (wie Phil 2,7 klar sagt, und worauf Rö 8,3 wenigstens hinweist), aber die dieser Existenz zugedachte Last bürdet er sich nicht selber auf—das widerspräche gerade dem kenotischen Zustand—,er ist nur bereit, sie sich in der 'Stunde,' die der Vater bestimmt hat, aufbürden zu lassen" (ibid.). [But it becomes at the same time visible, for what reason the humanity of the man Jesus does not need to be identical with the absolute suffering of the cross. For his existence is indeed entirely determined by the kenosis of God (as Phil. 2:7 clearly says, and to which Rom. 8:3 at least alludes), but he does not himself impose the burden intended for this existence on himself—this would certainly contradict the kenotic condition—he is only ready to let it be imposed on him in the hour which the Father determined.] See ibid., 208: "Jesus ist zuerst und vor allem der von Gott und—werkzeuglich innerhalb des Handelns Gottes—von

allen Menschen Preisgegebene." [Jesus is first and above all the one abandoned by God and—instrumentally within the action of God—by all men.]

33. "Daß das fleischgewordene Wort 'in sein Eigentum kam' (1,11), also nicht einfach (wie Karl Barth sagt) in die Fremde geht, sondern in ein Land, dessen Sprache er kennt: nicht nur das galiläische Aramäisch, das das Kind in Nazaret lernt, sondern tiefer die Sprache des Kreaturseins als solchen. Die Logik der Kreatur ist der Logik Gottes nicht fremd; man könnte sie einem Dialekt vergleichen, dessen Reinsprache bei Gott gesprochen wird."

34. "Weil Gott zu gehorchen und seinen Willen zu erwarten in der Grundverfassung der Kreatur liegt." One could gloss this as obediential potency.

35. "In der gnadenhaft geschenkten Kommunikation—bis zur Brüderschaft mit Jesus (Jo 20, 17; Rö 8,29; Hb 2,12)—wird durch alle Texte des Neuen Bundes hindurch unerbittlich der Abstand zwischen dem einen 'Meister und Herrn' (Jo 13,13) und den Jüngern und Nachfolgern gewahrt. Das müßte nicht sein, wenn die kenotische Bereitschaft zum väterlichen Willen nicht qualitativ anderer Art wäre als die aller freien Geschöpfe" (H III.2.2.201). [In the gracious gift of communication—to the point of brotherhood with Jesus (John 20:17, Rom. 8:29, Heb. 2:12)—the distance between the one "master and lord" (John 13:13) and the disciples and followers is relentlessly preserved through all the texts of the New Testament. This would not be necessary if the kenotic readiness for the Father's will were not qualitatively other in form than that of all free creatures.]

36. "Sonst wäre das Kreuz Christi nichts weiter als der Vollzug der rein kreatürlichen (etwa adamitischen) Haltung vor Gott, mit Übernahme der Existentialien des gefallenen Menschen, des 'Leeren, Ausweglosen, Zerrinnenden, Wesenlosen', das ihm zumal im Sterben bewußt wird" (H III.2.2.202). [Otherwise the cross of Christ would be nothing more than the carrying out of the pure creaturely (e.g. Adamic) posture toward God, with the adoption of the existentials of fallen humanity, of "exhaustion, hopelessness, wasting away, insubstantiality", which it becomes aware of especially in death.]

37. See Tillich's notion of new being in Christ, *Systematic Theology*, vol. 2, 118 ff. (Chicago: Chicago University Press, 1957).

38. "Jesus konnte dann vielleicht der Welt ein 'neues Existential einstiften', aber von hier bis zum stellvertretenden Tragen der gesamten Sünden der Welt durch den Einen, zur Wende der Äonen—'das Alte ist vergangen, siehe, Neues ist geworden!' (2 Kor 5,17)—bliebe ein weiter Weg" (H III.2.2.202). ["Jesus could then perhaps "introduce a new existential" into the world, but a long way remains from here to a substitutionary bearing of the collected sins of the world through the one, at the turning point of the eons: "the old is past, see, the new has come!" (2 Cor. 5:17).]

39. Chapter 5, I.A.

40. It may be tempting to see the specter of monotheletism here, but it is not necessary. The logic takes its starting point from the pre-Incarnational decision of the Logos, which is upheld through the earthly career of Jesus. What is said here could accordingly be upheld in either an orthodox or monotheletist context.

41. "Um in der Kenose reiner Raum zu sein für den Aufprall der Weltsünde" (H III.2.2.206). [In order in the kenosis to be a pure space for the collision of the sin of the world.]

42. "Abendmahl und Kreuz sind gemeinsam die 'Stunde', um deretwillen er gekommen ist."

43. "Wenn nun die Kenose und die auf ihr ruhende Existenzgestalt Jesu als Anspruch (Sendung)-Armut-Überlassung das Tragen der Weltschuld ermöglichte, so kann dieses Tragen sich nicht anders vollenden als in der Solidarität mit dem Todeslos aller" (H III.2.2.212). [If now the kenosis and Jesus' form of existence as claim (mission)-poverty-abandonment, which depends on the kenosis, makes possible the bearing of the guilt of the world, then this bearing can fulfill itself in no other way than in solidarity with the common fate, death.]

44. "Es wird sich erweisen, daß die dritte und letzte Folge des Wort-Fleisch, worin die beiden ersten Kennzeichen sich erst wirklich begegnen, auf diese Mitte: Wort als Unwort, als sich aufgebendes, aufhebendes Wort zuführt" (H III.2.2.131). [It will be shown that the third and last implication of the Word-flesh, in which the first two characteristics truly meet for the first time,

leads to this midpoint: Word as unword, as self-abandoning, self-dissolving word.] See *H* III.2.2.209 ff., *TL* II.98 ff.

45. "Thus one can construct above all a theological *aesthetique* ("Gloria"): God appears. He appeared to Abraham, to Moses, to Isaiah, finally in Jesus Christ. A theological question: how to distinguish his appearance, his epiphany among the thousand other phenomena in the world? How to distinguish the true and only living God of Israel from all the idols which surround him and from all the philosophical and theological attempts to attain God? How to perceive the incomparable glory of God in the life, the cross, the resurrection of Christ, a glory different from all other glory in this world?" Hans Urs von Balthasar, "A Rèsumè of My Thought," *Communio* 15 (Winter, 1988): 472.

46. "One can then continue with a *dramatique* since this God enters into an alliance with us: how does the absolute liberty of God in Jesus Christ confront the relative, but true, liberty of man? Will there perhaps be a mortal struggle between the two in which each one will defend against the other what it conceives and chooses as the good? What will be the unfolding of the battle, the final victory?" (ibid.).

47. Ibid. This problem is immediately linked to Christ: "That will be the problem of the two natures of Jesus Christ."

48. "Sollte sich aber göttliches, ewiges Wort in sterblichem Fleisch—auf wie geheimnisvolle Art auch immer—adäquat ausdrücken wollen, so könnte dies nicht durch den Menschen selbst geschehen, es sei denn so, daß er sein ganzes, fleischliches, sterblich-vergebliches Dasein zu einer solchen Selbstauslegung göttlichen Wortes zur Verfügung stellte, indem er sich als Ganzer, mit Geburt und Tod, mit Reden und Schweigen, Wachen und Schlafen, Erfolg und Vergeblichkeit und was sonst noch zum Wesen menschlichen Daseins gehört, wie ein Alphabet oder eine Klaviatur zur Auswortung *überließe.*"

49. "Ein steigendes Sich-überlassen an die Führung Dessen, der allein aus dem ganzen gelebten Dasein jenes endgültige Wort herausheben kann, das Gott zum Abschluß seines Neuen und ewigen Bundes braucht."

50. "Die 'Vollmacht,' das Hingegebene 'wiederzunehmen', ist nicht die Zurücknahme der Selbstüberlassung, sondern ihre innere Vollendung, sofern gerade der Gang in die letzte Enteignung der Selbstüberlassung mithinzugehört zur ursprünglichen 'Vollmacht', die sich darin von jeder sonstigen menschlichen, auch prophetischen, unterscheidet" (*H* III.2.2.136). [The "authority" to take up again that which was given up is not to take back the self-abandonment, rather it is its inner fulfillment, insofar as precisely the going out into the last condemnation of self-abandonment belongs together with the primal "authority," which thereby differentiates itself from every other human, even prophetic, authority.]

51. "Wo sonst nur noch Zwang und Unfreiheit herrscht. Von der früheren Terminologie her: nicht nur Anspruch und Armut, sondern auch die Überlassenheit (jenseits der Grenzen des irdischen Daseins) sind bei Jesus von seinem Gehorsam eingeholt; dies ist aber nur möglich, wenn seine ganze Seins- und Zeitstruktur untergriffen ist von dem freien Gehorsamsakt seiner Kenose. In diesem tiefern, nicht psychologischen Sinn ist er 'inter mortuos liber' (Ps 87,6 LXX)" (*H* III.2.2.214). [Where otherwise only coercion and unfreedom reign. In terms of the earlier terminology: not only entitlement and poverty, but also the abandonment (beyond the constraints of earthly existence) are for Jesus outrun by his obedience. But this is only possible if his whole being- and time-structure is undergirded by the free act of obedience of his kenosis. In this deepest, not psychological sense is he *inter mortuos liber.*]

52. "Himmel, indem gerade diese äußerste Entfernung des menschgewordenen Sohnes vom Vater auch unmittelbar (wie Joh[annes] sah) seine Rückkehr besagt, nämlich die Bloßlegung der ökonomischen Unmittelbarkeit zwischen ihnen, so sehr, daß der Gang in die äußerste Hölle im absoluten Nu der Auferweckung zeitlos in die letzte Intimität des Himmels umschlagen kann" (*H* III.2.2.217). [Heaven, as precisely this furthest removal of the incarnate Son from the Father also immediately indicates (as John saw) his return, namely the exposure of the economic

immediacy between them in such a way that the journey into the outermost Hell in the absolute instant of the resurrection can revert timelessly into the final intimacy of Heaven.]

53. "Das weist auf eine so göttliche und absolute Hingabe, daß sie seitens der Kreatur nur beantwortet werden kann mit dem vollkommenen Jawort der 'Magd des Herrn' (als Grundhaltung der Kirche), worin der Mensch Gott *sein läßt*, was er sein will, und sich von ihm schenken und einformen läßt, was und soviel er will" (*H* III.2.2.148). [This points to a self-giving that is divine and absolute to such an extent that it can only be answered from the side of the creature with the complete *fiat* of the "maidservant of the Lord" (as fundamental attitude of the Church), wherein humanity lets God be what he will and lets itself be endowed and formed by him, with what and to what extent he wills.]

54. "Gott ist das reine Für-sich-sein, das keines anderen Wesens bedarf. Sein unendliches Licht ist sich selber vollkommen, es verliert sich nicht naturhaft nach außen, sondern wird, wenn es mitgeteilt werden soll, nur durch freie Zuwendung geoffenbart."

55. Chapter 2, I, C.

56. Supra, p. 215 ff.

57. "Die Bewegung des Abstiegs öffnet einen lebendigen Beziehungsraum zwischen dem 'Orte' Gottes und dem 'Orte' des Menschen" (*H* III.2.1.44). [The motion of descent opens a living space of relationship between the "place" of God and the "place" of humanity.]

58. "Die Mittlerschaft Moses' wird, räumlich gesprochen, dahin führen, daß das oben auf dem Berg Geltende nun auch drunten (bei den Menschen) Geltung erlange" (ibid.). [Moses' mediation, spatially speaking, leads to the fact that what applies on high on the mountain now applies also below (among humanity).]

59. "Kommt bei der Weihe der Stiftshütte die Herrlichkeit endgültig und für ein zuständliches 'Wohnen'" (*H* III.2.1.45). [At the consecration of the tabernacle glory comes definitively and for an abiding "habitation."]

60. "Beides soll und muß gesagt werden: der Mensch steigt auf an den Ort Gottes ('Entrückung'), Gott steigt ab an den Ort des Menschen; in beiden Bewegungen, die nicht 'rein geistig' sind, sondern die sinnliche Sphäre einholen, vollzieht sich das Ereignis der Bundesschließung" (Ibid.). [Both are meant to be said and must be said: humanity ascends to the place of God ("rapture"), God descends to the place of humanity. In both movements, which are not "purely spiritual," but obtain the sensible sphere, the event of consummating the covenant fulfills itself.]

61. "Daß der ewige und geschichtslose Gott die zeitlichen und räumlichen Bewegungen der Menschen in ihrem Lebensraum mitvollzieht, nicht nur als Zuschauer und Lenker von oben, sondern als ein Mitfahrender und Miterfahrender auf der Ebene des Geschöpfs" (*H* III.2.1.46). [That the eternal and history-less God joins with the temporal and spatial movements of humanity in their habitat, not only as an on-looker and director from above, but as co-journeyor and co-experiencer at the level of the creature.]

62. This precisely because the divine being, as infinite, is not subject to limitation—it therefore follows that any limitation in the divine is giving something away.

63. "Nicht eigentlich in der Unbekanntheit Gottes liegt seine Entrückung, vielmehr in der Unfaßlichkeit, daß er, der Einzige (Is 43,10-12), der absolut Freie und Souveräne, sich den Andern, Vielen mitzuteilen geruht, ihnen Einlaß gewährt in den Bereich seiner Einzigkeit und Heiligkeit" (*H* III.2.1.164). [God's distance does not lie properly in his being unknown but in the incomprehensibility that he, the Unique (Is. 43:10-12), the absolutely free and sovereign, deigns to impart himself to the others, the many, permits them entry into the domain of his uniqueness and holiness.]

64. See note 62.

65. "Einmal damit Gott in sich selbst Leben, Liebe, ewiger Austausch in Fülle sei, der der Welt nicht bedarf, um ein zu liebendes Gegenüber zu haben, so daß er, die Welt schaffend, einen gänzlich freien Akt setzt, in dem er sich freiwillig und nicht zwangsmäßig an das begonnene und zu begleitende Werk bindet" (*TDg* II.2.484). [Firstly, in order for God to be himself love, life,

eternal exchange in fullness, who does not need the world in order to have an other to be loved, in such a way that he, creating the world, applies an entirely free act, in which he binds himself freely and without compulsion to the begun and to be accompanied work.]

66. *TDg* II.1.247

67. "Und wenn theologisch Gottes Wesen sich als 'absolute Liebe' (*autocharis*) dadurch erweist, daß er in sich der Sich-Verschenkende und Sein-Lassende ist, aus keinem anderen Grund, als weil dieses (grundlose) Geben das Gute und Sinnerfüllte ist—und darin das Schöne und Herrliche schlechthin—, dann kann auch sein Raumgewähren für seine freien Geschöpfe keinen anderen (grundlosen) Grund haben" (*TDg* II.1.248). [And if theologically the essence of God shows itself as "absolute love" (*autocharis*) through the fact that he is in himself the one giving himself away and the one letting be for no other reason than because this (causeless) giving is the good and meaningful thing—and therefore the beautiful and glorious *par excellence*—then his making space for his free creature also can have no other (causeless) cause.] von Balthasar references Gregory of Nyssa's *De Beatitudine* on "*autocharis.*"

68. "Raum für Freiheit aber erhalten sie nur, wenn der freilassende Gott in eine gewisse Latenz zurücktritt, wenn er, der von keinem Ort abwesend sein kann, ein gewisses Inkognito annimmt, worin er nicht nur scheinhaft, sondern wirklich der Freiheit viele Wege offenhält, indem er, der immer Wirkende, die Freiheit immerfort freisetzt" (ibid.). [But they only attain room for freedom if the emancipating God recedes into a certain latency; if he, who can be absent from no place, assumes a certain incognito, in which he not only in appearance but in reality holds open many paths for freedom as he, the one always working, delivers freedom evermore.]

69. "Wir haben diese beiden Momente zu betrachten: die Latenz und die Begleitung" (ibid.). [We have to consider these two moments: latency and accompaniment.]

70. See *TLg* I.136: "Nichts ist letztlich freier als die Liebe, die sich grundlos offenbart und verschenkt." [In the end, nothing is freer than the love that reveals itself and gives itself away without cause.]

71. "Sein Offenstehen für die Welt zeichnet in ihm die Grundverhaltungsweisen des Empfangens und des Schenkens, des Dienstes und der Schöpfung, der Gerechtigkeit und der Liebe vor, die alle nur verschiedene Ausprägungen der Hingabe sind" (*TLg* I.80). [Its openness for the world portrays in it the fundamental behaviors: reception and giving, service and creation, justice and love, which are all just different forms of self-giving.]

72. "Aber keine Notwendigkeit und kein philosophisches Gesetz vom Bau der geschaffenen Welt ermächtigt uns, den allerfreiesten Gnadenbeschluß der Kenose Gottes abzuleiten oder diese zu einem Weltgesetz auszudehnen" (*H* III.2.2.199). [But no necessity and no philosophical law of the constitution of the created world empowers us to deduce the absolutely free decision of grace of the kenosis of God or to extend it to a law of the world.]

73. "Und wenn es wahr ist, daß das ökonomische Hervortreten des innertrinitarischen Geheimnisses uns etwas vom Gesetz der immanenten Trinität verrät, so läßt sich trotzdem eine Notwendigkeit jenes Heraustretens keinesfalls aus dem innern Gesetz ableiten" (ibid.). [And if it is true that the economic emergence of the inner-trinitarian mystery reveals to us something of the law of the immanent Trinity, nevertheless a necessity of that going out can in no way be deduced from that inner law."

74. "Es muß allen Ernstes nach der imago Trinitatis in ente creato gefragt werden, auch wenn diese Frge in der Theologiegeschichte bisher nicht oft gestellt worden ist" (*TLg* II.159). [In all seriousness must there be an investigation of the *imago Trinitatis in ente creato*, even if this question has not often been asked in the history of theology to this point.]

75. "Um mit der leichter scheinenden Frage der Grundeigenschaften alles Seins, den Transzendentalien also, einzusetzen; da diese überkategorial das Sein im ganzen durchherrschen, mußten sie ja sowohl vom göttlichen wie vom weltlichen Sein prädizierbar sein" (*TLg* II.160). [In order to begin with the seemingly easier question of the fundamental characteristics of all being, thus the transcendentals. Because these hold sway through all of being super-categorially, they must indeed be predicable as much of divine as of worldly being.]

76. *TLg* II.160–61

77. "Diese Appropriationen werden im 'Hexaemeron' näherhin begründet, und zwar aus einem dreifachen Bezug des göttlichen Seins, das 'ex se et secundum se et propter se' existiert, was freilich innerlich erst aussagekräftig erscheint aus dem Vergleich mit dem weltlich geschaffenen Sein, welches 'ex alio et secundum aliud et propter aliud' existiert, sich somit einem ersten Ursprung (dem Vater), einem Urbild (dem Sohn) und einem vollendenden Ziel (dem Heiligen Geist) verdankt" (*TLg* II.161). [These appropriations are more fully explained in the *Hexaemeron*, and indeed from a threefold relation of the divine being, which exists *ex se et secundum se et propter se*, which in fact first appears innerly meaningful in the analogy with worldly created being, which exists *ex alio et secundum aliud et propter aliud*, which consequently owes itself to a first primal origin (the Father), to an archetype (the Son), and to a fulfilling goal (the Holy Spirit).]

78. "Hinzugefügt wird, daß diese dreifache Betrachtung des Weltseins das Thema des Metaphysikers ist, daß sie aber die erste Frage mit dem Naturphilosophen, der nach den Ursprüngen der Dinge fragt, die dritte Frage mit dem Ethiker, der nach dem Endziel fragt, gemeinsam hat, während die Frage nach dem Urbild, der Idee aller weltlichen Abbilder, also die Frage nach der Seinswahrheit, den Metaphysiker allein betrifft" (ibid.). [It is added that this threefold consideration of the being of the world is the subject matter of the metaphysician, that, however, it shares the first question in common with the natural philosopher, who seeks after the origins of things, and it has the the third question in common with the ethicist, who seeks after the final goal, whereas the question of the archetype, the idea of all worldly copies, thus the question of the truth of being, belongs to the metaphysician alone.]

79. "Aber die dreifache metaphysische Frage erhält ihre letzte Beantwortung erst, wenn das Absolute sich in seiner Dreieinigkeit offenbart hat" (ibid.). [But this threefold metaphysical questions achieves its final answer only when the absolute has revealed itself in its Trinity.]

80. "Das 'Breviloquium' verdeutlicht diesen dreifachen Bezug des geschaffenen Seins auf das göttliche durch die Transzendentalien: 'Denn jedes Geschaffene wird durch eine wirkende Ursache ins Dasein gesetzt, wird einem Urbild nachgestaltet und auf ein Endziel ausgerichtet, und ist dadurch ein Eines, ein Wahres und ein Gutes'" (ibid.). [The *Breviloquium* clarifies this threefold relation of created being to the divine through the transcendentals: "For every creature is established in existence through an efficient cause, is formed after an archetype, and is directed to one final end, and is therefore a single thing, a true thing, a good thing.]

81. "Nun können die Transzendentalien nicht einfach ausschließlich der göttlichen Wesenheit als solcher zugeschrieben werden, da die Imago und damit auch die Exemplarität für alles Erschaffbare Eigenname des Sohnes ist" (ibid.). [Now the transcendentals cannot simply be ascribed solely to the divine essence as such, for *imago* and therefore also exemplarity for every creatable thing is the proper name of the Son.]

82. "Wenn die Transzendentalien jedes, auch das untergeistige Sein durchwalten, so erlangen sie ihre Fülle doch erst, wo das Sein sich innerlich zum Geistsein lichtet, und wenn es wahr bleibt, daß vollendete Liebe auch eine vollendete Erkenntnis voraussetzt . . . dennoch die unvordenkliche Selbstentäußerung des Vaters zum Sohn hin selbst einer Liebe sich verdankt, die gedanklich über das Sein und seine Selbsterkenntnis hinausgeht" (*TLg* II.162). [If the transcendentals preside over every being, even subspiritual being, nevertheless they first obtain their fullness where being lights itself inwardly into spriritual being; and if it remains true that perfect love also presupposes perfect knowledge . . . nevertheless the unforeseeable self-outpouring of the Father to the Son is itself due to a love which theoretically exceeds being and self-knowledge.]

83. Von Balthasar quotes Gustav Siewerth on this point: "Liebe ist solchermaßen umfassender als das Sein selbst, das 'Transzendentale schlechthin', das die Wirklichkeit des Seins, der Wahrheit und der Güte zusammmenfaßt'" (ibid.). [Love is in such a way more all-embracing than being itself, it is the "transcendental *par excellence*" which encompasses the reality of being, truth and goodness."]

84. "Besinnt man sich aber nochmals auf den Prozeß der immanenten Hervorgänge in Gott, so sind ja beide Wege ungangbar: der eines Vaters, der den Sohn zeugte, um sich als Gott zu erkennen, wie der eines Vaters, der, weil er sich selbst vollkommen erkennt, den Sohn zeugt: das erste wäre hegelianisch, das zweite, ernsthaft durchgedacht, arianisch" (*TLg* II.162–63). [But if one again recalls the process of the immanent processions in God, both paths are indeed untravellable: the one of the Father who begets the Son in order to come to know himself as God, and the one of the Father who, because he knows himself fully, begets the Son. The first would be Hegelian, the second, earnestly thought through, Arian.]

85. "Deshalb kann die Unvordenklichkeit der Selbsthingabe oder Selbstentäußerung, die den Vater allererst zum Vater macht, nicht der Erkenntnis, sondern nur der grundlosen Liebe zugeschrieben werden, was diese als das 'Transzendentale schlechthin' ausweist" (*TLg* II.163). [Therefore the unpredictability of the self-emptying or self-outpouring which makes the Father to first be Father cannot be ascribed to knowledge, but only to groundless love, which proves this as the "transcendental *par excellence*."]

86. "Dies einzusehen ist nur möglich, wenn man mit Bulgakow von einer ersten innertrinitarischen 'kenosis' zu sprechen wagt, die keine andere ist als die positive 'Selbstentäußerung' Gottes in der Übergabe des ganzen göttlichen Wesens in den Prozessionen" (ibid.). [This can only be appreciated if one dares to speak with Bulgakov of a first, inner-trinitarian "kenosis," which is none other than the positive "self-outpouring" of God in the handing over of the whole divine essence in the processions.]

8
_____

Epilogue

Our study has illustrated from the philosophical side the momentous importance von Balthasar attaches to Incarnation—it is here that the Ideal Metaphysics of the exemplar pass over to and are fulfilled in the Historical Metaphysics of the one who is the concrete analogy of being, the embodiment and measure of every interval between God and humans. This focus on the Incarnate One was signaled from the start: *The Glory of the Lord* warns that the goal is the retrieval of an index of interpretation of the glory of God as it appears in this world. This glory is seen in its decisive form in the Incarnate Christ,[1] and this definitive theophany is to be understood not by reference to something external to the decisive event, but rather precisely in terms of its own native logic.[2] Therefore, the task was always to have been the explication of the ramifications of the Incarnation in terms of the eternal ground of the Incarnation in God (it always being understood that we only know this eternal ground through the definitive revelation accomplished in the Incarnation itself).

This creates a dynamic of "from Christ" and "for Christ" that will permeate both the Ideal and the Historical Metaphysics at every moment. The Ideal Metaphysic describes all being as coming from the Son and being directed back toward him;[3] thus, all creation both reflects its archetypal origin and points forward in myriad anticipations to the coming of the Anointed One. The Historical Metaphysic describes all being as from Christ in the soteriological opening of a new space of ontological affirmation accomplished by the redemption of human sin, without which redemption creaturely being was not free to be joyfully and existentially directed toward Christ and union with him in realization of the highest possibility of its being.

If therefore it is granted that all things must be referred to Christ, and specifically, in the aftermath of the decisive event of revelation in his earthy life, to the Incarnate Christ, then we necessarily have to deal with the double motion of this life. For Christ, as we have seen, descended into the deepest depths of an existence shattered by sin, but he did so precisely in order to ascend again, bringing the restored creation alongside him to new and glorious heights. In our last chapter, we saw the depth of the downward motion, and located that motion in the very character of God, in the groundless love that is most like itself when it groundlessly (without cause) gives itself away. If there were no Holy Spirit in the Trinity, the story could end there.[4] But because in God the divinity which is poured out in its entirety in Christ returns to God hypostatically (and therefore irreducibly and subsistently) in the love of the Holy Spirit, we must go on to speak of the ascension of Christ, which grounds the possibility of returning to God that being which was gifted to us in our creation. And because this return is made in the irreducibility of personhood, every question of absorption into an indiscriminate identity, of the loss of the many in the super-essential unity of the being of the One, is ruled out from the beginning.

The resurrection and ascension, in spite of their critical importance for the destiny of the creature and the fulfillment of the purposes of God, are not *hypostatic* changes for Christ, and therefore they do not inaugurate a change in the fundamental character of the metaphysics. Although, as we shall see, the ascension does in a certain way involve the creation of a new reality, it is a new reality within the metaphysics established with the hypostatic union of God and humanity in the Logos.

In this way, the logic of love, which calls forth its like in the beloved, demands that we add to our reflections of the point at which theological reality breaks into the metaphysical some comment about the transformation of all metaphysical reality into theological reality. This is the inner meaning of the fact that in the analogy of being the proportion of the Trinity is always dominant over the God-world proportion: this very fact signals that the destiny of creation is to be elevated into the divine, that the creaturely necessity to be explicated in terms of the divine being is not just epistemological or even merely ontological, but also existential.[5]

The destiny of earth is heaven, and the destiny of heaven is earth;[6] they have been set over against one another in order that they be able to draw near to one another.[7] Christ will prove and fulfill this by first filling an earthly life with eternal content and afterward making a place in heaven for the earthly life lived here below.[8] This opens the place of heaven for us for the first time—one might go so far as to say that this is the moment of the creation of heaven.[9]

Von Balthasar is clear that the issue at stake in return is not the transposition of earthly realities into heavenly realities, the crossing over from one cosmic sphere to another—rather, it is the conversion of the mortal world into an enduring, immortal world. This gives a properly cosmological signification to the ascension of Christ as that which archetypally (and eventually causally) institutes the transformation.[10] Embedded in this claim, von Balthasar thinks, is a twofold presupposition about the type of honor created persons will receive as they are taken up into their new, heavenly form: the first is that this must come as pure grace, as a gift which is not able to be expected; the second is that the creature must bring with it something of itself, something which will qualify the recipient as a "victor" who has overcome.[11]

Here the discourse forks: the necessity of the creature bringing something along with it becomes the grounding for a theology of the Eucharist which focuses on the way the Eucharistic presence opens for humanity and all creation a heavenly space in which to live.[12] This space is the first return of the cosmos to its origin, and it already surrounds us. The Eucharistic space thus opened not only welcomes all reality into itself, but conditions it: Everything that enters into that space partakes of its character,[13] grounding a "eucharistic permeability" of all subjects one to another that ultimately grounds the communion of saints.[14] Thus, as Christ pours himself out for us in the form of the Eucharist, creating within the transformed and ascended physicality of his existence room for our as yet untransformed, mortal existence, so do we analogously make room for others within our renewed hearts.

Von Balthasar would maintain that this Eucharistic reality is ontological, and so we are not merely speaking in figures or imprecisely here. However, we are certainly speaking *incompletely*, and this can hardly be the metaphysically robust *redditus* we have been seeking to complete the story of creation's journey.[15] For this reason one must take the other road opened to us. Returning to the claim that the type of honor created persons will receive as they are taken up into their new, heavenly form requires that this honor must come as pure, unexpected grace, we see the path opening before us to a discussion of that ultimate honor. This is to enter properly into the discussion of the nature of grace, and this alone can complete the picture we have been at such pains to describe.

At this point, the *Theodrama* cannot carry us forward, for its concerns do not allow it to penetrate deeper than the world's existence in the divine in the most economic terms. Accordingly, although at this point in the discussion von Balthasar has opened the fundamental philosophical question of the way in which creaturely being is embraced by uncreated being, he goes on to treat it with respect to its origin in the archetype on the basis of the Platonic notion of "ideas."[16] *Theodrama* never progresses further than the existential condition of a created freedom embraced within an unconditioned and unconditional

200 | Christic and Analogy

freedom. Theology in the mode of the *Good* stops short of achieving the ultimate goal.

Similarly, *Theologic* stops surprisingly short: after speaking of the return to the Creator in terms of a fundamental openness between the One and the many,[17] the discourse shatters on the unsearchable depths of God[18] and can ultimately only gesture toward the glory of the invisible Father.[19] Theology conditioned by the transcendental *True* pulls up short due to the abiding mystery of God, which is revealed precisely as that which remains protected by inner mystery.[20]

The Glory of the Lord too can only speak in its final volume of a "departure toward God";[21] the New Testament horizon restrains the discourse, limiting it to the transition from Old to New Covenant and the glory of God appearing in the Church, with only occasional and heavily veiled glimpses beyond the conditions experienced this side of creation's exaltation. The great hope it offers is not the eschatological return, but the reality of the Church within the confines of the existential difficulties of a world dominated by sin.[22] Even the great opening volume ends with no more than a glance at the reality of the final consummation of grace.[23] Theology in the mode of the *Beautiful* equally falls short.

To make sense of this, we must turn to the *Epilog*. Here, von Balthasar warns us that although throughout the Triptych being is shown increasingly to be epiphanic, nevertheless the "deepest mystery of being" came into view only imperfectly.[24] What does arise from all of this, however, is the miracle of fruitfulness, which is immediately linked to death, to the necessity of sacrifice.[25] This link grounds the self-understanding of the church as body and bride of Christ in Christ's act of self-surrender.[26]

At this point, another road to the sacraments has been opened.[27] If we eschew this path for the sake of the examination of the nature of grace, we are led immediately back to the cross, and to the "marvelous exchange."[28] The last word reaches no higher than the real possibility of an ultimate rejection of the gift of God and the hope that love brings that such a tragedy will not materialize.[29] Even here at the end, we seem to encounter a dead end.

The *Epilog* has at least given us the possibility of understanding why the variously modulated theological discourses fall short at this precise point. There is every indication that we are approaching the limit concept for the transcendentals of being. And our investigations in the last chapter have prepared us for the realization that there is something greater than the transcendentals, something which trumps even their universality: the transcendental *par excellence*, love. It would therefore seem to be a reasonable conclusion that each of the works must fall short of the explication of grace insofar as this, being absolutely undeducible and totally free, does not submit to the logic of being as such, but rides above it as the most likely (and yet not necessary) act of thoroughly free being.

The transition from philosophy to a theology grounded in Biblical revelation is what von Balthasar calls in the *Epilog* a threshold.[30] Beyond this threshold are the "mysteries of Christianity," which are precisely those things that cannot be derived from religious philosophy.[31] Therefore, even the *Epilog* can only hint at them. But for von Balthasar, that which is underivable is that which is free. Therefore, beyond the confines of being controlled by the transcendentals, beyond the transition from metaphysics to theology, in the realm that philosophy can only term the *One* because it is ignorant of the trinitarian depth that is the rule there, there exists only the eternal, hypostatically expressed, co-equal trinitarian love.

It is at this point that von Balthasar, after so much speech, falls silent. Yet he has not left us without resources. Clearly, the understanding of grace that must be developed is utterly free and therefore to the highest imaginable extent an act of love. And we have learned that all acts of love are kenotic—not just characterized by self-sacrifice but by the gift of one's self. Thus even deifying grace must be seen to be in some significant sense the gift of God's being to us, a sharing of Godself in order to elevate us as high as contingent, dependent creatures may be elevated. It is along these lines that any Balthasarian understanding of grace must be motivated.

At any rate, our study of the metaphysics of von Balthasar can progress no further. At this point, the theological analysis of von Balthasar would have to begin. We have already indicated (for example, in the brief discussion of eucharistic reality in this epilogue) some of the directions possible within the Balthasarian framework. The task of pursuing these highly suggestive avenues must, however, remain the work of another project.

Notes

1. *H* I.26
2. *H* I.117
3. A dynamic which mimics the trinitarian motions, for the Father is established by his groundless self-giving to the Son, and the Holy Spirit in the unifying act of love is infinitely "for" the Son and the Father.
4. This is not strictly true. Even the Son loves the Father, and thus returns all that he is to the Father in absolutely free love. Without some sort of *redditus*, the Son is not able to love the Father with a co-equal, consubstantial love—this can be accounted for must easily in an Arian

context, though it could also be explicable in Modalist terms. It remains in either case well outside the bounds of orthodoxy.

5. That is to say, if we wish to know about the creature intellectually, or if we wish to explain its being (or its being such a way and not another), these questions are all correctly answerable only in relation to the divine archetype—in the realm of the Historical Metaphysic, that means not just Christ, but the Incarnate Christ. In addition to all of this, it is also true that any understanding of the destiny of the creature (in its choosing and in its submitting or lack thereof) must also be referred to the trinitarian dynamics of the life of God as imaged in Christ.

6. This last is secured if we remember that God does not live in heaven, which is a place, but is the *locus* (metaphorically speaking) of blissful, eternal joy above the heavens (for example, *TD* V.111).

7. "Himmel und Erde sind füreinander da, ihre ursprüngliche und durchgehaltene Distanz ist um ihrer Bewegung aufeinander zu geschaffen" (*TDg* IV.343). [Heaven and earth are there for one another; their original and abiding distance is to to create their movement toward one another.]

8. "Aber der vollendete Ausgang aus Gott und die vollendete Rückkehr in ihn erfolgt doch für alle einmalig in Christus, der als Ewiger ein irdisches Leben lebt und dieses mit Ewigkeitsgehalt füllt, um, zum Vater im Himmel zurückkehrend, das irdische gelebte Leben in der Ewigkeit einzubergen" (ibid.). [But the complete *exitus* from God and the complete *reditus* into God happens for all things definitively in Christ, who as the eternal one lived an earthly life and filled it with eternal content in order, returning to the Father, to recover the earthly lived life in eternity.]

9. "Das Gehen Jesu Christi zum Vater kann verstanden werden als die Erschaffung des Himmels, das heißt einer neuen Dimension dieser Schöpfung Gottes, in die hinein sich Mensch und alte Schöpfung zu wandeln beginnen: sie beginnen, bei Gott anzukommen" (*TDg* IV.344). [The going of Jesus Christ to the father can be understood as the creation of heaven, that is, of a new dimension of the creation of God, into which humanity and the old creation begin to transform: they begin to arrive at God.]

10. "Aber es geht nicht um einen bloßen Wechsel zwischen kosmischen Sphären: von der sublunaren zur unvergänglich-planetaren, vielmehr um eine Verwandlung der sterblichen Welt gerade durch die Radikalität des Todes hindurch in eine unvergängliche. Das Christusereignis ist hierin das anführende (*archēgos* Apg 3,15; Hebr 2,10; 12,2) nicht nur als ein personales, sondern auch als ein archetypisch-kosmologisches" (*TDg* IV.346–47). [But it is not about a simple change of cosmic spheres: from the sublunary to the imperishable planetary, but rather it is about a transformation of the mortal world precisely through the radicality of death into an immortal one. The Christ-event is herein the head, not only as a personal reality, but also as an archetypal-cosmological reality.]

11. "Daß der Vater die vom Sohn an seinen Ort 'geholten' Menschen 'ehren' wird (Joh 12,26), setzt immer beides gleichzeitig voraus: daß hier reines Gnadengeschenk über alles Erwartbare hinaus verabreicht wird, aber daß dieses Geschenk, um den Beschenkten nicht zu beschämen, an irgend etwas anknüpft, was er selbst mitbringt, in der Sprache der Bibel: irgendwie 'verdient' hat. In bestimmter Weise muß der Begnadete zu den in der Apokalypse als 'Sieger' Bezeichneten gehören, um der wundersamen Dinge, die Gott ihm schenken will, teilhaft zu werden" (*TDg* IV.347). [That the Father will "honor" the people "brought" by the Son to his place presupposes both things simultaneously: that here a pure gift of grace, beyond all expectation, will be given, but that this gift, in order not to shame the receiver, begins in something that [the creature] brings with it; in the speech of the Bible: he has in some way "deserved" it. In a particular way the graced one must belong to the ones called in Revelation "victors" in order to become partaker of the wonderful thing that God wants to give him.]

12. *TDg* IV.349 ff.

13. "Aber da die eucharistische Wirklichkeit die neuen Räume (und Zeiten) der verklärten Welt freigibt, können die in diese Eintretenden nicht anders, als auf analoge Weise an dieser

verströmten Existenz teilzunehmen: jeder ist er selbst, indem er sich gleichzeitig für alle andern durchwohnbar macht" (*TDg* IV.349).

14. "Diese eucharistische Permeabilität aller Subjekt füreinander und sogar für die noch sterbliche Existenz ist das Grundexistential der *Communio Sanctorum*, und dies wesentlich ohne Tangierung des Freiheitsgeheimnisses jeder Person" (*TDg* IV.350).

15. von Balthasar acknowledges the point: "Aber sind diese theologischen Sichten nicht übereilt, solange die philosophische Grundfrage nicht geklärt ist, wie eine Einbergung des endlichen und zeitlich-räumlichen Seins in das Absolute überhaupt denkbar ist: ohne pantheistische Absorption einerseits und ohne ein bloßes Nebeneinanderbleiben andererseits?" (*TDg* IV.352). [But these theological dimensions are not rash as long as one does not throw out the philosophical first question of how an ingathering of finite and temporal-spatial being in the absolute is at all thinkable without on the one hand a pantheistic absorption, and on the other hand a simple setting alongside one another?]

16. Ibid.

17. *TL* III.399–404

18. *TL* III.405–8

19. *TL* III.409–10

20. *TL* I.290

21. "Der Aufbruch zu Gott" (*H* III.2.2.455).

22. *H* III.2.2.507

23. *H* I.656–57

24. "Bei der Besprechung der Transzendentalien ist das tiefste Geheimnis des Seins nur unvollkommen in Sicht gekommen. Alles Seiende erschien als wesenhaft und zunehmend epiphan: sich-zeigend, sich-gebend, sich-sagend, wobei alle drei Modi jeweils, die andern beiden einschließend, als Inbegriffe hervortreten konnten" (*Epilog*, 86). [In the discussion of the transcendentals, the deepest secret of being comes into view only imperfectly. All beings appear as essentially and increasingly epiphanic: self-indicating, self-giving, self-saying, in which all three modes can emerge at any one time as the epitome, conditioning the others.]

25. Ibid.

26. *Epilog*, 89

27. *Epilog*, 90 ff.

28. *Epilog*, 94

29. *Epilog*, 97–98

30. *Epilog*, 7

31. Ibid.

Bibliography

Anselm. *Cur Deus Homo*. London: Frederic Norgate, 1885.

Aristotle, *The Complete Works of Aristotle*. 2 vols. Edited by Jonathan Barnes. Princeton: Princeton University Press, 1984.

Aquinas, Thomas. *Summa Theologica*.

Augustine. *De Civitate Dei*. 2 vols. Edited by Emanuel Hoffman. Prague: F. Tempsky, 1899.

Babini, Ellero. "Jesus Christ, Form and Norm of Man according to Hans Urs von Balthasar." *Communio* 16, no. 3 (1989): 446–57.

Barth, Karl. *Church Dogmatics*. 14 vols. Edited by G. W. Bromiley and T. F. Torrance. Translated by G. W. Bromiley. Edinburgh: T&T Clark, 1975.

Bieler, Martin. "Meta-Anthropology and Christology: On the Philosophy of Hans Urs von Balthasar." *Communio* 20, no. 1 (1993): 129–46.

Bonaventura. *Opera Omnia*. Edited by PP Collegii a S. Bonaventurae. 10 vols. Roma: Quaracchi, 1882–1902.

Bowman, Leonard J. "The Cosmic Exemplarism of Saint Bonaventure" *Journal of Religion* 55 (1975): 181–98.

Casarella, Peter, "*Analogia Donationis:* Hans Urs von Balthasar on the Eucharist." *Philosophy and Theology* 11, no. 1 (1998): 147–77.

———. "Experience as a Theological Category: Hans Urs von Balthasar on the Christian Encounter with God's Image" *Communio* 20, no. 1 (1993): 118–28.

Chadwick, Henry. *Augustine*. Oxford: Oxford University Press, 1986.

Chapp, Larry. *The God Who Speaks: Hans Urs von Balthasar's Theology of Revelation*. San Francisco: International Scholars, 1996.

———. "Revelation" in *The Cambridge Companion to Hans Urs von Balthasar*. Edited by Edward T. Oakes and David Moss, 11–23. Cambridge: Cambridge University Press, 2004.

de Lubac, Henri. "A witness of Christ in the Church: Hans Urs von Balthasar." *Communio* 2, no. 3 (1975): 228–49.

Denzinger, Henricus. *Enchiridion Symbolorum Definitionum et Declarationum de Rebus Fidei et Morum*. Barcinone: Herder, 1973.

Derrida, Jacques. *The Gift of Death.* University of Chicago Press: Chicago, 1996.

———. "Structure, Sign, and Play in the Discourse of the Human Sciences." In *The Structuralist Controversy: The Languages of Criticism and the Sciences of*

Man: Fortieth Anniversary Edition. Edited by Richard Macksey and Eugenio Donato. Baltimore: Johns Hopkins University Press, 2007.

Dickens, W. T. *Hans Urs von Balthasar's* Theological Aesthetics: *A Model for Post-Critical Biblical Interpretation.* Notre Dame: Notre Dame University Press, 2003

Dörrie, H. "*Formula Analogiae:* An Exploration of a Theme in Hellenistic and Imperial Platonism." In *Neoplatonism and Early Christian Thought,* 33–49. London: Variorum, 1981.

Dupré, Louis. "The Glory of the Lord: Hans Urs von Balthasar's Theological Aesthetic." *Communio* 16, no. 3 (1989): 384–412.

Escobar, Pedro. "Hans Urs von Balthasar: Christo-logian." *Communio* 2, no. 3 (1975): 300–16.

Fisichella, Rino. *Hans Urs von Balthasar: Dinamica dell'amore e Credibilità del Cristianesimo.* Roma: Città Nouva Editrice, 1981.

Guardini, Romano. *Systembildende Elemente in der Theologie Bonaventuras.* Leiden: Brill, 1964.

Healy, Nicholas J. *The Eschatology of Hans Urs von Balthasar.* Oxford: Oxford University Press, 2005.

Heidegger, Martin. *Being and Time.* Translated by John Macquarrie and Edward Robinson. San Francisco: Harper & Row, 1962.

———. *Introduction to Metaphysics.* Translated by Gregory Fried and Richard Polt. New Haven: Yale UP, 2000.

Henrici, Peter. "The Philosophy of Hans Urs von Balthasar." In *Hans Urs von Balthasar: His Life and Work.* Edited by David Schindler. San Francisco: Ignatius, 1991.

Howsare, Rodney. *Balthasar: A Guide for the Perplexed.* T&T Clark: London, 2009.

Kay, Jeffrey. "Aesthetics and A Posteriori Evidence in Balthasar's Theological Method." *Communio* 2, no. 3 (1975): 289–99.

Kerr, Fergus. "Balthasar and Metaphysics." In *The Cambridge Companion to Hans Urs von Balthasar,* edited by Edward T. Oakes and David Moss, 224–38. Cambridge: Cambridge University Press, 2004.

Kilby, Karen. *Balthasar: A (Very) Critical Introduction.* Eerdmans: Grand Rapids, 2012.

Liddell, Henry George and Scott, Robert. *Greek-English Lexicon.* Oxford: Oxford University Press, 1940.

Lindbeck, George. *The Nature of Doctrine.* Philadelphia: Westminster, 1984.

Losel, Steffen. "Love Divine, All Loves Excelling: Balthasar's Negative Theology of Revelation." *The Journal of Religion* 82, no. 4 (October 2002): 586–616.

Löser, Werner. "Being Interpreted as Love: Reflections on the Theology of Hans Urs von Balthasar." *Communio*16, no. 3 (1989): 474–90.

Louth, Andrew. "The Place of *Heart of the World* in the Theology of Hans Urs von Balthasar." In *The Analogy of Beauty*, edited by John Riches, 147–63. Edinburgh: T&T Clark, 1986.

Marion, Jean-Luc. *God without Being*. Translated by Thomas A. Carlson. Chicago: Chicago University Press, 1991.

McGregor, Bede and Norris, Thomas, eds. *The Beauty of Christ: An Introduction to the Theology of Hans Urs von Balthasar*. Edinburgh: T&T Clark, 1994.

Mongrain, Kevin. *The Systematic Thought of Hans Urs von Balthasar: An Irenaean Retrieval*. New York: Crossroad Publishing Co., 2002.

Nestle, Eberhard et al. *Novum Testamentum Graece*. Stuttgart: Deutsche Bibelgesellschaft, 1993.

Nichols, Aidan. *A Key to Balthasar: Hans Urs von Balthasar on Beauty, Goodness, and Truth*. Baker: Grand Rapids, MI, 2011

———. "The Theo-logic" in *The Cambridge Companion to Hans Urs von Balthasar*, edited by Edward T. Oakes and David Moss, 158-171. Cambridge: Cambridge Univ. Press, 2004.

Oakes, Edward T. *Pattern of Redemption: The Theology of Hans Urs von Balthasar*. New York: Continuum, 1994.

O'Donnell, John. "Truth as Love: the Understanding of Truth according to Hans Urs von Balthasar." *Pacifica* 1:2 (1988): 189-211.

O'Donoghue, Noel. "A Theology of Beauty" in *The Analogy of Beauty*. Edited by John Riches. Edinburgh: T&T Clark Ltd., 1986, 1-11.

O'Hanlon, Gerard F. *The Immutability of God in the Theology of Hans Urs von Balthasar*. Cambridge: Cambridge Univ. Press, 1990.

O'Meara, Thomas. "Of Art and Theology: Hans Urs von Balthasar's Systems." *Theological Studies* 42 (Je 1981): 272-276.

O'Regan, Cyril. "Balthasar: Between Tübingen and Postmodernity." *Modern Theology* 14:3 (July 1998): 325-353.

———. "Von Balthasar and Thick Retrieval: Post-Chalcedonian Symphonic Theology." *Gregorianum* 77:2 (1996): 227-260.

Plato. *Plato: Complete Works*. Indianapolis: Hackett Publishing Co, 1997.

Roten, Johann. "Hans Urs von Balthasar's Anthropology in Light of His Marian Thinking." *Communio*20:2 (1993): 306-333.

Saward, John. *The Mysteries of March: Hans Urs von Balthasar on the Incarnation and Easter*. Washington, D.C.: Catholic University of America Press, 1990.

Schindler, D.C. *Hans Urs von Balthasar and the Dramatic Structure of Truth: A Philosophical Investigation*. New York: Fordham Univ. Press, 2004.

Scola, Angelo. "Nature and Grace in Hans Urs von Balthasar." *Communio*18:2 (1991): 207-226.

Simon, Martin. "Identity and Analogy: Balthasar's Hölderlin' and Hamann" in *The Analogy of Beauty*, edited by John Riches. Edinburgh: T&T Clark Ltd., 1986, 77-104.

Tillich, Paul. *Systematic Theology*. 3 vols. Chicago: Chicago UP, 1951.

van Driel, Edwin Christian. *Incarnation Anyway*. Oxford: Oxford University Press, 2008.

von Balthasar, Hans Urs. *Cosmic Liturgy: The Universe According to Maximus the Confessor*. Brian E. Daley, trans. San Francisco: Ignatius, 1988.

———. *Epilog*. Trier, Johannes Verlag Einsiedeln, 1987.

———. *The Glory of the Lord: A Theological Aesthetics*. Translated by Oliver Davies et al. 7 vols. Edinburgh: T&T Clark, 1982-89.

———. *Heart of the World*. Translated by Erasmo S. Leiva. San Francisco: Ignatius, 1979.

———. *Herrlichkeit: Eine Theologische Ästhetik*. 5 vols. Freiburg: Johannes Verlag Einsiedeln, 1961-69.

———. *In the Fullness of Faith: On the Centrality of the Distinctively Catholic*. San Francisco: Ignatius, 1988.

———. *Love Alone is Credible*. San Francisco: Ignatius, 2004.

———. *Presence and Thought:An Essay on the Religious Philosophy of Gregory of Nyssa*. San Francisco: Ignatius, 1995.

———. "A Résumé of My Thought." *Communio* 15 (Winter 1988): 468-73.

———. *Theodrama*. 5 vols. San Francisco: Ignatius, 1988-98.

———. *Theodramatik*.Freiburg: Johannes Verlag Einsiedeln, 1973-83.

———. *A Theological Anthropology*. New York; Sheed and Ward, 1967.

———. *Theologie der Geschichte: Ein Grundriss*. Freiburg: Johannes Verlag Einsiedeln, 1959.

———. *Theologik*. 3 vols. Freiburg: Johannes Verlag Einsiedeln, 1985-87.

———. *Theologic*. 3 vols. Adrian J. Walker and Graham Harrison, trans. San Francisco: Ignatius, 2000-05.

———. *A Theology of History*. New York: Sheed and Ward, 1963.

———. *The Theology of Karl Barth*. New York: Holt, Rinehart and Winston, Inc, 1971.

———. *Truth is Symphonic: Aspects of Christian Pluralism.* San Francisco: Ignatius, 1987.

Wigley, Stephen. *Balthasar's Trilogy.* T&T Clark: London, 2010.

Williams, Rowan. "Balthasar and Trinity" in *The Cambridge Companion to Hans Urs von Balthasar*, edited by Edward T. Oakes and David Moss, 158–171. Cambridge: Cambridge Univ. Press, 2004.

Wipple, John. *The Metaphysical Thought of Thomas Aquinas.* Washington, DC: Catholic University of America Press, 2000.

Index

CPSIA information can be obtained at www.ICGtesting.com
Printed in the USA
BVOW01s1302140813

328383BV00004B/20/P